CLEANER'S BOY

A RESISTANCE ROAD
TO A LIBERATED LIFE

PATRIC TARIQ MELLET

Tafelberg

Tafelberg
An imprint of NB Publishers
A division of Media24 Boeke (Pty) Ltd
40 Heerengracht, Cape Town, 8000
www.tafelberg.com

© 2022 Patric Tariq Mellet

All rights reserved.
No part of this book may be reproduced or transmitted in any form or by any electronic or mechanical means, including photocopying and recording, or by any other information storage or retrieval system, without written permission from the publisher.

Set in 11.5 on 15.5pt Ehrhardt MT
Cover design by Mike Cruywagen
Book design by Melanie Kriel
Edited by Tracey Hawthorne
Proofread by Gillian Warren-Brown

Printed and bound by CTP Printers
First edition, first impression 2022

ISBN 978-0-624-09365-7
ISBN 978-0-624-09366-4 (epub)

'The wind carries stories from afar to the ears of those who are attuned to listening.'

– ǁKabbo, San storyteller of the ǀXam community

CONTENTS

Prologue   9

1	**Fairyland:** Origins in the grey	13
2	**Hell:** The sojourner child	34
3	**Youth:** Early learnings and part-time work	51
4	**Manhood:** Tyranny and protest	65
5	**Repression:** The first clashes	79
6	**Exile:** Into Botswana	100
7	**Lusaka:** Cutting my ANC teeth	116
8	**Shishita:** The cleansing	132
9	**Displacement:** Beginning again in the UK	145
10	**London:** The liberation printer	158
11	**Homecoming:** Preparing for freedom	171
12	**Settling:** Shifts and transitions	185
13	**Contributions:** Working for the people	199
14	**Challenge:** Tackling corruption and criminality	217
15	**At rest:** Learnings from a lifetime in the struggle	238
16	**Identity:** The heritage whisperer	254

Acknowledgements   263
Index   264
About the author   272

PROLOGUE

Between what I see and what I say,
Between what I say and what I keep silent,
Between what I keep silent and what I dream,
Between what I dream and what I forget:
– Poetry. It slips between yes and no.

Octavio Paz, A Tree Within

In 1997 I became Patric William Tariq Mellet at the stroke of a bureaucrat's pen.

That was the year the department of home affairs acceded to my request to have my paternal surname restored to my children and me. For 41 years I'd been known by neither of my parents' surnames, but as 'De Goede'. I'd gone through momentous times with this persona and identity, and suddenly 'De Goede' was no more – 'De Goede' was dead. All that remained as a reminder was a nickname, 'Zinto', given to me by comrades who'd humorously interpreted 'De Goede' as 'things' or 'dinges' – 'zinto' in isiXhosa.

This book tells the story of both personas, and of the road I took as I navigated my way through life. It also tells the story of my life within a racist system for a great part of my youth, where my struggle with my identity was what Mariah Carey calls, in her ballad 'Outside', 'neither here nor there . . . somewhere halfway / feeling there's no one completely the same'. In South Africa, this was the grey world of the 'halfnaatjie' (literally, 'half seam', referring to two halves of something stitched together). I had a deep longing for resolution, and to see and enjoy identity outside of a 'race' paradigm.

Like the Mexican poet and Nobel laureate Octavio Paz (1914-1998) unpacks the poetry of life – the world between yes and no, here and there – so has my life unfolded. I did follow my dreams – dreams much greater than wishes for myself – and, by choice, took the road less travelled, a resistance road, in the hope of a liberated life for myself and my country. My life has been filled with complexity and hardships, yet my story remains that of a simple man who has lived through extraordinary events, and who thinks of his experience as a fortunate life.

Life for me has been dominated by my choice to follow a resistance road, which I believe, in the evening of my days, has delivered a liberated life. It's rooted in the fact that I didn't passively accept being a low-born, down at heel, nor did I just go with the flow; I refused to be cowed by the social engineering of identity, and the evil and repression of those times.

In embarking on telling my story, my earliest memory was an identity marker that came about because of my single mother's work as a laundry and dry-cleaning shop assistant in District Six. The customers and everyone else in District Six called her 'Cleaner's' and I, the little boy often at her side, was called 'Cleaner's boy'.

I dedicate this story to my mother, whom I tried to but perhaps could never fully understand. For much of my life she was absent, though her spirit always loomed large; I missed her as much in life as I have since she passed.

I dedicate this book, too, to all those I've had as companions along the way, who faced similar challenges and had to make difficult decisions. This includes my children, Dylan, Manuel and Vuyo, whose lives were negatively impacted because of their parents' activism.

Most of all, I dedicate this book to the many in my generation whom I knew, and who lost their lives along the resistance road.

Patric Tariq Mellet
Cape Town, June 2022

1

FAIRYLAND: ORIGINS IN THE GREY

I glanced across the room at my mother, rocking in the chair, with that faraway look on her face. She'd disappeared again, into the sands of time – something I'd become accustomed to. When disappearing into her yesterdays, Mom had the habit of twisting and turning a hanky in her hand.

My mother's mother, Ma-Huntley, was of mixed parentage – Englishman and 'Coloured'. Her father, Willie Huntley, was an Englishman, a military man who'd been heavy-handed with his children. Mom had told me how they were punished for little wrongs by being beaten with a leather belt, and explained how he would put them in wet hessian bags, which he then hoisted up off the ground with a rope and pulley in a dark room, locking them in. Huntley ultimately abandoned his family and went back to England, so my mother's eldest sister, Aunty Doll, and her brother Bill went out to work and assisted Ma-Huntley to run the home.

Bill, following his father's example, also ruled the roost with an iron fist. He was a tough, no-nonsense trade-union man at work and had a bit of an alpha-male personality. He made sure all his siblings handed over their wages to their mother when, one after the other, they left school with a rudimentary education and went into factory work.

For my mother, Annie, this happened when she turned thirteen. Her first job, as an apprentice seamstress for a family-run sweatshop factory, was remunerated at a shilling (ten cents) a day, for a ten-hour working day, seven days a week. (Its value equivalent today would be around R3.50 per day.) She thought that her Jewish boss was kind because he let her attend holy mass on a Sunday before going to work.

(In the first two decades of the twentieth century, some poor Jewish immigrants from Eastern Europe, via England, came to South Africa. With borrowed money they set up sweatshop factories and, through exploitative labour practices, within one generation had become wealthy. In our areas while growing up there were left-wing Jews who supported working-class struggles, and there were also exploitative colonial Jews who were part of the oppressive machinery. This also took a Zionist versus non-Zionist character.)

My mother and Aunty Doll had a very strong bond despite their thirteen-year age difference. Mom suffered from what is today called the 'middle-child syndrome' – she felt that her mother always found fault with her. When Ma-Huntley and Mom butted heads, it was always Aunty Doll who intervened to make the peace.

One time after a mother-daughter conflict, Ma-Huntley locked my mother out of the house. Aunty Doll came home from work to find my mother sitting on the stoep outside, sobbing. After being apprised of the problem, Aunty Doll said that she knew what to do about it.

Hooking her arm through my mother's, she took Mom to stand outside the kitchen window, where she struck up a hearty rendition of 'That Wonderful Mother of Mine': 'The moon never beams without bringing me dreams of that wonderful mother of mine. The birds never sing but a message they bring of that wonderful mother of mine. Just to bring back the time that was so sweet to me, just to bring back the days when I sat on her knee. You are a wonderful mother, dear old mother of mine!'

It melted the heart of Ma-Huntley, who let them back into the house and made some tea.

Both Mom and Aunty Doll married early in life, Aunty Doll to a man with Indian roots by the name of Christian Clarke van Rooy from Woodstock in Cape Town (and they had a loving marriage until Uncle Christian's relatively early death), and my mother to a man called Alan de Goede (a short and difficult marriage).

On 13 March 1956 I was born into a whirlwind of turbulence which, over time, I learnt would never pass.

* * * *

I'd grown up hearing my mother's stories, and the variants of them within our extended family. One of these was of what I call 'the time of the green colour of blood' – referring to the accident in which my mom's little niece Joan, her sister Doll's first child, was killed. And I could imagine it quite vividly. The squealing creak of the wire-mesh front gate grinding and gnawing, iron hinge on iron. Four-year-old Joan swinging back and forth, head thrown back, with a smile from ear to ear, not a care in the world. Her dress – the fateful green dress – billowing as each swing of the body became the swing of the gate, responding to her rocking back and forth. Each movement accompanied by her rhyme, 'Jan Spanspek spring oor die hek, dan briek hy sy nek, en hy sê dis ek.' (Little Johnny Melon jumped over the gate and broke his neck, and then he blamed me.)

From the kitchen, Ma-Huntley's voice sliced through the bliss. 'Jo! You riding the gate again. How many times must I tell you not to ride the bladdy gate! We need some bread from the shop.'

Playtime ended abruptly as the clock struck ten minutes to five. The two kids, my mom, Annie, fourteen years old, and her little niece Joan, were given a pleasant chore – an errand to the shop.

Hand in hand, they skipped all the way, and soon they stood in front of the shopkeeper, who knew them well. They were swaying from side to side and giggling.

Annie poked little Joan in the side, saying, 'You ask the uncle.'

'Uncle Babbie, my Ma say I must buy from uncle a loaf of bread. On the book, please uncle.'

'And pasella kanala, uncle,' Joan piped up. 'Taramakassie, Uncle Babbie.'

(This was our own colloquial language, a working-class patois of English and Kaaps. 'On the book' means on credit – written down in the book; 'pasella' and 'kanala' both mean something extra for free; 'taramakassie' is thank you; and 'Babbie' is the Cape-creolised version of Baboo, a respectful Hindi word for 'sir'.)

Soon, bread in hand, pasella sweets in mouth, they set off back home, carefree on that road.

The still of the afternoon was broken by the screeching of brakes as a car mounted the verge. There was a thud, then grinding and gnawing. Iron ripped through flesh. A scream, then silence. And the dress – the fateful green dress – torn and limp and splattered with blood. Blood-stained green, fateful green.

The loaf of bread soaking up the blood like a sponge.

The blood and the dust, the arrested scream: a lifeless child and another child, my mom, sobbing. Alive, but branded for life with stigmata wounds, ever-bleeding in her heart.

The rich drunken driver and his girlfriend blamed young Annie. They said she'd let go of Jo's hand, that Jo had darted into the road. The driver slipped some cash to the policeman to make it all go away. Case closed.

The colour green, generation after generation, became a family taboo. No green clothes, curtains, tablecloths or objects were allowed in our homes. Green is the colour of our blood.

And the ditty, with a twist, lodged in my mother's head: Hy't haar nek gebriek; dan sê hy dis ek.

My mother was forever haunted by the events of that day in 1932 when little Joan's hand was ripped from hers. She harboured doubt, a sense of guilt, planted in her mind by the driver of the car. After years of hearing different versions of the story from her and other family members, I found the archived death certificate, which confirmed all the basic facts of the events of that day: that Joan van Rooy, aged four, had died 'due to concussion of the brain from a fractured skull caused by the deceased being knock over by a motor car driver'.

Aunty Doll was to have five more children, most of whom were grown when my uncle Christian died in 1952, just as apartheid laws were being ushered in. The children were physically a mixed bag, with features ranging from blonde hair, blue eyes and pale complexions, to dark hair, Asian eyes and the deepest, darkest skin. Up until then, those with birth certificates, even though not looking white, were registered as 'European' in a system that wasn't strictly policed; apartheid, of course, would want the children classified according to the dictates of racist ideology. Aunty Doll realised that her children and grandchildren were going to be differently classified under apartheid, and that some of them would find it impossible to 'play for white'. She didn't want her brood to become antagonistic to each other and live in different worlds of ambiguity.

The apartheid system ripped through our family, leaving emotional carnage in its wake, splitting us up and flinging us into different worlds and territories. This was the pain that hovered over my childhood days.

* * * *

My mother was a single parent and a working woman. When she retired at 60, she was earning R15 a week, which, calculated to allow for inflation, was more or less the same wages that she'd earned as a child labourer at thirteen when she'd first gone out to work.

Mom had married young and had four children, one of whom, Alan, had died, and three, John, May and Henri, who were grown by the time I was born. My mother and Alan de Goede had separated in the 1940s and were divorced some time in the early 1950s.

My mother met my father, a leather worker and shoemaker, who worked for Balley's, which was near Sweet-Orr, an industrial clothing manufacturers in Woodstock where she was working at the time. She was 40 years old when she gave birth to me. For most of my life I had no contact with my father; my mother raised me to believe he'd died in a car accident. When Mom went to buy vegetables at Salt River Market, she would take me past the spot at the Salt River traffic circle, alongside the Locomotive Bar and Hotel, and describe the horrific motorcar accident in which my father lost his life.

Mom, who went by her maiden name of Huntley, told everyone that she was a widow and even wrote this on official forms, but neither the husband from which she was divorced nor my father was dead. She only used the name 'Mrs De Goede' when dealing with my foster carers and school. I was born at home and not in a hospital, and I never saw any birth certificate. For my entire childhood, she used 'De Goede' as my surname – with no explanation – although by the age of twelve I'd come to understand that it wasn't the name of my biological father.

My mother made things up and seemed to believe her own stories. This resulted in much confusion for me as I grew older and began seeing the holes in her yarns – and it left me somewhat without identity.

My parents were never married to each other, but my father had three wives in his lifetime (one at the same time as his relationship with my mother) and eight children of which we know; he had relationships with too many women to count and it's likely that there are other children of whom we don't know. Though I grew up as an only child, late in my life I came to know that I was one of twelve – at least.

When I was a toddler, not yet two years old, I was in an accident at home. Our three-legged primus-burner was on a rickety table, with a big pot of simmering milk perched precariously atop in preparation for making custard. I wanted a turn to stir the pot, and in trying to do so, pulled the burner from the table. The boiling contents of the pot spilt all over my neck, chest and arms.

Screaming my lungs out, I was rushed to hospital, where I had skin grafted from my thigh to patch up the third-degree burns. I remember the trauma clearly. I stayed in hospital for almost three months. To this day I have thick keloid scars and in places scar contractures across my chest, with a huge hole-like indention in the centre that resembles a feline; I refer to this scar as my 'gatto' – my cat. I have the same type of keloid scarring on my arms and neck. When I look in a mirror, the burnt cat's face stares back at me. It acts as a kind of gateway into a labyrinth of memories.

It was during this tumultuous time that my mother caught my father – a real skirt-chaser – partying with a group of young women in a garage. That was when, twenty months after my birth, my father vanished from my life.

My mother never recovered from my father's betrayal and was, for the rest of her life, antagonistic towards men in general. If invited into a married friend's home, she would first ask whether 'mister' – the husband – was at home, and if he was, she would make up an excuse as to why she couldn't stop over.

The only childhood memory I have of my father is when he lifted me onto his shoulders when he and my mom danced. The Luther Vandross song 'Dance With my Father' still grabs me in the gut whenever I hear it.

* * * *

My family were poor working people residing in the old districts of Cape Town, regarded as 'grey areas' in the parlance of the political world that governed our existence. This referred to the people of multi-ethnic roots who lived in District Six, Woodstock, Salt River, and the small adjoining partly industrial area at the edges of Observatory hugging Salt River. Outsiders may have painted us as a mix of 'poor whites' and 'poor Coloureds', but we didn't see ourselves as separate, nor in terms of colour or race. We were just poor people, and we were one people. We interrelated across colour lines, sharing bloodlines and experiences. Though our districts were called 'grey areas', there was everything colourful about us – we were grey only in the imagination of our apartheid overlords.

White poverty in the City of Cape Town and its immediate surrounds, District Six, Woodstock, and Salt River, has a long history going back to the seventeenth-century uneducated class of European unskilled labourers called knechts. Most notable was the fact that many of these assimilated into the Free Black population as a result of marriages or liaisons which crossed the colour line. This class of poor Europeans in the city of Cape Town and surrounds began to increase exponentially from the 1830s into the twentieth century, with poverty and slums becoming highly visible.

The poverty had its roots in the demobilisation of many British soldiers who bought their discharge to remain in the Cape, but were largely penniless and lacked skills, plus the mass importation of many impoverished British families facing similar conditions who did not want a rural farm life. Added to this were those called remittance men, banished to the Cape for bringing their families into disrepute, as well as the large importation of over 700 British orphan indentured child-labourers, ship-jumpers, St Helenians (white and non-white) and single white women recruited to be house servants, but who on arrival found themselves workless and homeless, and who turned to prostitution as a means to survive.

From the 1840s onwards, decade by decade, right into the twentieth century, these social problems resulted in the formation of many charities, temperance societies, and welfare organisations to assist in managing this poverty explosion. Slums began to develop in Roggebaai and other parts of Cape Town, and in the colony's then second-largest city, Woodstock, to the extent that up to six families were living in sub-let houses with four or five rooms, and poor whites were even living in shacks, sheds and stables in abject poverty. Three out of every four Europeans in Cape Town were tenants, and most were unemployed or employed part time. Alcoholism, prostitution and crime skyrocketed in Cape Town to such an extent that court sentences regularly involved the deportation of these poor whites to the New South Wales penal colonies in Australia.

At the same time, many of the enslaved who'd been formally emancipated after their compulsory four-year apprenticeships by 1838, also moved to Cape Town, as did the 'Liberated Africans' also known as 'Prize Slaves' right through to 1870. Many of the poor European immigrants married or had common-law relationships with local women of enslaved ancestry in these slum neighbourhoods. This increased the number of people deemed by those doing 'race determination' as being of ambiguous race. The majority of the poor whites in our neighbourhood had this background.

In the early twentieth century, refugee Afrikaners from the Boer War and 'bywoners' (share-croppers), plus farmers' children and grandchildren who were trying to make a living on the subdivided farms of the older generation, began to constitute a different poor-white problem. These were whites forced through livestock sicknesses, market forces and overcrowded farms to try and turn around their conditions in urban areas. The latter, largely uneducated, settled mainly in the northern suburbs of Cape Town and did not mix with non-white people, as was the case of the former.

In the heart of District Six stood seven stone steps, which became one of the symbols of the neighbourhood that live in the hearts of all who loved, played and worked in 'the District'. For me in later life, those seven steps came to symbolise the seven tributaries that make up 'Coloured' or Camissa African identity: the roots of indigenes (indigenous Cape people – the San, Khoe, Gqunukhwebe and Xhosa); enslaved Africans and Asians; nonconformist Europeans; 'Free Blacks' (free non-white migrants and freed slaves); 'Orlam' (Khoe, San and some Xhosa who had over time been forced off their lands by wars and had retreated to the Kai !Gariep territory), 'Drosters' (escaped slaves), 'Maroons' (Europeans and Asians who were shipwrecked along the Wild Coast and integrated into African societies); or runaway Europeans from the Cape Colony, usually criminals, black exiles and refugees; and black sailors, indentured labourers and economic migrants.

It was in District Six as a child that I came to understand the violation of apartheid. It was there that I first heard the names of those who stood up for the poor and against colonialism and racial oppression – Abdurahman, Kadalie, Mangena, Plaatje, Gool, Kotane, Gomas, La Guma, Mandela, September, Kahn, Alexander, Snitcher and many more. They were a mix of liberals, socialists, communists, trade unionists and African national liberationists. The stories of these great people, together with the daily reminders of the poverty around me, the effect of apartheid on my family, and the declaration of District Six as a 'whites only' area, followed by its physical destruction, lit a fire within me to struggle against the aberrations and atrocities of apartheid. This is where one of my identities – the resistance man – was born.

District Six was a place that made people think. It was creative and had a great culture and character despite the austerity. It was full of life. So many characters remain fixed in my mind, the music, the smells, the fahfee (Chinese numbers betting) and gambling on the gee-gees (horses), religion and politics, and the many forms of cultural expression that blended into a unique Cape-creole culture.

Mom worked at Lawson & Kirk's Hanover Street laundry and dry-cleaners. It was next to a groceries and general dealer. The shopkeepers' family home was adjacent to the shop. Their house was directly opposite a steep road going up in the direction of Clifton and Stone streets. On one occasion, a Bedford lorry had a brakes failure and hurtled down the steep street, crossed Hanover and crashed into the family home, killing a woman who lived there.

Shortly after this event, Lawson & Kirk was taken over by Nannucci Brothers. My mom worked in various outlets, including one at the top of Hanover Street near the large and imposing Avalon bioscope, and later in Salt River, opposite the Locomotive Hotel and Bar.

At an impressionable age, District Six offered me, a sojourner child who'd already gone through the mill, a broad identity with enough colour to blot out the painful greyness of institutionalised life. Many residents called it Fairyland. Whiling away the hours at play among the laundry bags, I would listen to the conversations of customers as my mother worked. At other times I watched the theatre of life playing itself out on the pavement outside, from my vantage point at the large windows. Etched in the faces, dress and behaviour of the passers-by were elements of all the wonderful roots of peoples, faiths and cultures of the world. This was my world.

Sometimes my mother sent me down the road to the barber shop in Tyne or Sydney Street for a haircut. It cost a bob (a shilling, or ten cents). I would say, 'My mommy says I must ask for a crew-cut,' and the barber, a kindly and knowledgeable Muslim man with a special flair, would know what to do. He would pull out a plank, which he placed across the armrests of the barber's chair, and I would sit on this plank so that I was at the right height for him to cut my hair. The barber would square off the edges of the style with his blade, and if there were any loose hairs left dangling, he singed them away with a Zippo-type cigarette lighter. He was a real craftsman.

While the barber did his work, an old hadji would talk to me about the holy prophet Mohammed and the friends of the prophet, such as Bilal the slave, who was given the privilege and coveted position of singing the athaan, the call to prayer. Even to my young mind it became abundantly clear that the Catholic faith, in which I'd been brought up, and this kindly old hadji's faith, were one and the same. And when Mrs Margolis came and rested in the dry-cleaner's shop after her long walk to the top of Hanover Street and spoke to my mother, I noted that this old Jewish woman's beliefs and my own were also one and the same. It didn't make sense to my child's mind that we thought of each other as different. In the District, I took in different messages, learning from Muslims, Jews, Christians, Chinese Buddhists, the shamanist doekum or dukun, and communists.

My mother was a member of the Laundry Workers, Cleaners and Dyers Union, a constituent of the left-wing South African Congress of Trade Unions (SACTU), which had a formal alliance with the African National Congress (ANC) and the South African Communist Party (SACP). This is how I was first introduced to unions, and later I went with my mom to her union meetings. To be a unionist was a source of pride for many working people, with the union's leaders carrying the same esteem as the parish priest in our world. Mom went to union meetings like she was going to church, for the company of others, and the tea and sandwiches.

I hardly understood all the dimensions involved, but here the first tiny elements of class consciousness filtered into my thinking. There were no rich people at union meetings – only working people. It was a level ground. I learnt that a social-advancement outlook could both explain poverty and deprivation, and offer an alternative way of living and doing business that gave dignity to working people.

When my mother needed legal help, she went to Harry Snitcher, a communist lawyer, for advice. Many of the trade union people were also communists, so when the apartheid regime talked about 'the communist danger', it just didn't make sense to people like us. These were the people who were doing good among us, with no financial reward, and who were often on the receiving end of much harassment.

* * * *

When I was growing up, my mother was always telling people that I wanted to be a priest. Throughout my childhood she nurtured this dream, and that she would be the priest's housekeeper.

There was a tailor who was a hadji who said that I should come to him one day in the future to have my first priest's habit made. One day he surprised my mother with a Klopse suitjie (carnival suit) for me.

The Klopse Carnival, which whites and middle-class people classified as 'Coloured' would call the Coon Carnival, was an annual week-long celebration starting on what we called Tweede Nuwe Jaar – second new year, or the day after New Year's Day. Traditionally that was the day on which the enslaved, who worked hard on New Year's Day, got the day off.

The tailor asked if I could join his troupe at the new-year minstrel festival, but my mother said no, because the skollies (gangsters) got out of hand sometimes and who would look after me? The hadji gave my mother all sorts of assurances, but she still said no, so no it was.

My mom's fear of skollies wasn't irrational. It's true that there were lots of gangsters and they could be nasty, even to children. On the other hand, when I walked up Hanover Street on my own to find my mother, there were gangsters who would often walk me all the way up to the dry-cleaner's shop, and on many occasions our local skollies actually helped my mother out.

Once, a skollie from another area came into the laundry shop with a knife in his hand and demanded the till money, which she handed over. In those days the company made the worker pay in from their wages any money that was lost, and the local guys knew this. A District skollie standing on the opposite side of the road saw what was happening and crept into the shop, pulled out his flick-knife and plunged it into the man's side. Dragging the injured man outside, the local skollie waved to my mother, gave her a toothless smile, and said, 'Don't worry, Cleaner's, I know this moegoe. You moss our Cleaner's. He should know better. Any time, Cleaner's. Any time. At your service.'

It was usual for skollies to prey on female workers around the Grand Parade, on 'movie snaps corner' opposite the post office (so called because street photographers took pictures of pedestrians, then gave the subject a receipt, and they could then buy their picture at the shop at that corner) and the bus stop for the Lower Main Road, especially on Friday – pay day. One Friday, a skollie grabbed my mother's bag, cutting the shoulder strap to free it, and injuring her arm in the process. He dashed off, but one of the skollies from the laundry shop area of Hanover Street saw this and gave chase. He clobbered the thief and returned my mother's bag with her pay packet intact.

When my mom took me with her to work, regardless of the regulations not allowing children to accompany workers, everyone cooperated in pulling the wool over the eyes of the company inspectors. Sometimes the shopkeeper next door or one of the other regular customers would hide me – District Six was a 'kanala' (gifting) and 'help mekaar' (help each other) society. That was how I came to know the many situations in District Six that remain to this day in my head: the general dealer, the record shop, the barber, the fishmonger. Sometimes I was sent to an aunty so-and-so from Aspeling Street or Pontac Street, then I would sit all day, watching food being prepared and listening to skinder (gossip) while I waited for my mother to come and fetch me. We would sometimes have supper with the people who cared for me before going home.

When the company inspector came to the shop, my mother was tipped off by the laundry van drivers. She would ask uncle Izak, the Nannucci driver, if I could accompany him in the van. On occasions I would join him in the delivery van for the whole day, travelling through District Six and the Bokaap where he had friends. We also went to other areas of the city, including white neighbourhoods.

The memory of Uncle Izak struck a chord in me some years later when Steve Biko, the leader of the black consciousness movement in South Africa, spoke to our generation of youth. In 1976, Biko, giving critical testimony in a landmark trial – and speaking in public for the first time since his banning in March 1973 – articulated for so many of us the misery and pain of apartheid, and our hopes and dreams. When he told the story of the Indian man who worked as a dry-cleaners' delivery-van driver, it was like he was talking to me personally, about Uncle Izak.

Uncle Izak always helped me choose and buy presents for my mother on her birthday or on Mother's Day. She used to give me two shillings, for her own present, but he would occasionally add to this so that I could afford to make the best purchase.

On one occasion, I'd gone off with Uncle Izak to buy a birthday gift for my mother, and he'd dropped me at the Castle, so I had to walk up Hanover Street to the laundry shop. Proudly in my hand I had a plastic purse that I'd bought for my mother. It still had the tissue paper in it, so it looked like a purse that had money in it. A skollie pushed me over and stole the purse, and I was very upset when I reached the laundry shop.

I explained to Mom what had happened. She said not to worry, 'it's the thought that counts'. But she also said I couldn't stay because she was still expecting the inspectors, and she then sent me to sit with Aunty Dora, who ran the snack counter at the Avalon bioscope. (After churches and mosques, bioscopes had iconic status and drew the most crowds, offering, for just a little while, another world.)

While sitting behind the Avalon snack counter, I saw the skollie with the purse in his hand. I told Aunty Dora and she got the man working at the door to grab the guy. The doorman smacked him over the head, saying 'Hoekom het djy Cleaner's se laaitie se present gesteel?' (Why did you steal Cleaner's kid's present?) So I got the purse back.

* * * *

It was around the time of the break-up of my parents' relationship in the mid-1950s that my Aunty Doll, a widow by then, gathered her brood and fled apartheid South Africa to England. She believed that her children and grandchildren would stand a better chance of a normal life in London, and used her long-lost father Willie Huntley's nationality to gain entry to the UK.

Aunty Doll, who was my mother's stability, left my mother in a predicament. A single parent with a baby to look after, she had to also work, and she was devastated that her closest family had left her on her own to navigate her way forward in this crazy South Africa.

After getting over a nervous collapse, she had to find a home for herself – but wherever she went, the landlady wouldn't want a child too. I was thus placed in a series of foster homes. The first, where I spent a year, was with one of my mom's former workmates from the factory. Gracie and her husband Alex were good people who couldn't have children of their own. Uncle Alex unfortunately was overcome by an aneurism in the bathroom one night and died, and my mother had to find another home for me.

The next one was with her cousin Macky Genau's family. Six months later my mother took me back and tried again to look after me herself, but didn't manage. In desperation, she put an advertisement in the weekly Catholic newspaper, the *Southern Cross*: 'Well behaved five-year-old boy needs foster home with practising Catholic family. Mother is a single working mother of modest means.'

The morning of Thursday 22 December 1959 started much like any other in my recent memory: I went off with my mother to her workplace, the laundry shop in District Six. There was excitement in the air – 'Christmas was coming; the goose was getting fat.'

One by one the customers cheerily entered the shop to collect their clean laundry. 'Good morning, Cleaner's. Hope you have a Merry Krismis, Cleaner's. And you too, Cleaner's Boy.' With each of the customers, a penny or two would fall *clink-clink* into the Christmas bottle for the poor on the counter – the money went to the St Vincent de Paul Society, a Catholic welfare organisation.

Uncle Izak then came to pick me up, as he often did, to take me for a drive to help my mom out when the company inspectors came to check up at the laundry shop. In the District I was able to sit up front with Uncle Izak, but outside of the District I had to hide in the back of the van among the laundry bags. Uncle Izak said that he would get into trouble because people would think he'd kidnapped a little 'white' boy.

This time Uncle Izak drove me down Hanover Street straight on to Electricity House in Strand Street, where my elder half-sister, May, worked for the city council. They were having a Christmas party for the workers' kids, and I got a bright red fire-engine from Father Christmas and there were sweets and Coo-ee cold drinks and joyfulness filled the air.

Then May walked me down to the Parade to meet up with Mom – they'd both got a half day off. When I said goodbye, May hugged me, tears rolling down her cheeks.

'Why is May crying, Mommy?' I asked, as my sister hurried away.

'May is happy, boy. It's Christmas,' she responded. And, indeed, as we waited at the bus terminus on the Grand Parade, customers from the laundry passed by, and one after the other all boomed out, 'Merry Krismis, Cleaner's! And you too, Cleaner's Boy!'

We took the bus to Salt River, where we changed buses, and then there was a long trip to Bellville. Whenever I asked Mom where we were going, she said, 'Stop asking so many questions.' We walked for a long time up a road towards Durbanville, until we left the houses behind. Between Bellville and Durbanville it wasn't built up into the huge commercial and residential areas that are there now; then, it was just bush.

I was exhausted. Mom looked sad. She said that there were lots of children at the house of the nice people we were going to visit.

It was late in the afternoon by the time we came to the top of a dirt road sloping down to a cluster of five houses with an expanse of bush around it. As we walked down the road, we met kids playing cricket. At one of the houses we were greeted and welcomed by a tall man with a woman at his side. I would come to know them as Uncle Jimmy and his wife Aunty Gilda.

I was told to go play with the kids, who'd all trooped into the house to meet us.

A short while later I heard a bit of a commotion down the passage. I ran down, to see my mom at the door saying goodbye to the people. She was crying.

I realised what was happening and I grabbed Mom's leg. The people were pulling me, and I was crying. It was like a tug-of-war.

Mom sobbed, 'Goodbye, boy,' and I screamed, 'Mommy! But it's Krismis! Krismis, Mommy!'

* * * *

I spent two years with that tight-knit family, seeing what a real family life could be like. I was part of the family and not part of the family at the same time. I lived in my own world within their world, an outside observer inside a real family.

Then, when I was seven years old, as suddenly as I'd been placed there, my mother removed me from their care. She had apparently had an argument with them.

I briefly went to live with my mother again, who by this time was boarding with May and her family. The continuous arguments signalled that this wasn't to last long either, however, and soon we were homeless again and my mother had yet another of her nervous breakdowns.

There was never much money and life was very basic. Mom would lay-by clothes and shoes for me in an annual ritual whereby I could choose the clothes and shoes at a shop, and the store owner would keep them until Mom had paid off all the instalments. Bridge Stores in Salt River was one of the shops where we bought clothes under this arrangement.

We had little money for entertainment, and one of our occasional outings would be window shopping. Mom would say, 'Boy, do you feel like going window shopping? Come, wash your face and hands, and be sure to use the rag with soap.' And off we would go to town, where we would walk slowly around, looking at things we couldn't afford displayed in shop windows. But we enjoyed the outing and fantasising about being able to buy this or that.

Mom was dead against getting into debt and didn't believe in hire-purchase. It was a trade union thing that we were taught in those days: that workers shouldn't become debt slaves. Mom said that people of our class had to be disciplined and learn to go without rather than be in debt. That way, we'd be free. I would sarcastically chirp 'and miserable'. I would always say to Mom, 'Why can rich people have what they want, and poor people can't?'

She would say, 'Carry on with that line of thinking, boy, and they will put a rope around your neck, and you will swing.'

As I grew older and became more political, Mom would often warn me not to talk smart about the government and the well-off white people. 'Walls have ears, mastermind,' she would say. But she had her own disdain for politicians, and would always refer to the toilet as 'the house of parliament'. She would chuckle and say, 'That's where all the members hang out,' in reference to the dicks that were in parliament.

My mother would also tell me in my teens to stop proudly saying that my grandma was black because it would get us into trouble – 'they will put a rope around your neck and you will swing'. In her younger days the issue of colour didn't matter but in her older years she saw that I was heading for trouble with my outspokenness and my embrace of what was seen as black politics.

* * * *

When I was about eight years old, Sister Mary Martin of the Holy Cross nuns from Nile Street in District Six came into my life. The Swiss German nun, and her sibling and fellow-nun, Gertrude, would bring laundry to the shop where my mother worked, and Sister Mary Martin would look after me often as a favour to my mother.

Sister Mary Martin introduced me to St Martin de Porres and awakened me to the stories of the slavery experience. There was a statue of the saint in her room, and she had this way of throwing him stolen glances of admiration. There was a kind of electricity between the two of them – a white German lady and a long dead black man, in apartheid South Africa. Drifting into sleep near her, I would see her kneeling and talking to the saint, with her eyes fixed almost trance-like on his face. The flickering candlelight showed a glowing look on her face and a slight trace of a smile, and, feeling safe and contented, I would drift off to sleep.

I'd never seen a statue of a black saint before; you just don't see black saints and angels in churches. 'Sister, who is that?' I asked.

'That's my namesake,' Sister Mary Martin responded. 'He was from a city called Lima in Peru. He was born in the sixteenth century and died in the seventeenth century – a very long time ago. But if you have him as your friend, you'll find that nothing is impossible for him to help you with.' As she was talking, she was beaming. 'Let's kneel and talk to

Martin for just a few minutes, and then I'll tell you more about him and answer all your questions.'

She lit a candle, knelt, and said, 'Saint Martin, I've brought this young boy to meet you. His mother has fallen on hard times and has asked for my help. She's unable to care for him on her own and I'm asking you to care for them both. This boy, Patric, has been homeless most of his life, and cared for by a few families, and he has no friends. He would really like you to be his friend and for you to give him a helping hand.' Sister Mary Martin then turned to me and said, 'Patric would you like that? Ask Martin to be your friend and walk by your side.'

This may have seemed a normal enough conversation, except for one thing. Mary Martin was talking to a statue of a man who'd been dead for 400 years, and was asking me, a streetwise kid, to join in a situation that seemed to be from a make-believe world. Oh, I was used to saints by this stage in my life, and I was used to praying mantras, but not this kind of personal 'meet Martin' conversational stuff. And like he was really going to help me get through the kind of daily trials and tribulations that I went through?

Stunned, I kept silent.

'Go on, then,' Sister Mary Martin said, with a cherubic look on her face.

I looked up at the statue, and I swear I saw the fella wink as I blurted out the coaxed words, 'Please, Saint Martin, can you help me and be my friend . . . I really need help and someone to look after me.'

'Now, that wasn't hard to do,' said Sister Mary Martin. 'Just be sure to spend some time talking to Martin every night before you go to sleep.' She gave me a holy-card picture of San Martino de Porres Velázquez, then she sat me down and told me the whole story about St Martin.

His mother was an African woman who'd been enslaved. A Spanish military officer of some standing took his mother as an informal second wife and freed her from bondage. But Martin had grown up poor, homeless and an outcast before being given a home as a servant in a Dominican monastery. The penny was beginning to drop: Sister Mary Martin was trying to tell me that Martin and I had had similar life experiences.

'What does being enslaved mean?' I asked.

If Sister Mary Martin was taken aback by such a forthright question from a child, she didn't show it. Instead, she said, 'Do you see how hard your mother works for little pay? Now imagine having to work hard every day for no pay at all. And imagine that someone can buy or sell your mother, and that she had no freedom, and is owned by someone who can punish her and hurt her as he pleases. That's what it means to be someone's slave.

'The enslaved people were forcibly taken from Africa and Asia and packed into ships on voyages where many died. They were taken to new lands by Europeans and made to work hard under whippings and other cruel conditions. Often, they were chained and endured bad punishments.'

Sister Mary Martin said this with tears in her eyes. She looked at me and said, 'Most of your community here in District Six are the great-grandchildren of people who were brought from other parts of Africa and from Asia as slaves. You should learn more about slavery as you grow older if you want to understand more about why people are so poor and struggle against hardships now.'

I came to embrace this saint – the patron saint of the poor, and of those of multi-ethnic ancestry, like us Camissa Africans, of medics and health workers, of anti-racists, of homeless and abandoned children and orphans, and of veterinarians and those engaged with animal welfare – as a lifelong friend and muse, and called him Marty. Marty was said to be a shamanic figure and mystic with healing powers, and powers of bilocation – the ability to be in two places at the same time – and of levitation.

Marty became a regular part of my life; some would say he was my imaginary friend. As a kid in foster care and institutions, it was a great thing that Sister Mary Martin had done in introducing me to Marty, who became a friend, guide and muse. That conversational approach to which Sister Mary Martin had introduced me continued between us over the years.

It was also the first steps that led to my adoption later in life of a syncretic faith, with Catholic, Muslim, Buddhist and Afro-Asian shamanistic animist influences. This syncretism can be found all over the world along the old slave routes, within descendant communities. District Six too had such a mix of faiths, which influenced me from childhood into adulthood.

Marty filled an empty space within me with a much-needed voice of wisdom, and his story and his mother's story started me on journeys that linked me into an amazing ancestral world, and so much information and experiences that I was able to bring to greater audiences. What an amazing gift to have received via the serendipity of a woman responding kindly to my mother reaching out to her for help.

2

HELL:
THE SOJOURNER CHILD

One day, without warning, I was dropped off at the children's asylum where I would stay under conditions of near-incarceration for four excruciating years.

When I cast my mind back, I see myself as a small boy, with a little case in my hand, standing outside a spooky-looking building, feeling bewildered. My mother was sobbing, a repeat scenario that had occurred four times before in the short but winding eight years of my life to that point, as she handed me over with a little push to the stern-faced lady dressed in white – a nun of the order of the Sisters of Nazareth.

It was six by all clocks and the Angelus bells tolled as I stumbled forward. The nun grasped my hand, and with her other hand gesticulated to my mother that she should go. There was no goodbye. She shooed Mom away as though she were a pesky rodent – and then stood still as the bells chimed out while she started muttering a prayer, one I would learn by heart and repeat over and over again in my time there: 'The Angel of the Lord declared unto Mary: And she conceived of the Holy Spirit. Hail Mary, full of grace, the Lord is with thee . . .'

Finally breaking off her mantra, the nun released my hand to sign herself with the cross. Then, nearly yanking me off my feet, she grabbed me by the ear and began marching me down a long, echoing corridor. 'Come on you, little rascal, little mommy's boy,' she said. 'We don't like softies here. You will learn. By Jove, you will learn. Your mother says you want to be a priest. Just know this: I don't tolerate little holy Joes and pansies. Get on with you. Jesus, Mary and Joseph be my witness, you will learn, softie.'

Overcome with confusion and pain, I allowed myself to be dragged along. I could hear children's voices.

Suddenly I was pushed, stumbling, into a room.

Everyone suddenly went quiet.

'So where were we, before this little softie's wretched mother disturbed me?' the nun asked, casting her eyes around the little knot of about 25 evidently frightened children, ranging in age from about six to twelve. 'Oh yes! We were trying to get to the bottom of who it was that threw his food in the pig's pail. Is anyone ready to talk?'

When nobody said anything, the nun suddenly shouted, 'It looks like I will need to loosen your tongues!' From under her flowing white robes, she whipped out a hard black plastic rod. 'Line up! Out with your hands, knuckles up!' I was standing, staring, terrified, and she turned to me. 'You too, softie.'

Three astonishingly painful whacks on my knuckles, for an infraction for which I couldn't possibly have been responsible, were my introduction to this house of pain.

Today Nazareth House in Vredehoek, Cape Town, is a reformed institution that does good work, but in my time and for over a century before, it was a place of horrific abuses. Welfare societies sent children to Nazareth House as a 'place of care'; it was anything but. The 'Huis' was on large grounds in the centre of which was a ghostly-looking Victorian-style building and church. The stone-walled main building accommodated dying people in a hospice (men and women in separate wings), abandoned babies in a nursery, and needy children of various ages, also separated by gender.

We children were from an array of difficult circumstances, poor dysfunctional families, and the racially ambiguous world of the grey areas. Many were on their own in a difficult world. Most of the kids had been born old, and had seen and experienced things that no child should ever have to. Two young boys I knew from Lower Woodstock, for instance, had seen their mother being murdered in front of them – she'd been turning tricks and was murdered by a john in her bath. The children had received no counselling, and were dumped at the Huis by welfare officials.

The assumption of welfare officers was that children's asylums, especially church institutions, foster families and adoptive families offered a better deal than families considered dysfunctional, but these alternatives could prove to have even worse outcomes. Under the guise of 'caring institutions', the most abusive situations thrived, and the children had nobody to talk to or turn to for help.

Welfare officers sniffed out those in need of 'salvation and care', which exacted a great price. These officers, who were both needed and despised in our area, were seen as white upper-class people who looked down on us as low-born, ever ready to chastise poor mothers and remove children for reasons supposedly in the best interests of the child.

In our grey-areas scenario, welfare officers also engaged in apartheid social engineering, where children were taken away from their family if they were 'too light' in complexion and with 'European' features, if their family was considered 'Coloured'. And the opposite also applied, to a child who looked too dark in families that were light in complexion. It was considered 'in the best interest of the child' to remove a child from families where they 'did not belong'. This was the ambiguous world of those of us called 'halfnaatjies' – the people with 'the touch of the tar', as our families were labelled on the streets.

Racial integration, using the same amenities, living in the same house or areas, fraternising, and mixed sexual relations were from 1950 all considered unlawful, and there were laws that minutely detailed these offences. It was deemed criminal delinquency not to take 'race separation' and 'race purity' seriously, and grownups in our poor mixed society were seen as childlike offenders who had a criminal inability to tell right from wrong. Churches played a big part in this twisted approach.

* * * *

My main job, with one other boy, for all my years at the Huis, was to scrub half of the two-metre-wide hospital-style passage running through the complex. It was about 26 metres in length in total; our job was to scrub the half in the male section of the building, plus a small tiled external landing and stone stairs leading to a tarred roadway.

Every Saturday, and sometimes during the week, summer or winter, I would be on my hands and knees with a scrubbing brush, soap and a metal basin filled with water. The task would take all day, from 7 am to 3 pm – and for supposedly missing dirty spots, we were beaten with a hard plastic rod, sometimes kicked or punched, and had our ears pinched until the skin came off. I remember many an occasion when I was kicked flying into the basin of dirty water on the passage floor, with the rod raining blows on my head and back, leaving purple welts.

A cardinal sin was missing a black streak left behind by the rubber heel of a shoe. We learnt that Vim scouring powder, filched from the kitchen, would deal with these marks where sheer elbow grease wouldn't – but the nuns were always one step ahead of us. Staring us in the eye, the sister would stoop and run her finger across a dried tile, then rub her finger across her thumb, alert for the grittiness of dried Vim. If she felt it, the beating began.

Other children cleared rocks from the fields, washed windows, polished wooden floors, scrubbed the floor of the eating hall and scullery, cleaned the rubbish bins, emptied the pigs' pails or (mainly the girls) worked in a Dickensian laundry that serviced the entire establishment. There were no cleaners, servants or groundsmen: we, society's throwaway children, were the labourers.

Rich benefactors of the institution sometimes came to use the chapel and grounds for weddings and other occasions, when we children were expected to render service, or we'd be locked away so that we weren't an embarrassment. We were known by a number and a surname only, and we had no personal possessions. We were dressed in a kind of prisoner garb – khaki, with brown jerseys – and we usually went barefoot.

The motto of our carers was 'spare the rod and spoil the child'. The two nuns caring for the boys each carried one of those hard plastic rods, about 40 centimetres long, up the sleeve of her habit, out of view. When a beating was required, she would let it slide down into her hand and strike, all in one movement. And the nuns were indiscriminate about beatings, frenziedly striking the defenceless children on their legs, arms, back, buttocks and head. Those Irish women, emotionless and tough, hypocritical and in some cases actually mentally deranged, were acting out the same regimen they'd endured as children. I once watched a nun bash a child viciously and repeatedly on the head with the metal handle of a knife until blood poured out.

Along with the beating would go a litany of religious cursing – 'by Jove', 'Jesus, Mary and Joseph', 'God damn you to hell', 'you little son of a harlot'. Those of us with mothers would hear that they were worthless fallen women, 'sluts', 'whores', 'trash', 'good-for-nothings'; children whose mothers had died had 'got what was coming to them'.

In the basement was a row of toilets without doors, and a row of open cold-water showers. Boys older than seven had to shower in cold water, even in the dead of winter – the nuns believed that warm water would sexually stimulate males. We also had to wear a thin green cloth called a slip around our waists, as nudity wasn't allowed.

If we were sick, we went without food, because it was believed that if you were sick, you lost your appetite, and thus, anybody with an appetite couldn't be sick.

Every Sunday two slices of fresh bread per child were stacked on a wooden tray and handed out. At the end of the meal, all unconsumed bits were collected, and the following morning those messy pieces were put on the wooden tray again, the balance being made up with slices of bread. As each day passed, there would be fewer and fewer slices and more and more of the mess of bits and pieces. At the end of week, whatever was left was added to a 'pudding' that was served after Saturday dinner.

Sometimes, in desperation, kids threw away rotten food rather than eat it. There were two separate bins, one for general rubbish and one for organic leftovers, or the 'pig pail', as it was called. Whichever bin the food was found in, it would already be covered with muck. The discarded food would be taken out of the bin and the 'culprit' would be forced to consume it in front of everyone. The child would almost always vomit in the process, and he would be forced to eat the vomit too.

A favourite form of mass punishment by the nuns was interrogation sessions over ridiculous infringements, where we would be collectively beaten on our knuckles with the hard plastic rod, on the hour, while having to stand still in one spot and in rows for hours on end and sometimes days in succession. The flesh would be pulled from our ears, we would be yanked up off the ground by our hair, and often we were beaten with a fist in the face. I once lost a tooth that way.

Ultimately the culprit would be outed, or a fall guy would take the culprit's place. Then, in addition to the culprit getting severely thrashed and punished in other ways, we would all get beaten again for not having given up the culprit sooner.

Welfare officials who came to inspect the institution would have the wool pulled over their eyes with elaborate tricks and showmanship by our carers. Welfare department financial grants were at stake. Before the child welfare came, the nuns handed out normal clothes and shoes for us to wear. All the tin cups and plates were stored away, and tablecloths, cutlery and proper plates, cups and tablecloths were laid out; flower arrangements appeared. It was like setting up a film set. Immediately after the officials had left, the clothes would be taken back and all the plates, cutlery, tablecloths and floral arrangements were removed and returned to storage.

A few children, me included, were coached on what to say, and threatened in advance with violence if we gave the game away to the welfare inspectors. The carers would stand behind the welfare officers when they spoke to us, and the nun would show us her fist or bare her teeth if we were thought to be creating a problem and not smiling.

There was little time for play or for us just to be children. On the rare occasions that we weren't doing manual chores, we'd be herded onto a field, where we would stand around talking to each other, walking up and down, scavenging for vrietangs, suurangs and denne pitjies in the grass – the soft buds of groundcover, the sour stems of wild sorrel and pine-cone kernels, collectively known as veldkos (field-food). It was like a prison-yard scenario: there were no balls to kick around, or anything else for us to do. Sometimes some of us would be sent to the kitchen to bring food, then we'd eat sitting on the ground.

Alternatively, mainly in winter, we were locked in the dimly lit basement, where we sat in a square and had to take turns telling stories or singing or making up jokes, or sometimes having boxing matches. The stories, songs and jokes would often reflect the child's social reality back at home.

This was the kind of song a child about my age might have sung.

I was standing on the corner
With my blue suede shoes.
Along came a copper,
Singing the blues.
He looked to the left,
He looked to the right,
Then he took out his dagga pill
And he asked me for a light.
It's a ducktail boogie,
A ducktail boogie,
Yeah, yeah.
I was standing on the corner
With my razor and coat.
Along came a copper
So I slit his throat.
But the copper woke up.
He put me to sleep
And I was taken for a ride
in the Boere's jeep.
It's a ducktail boogie,
Yeah, a ducktail boogie,
Yeah, yeah, yeah.

In that same basement the exercise of 'pairing shoes' took place, when charities collected and passed on secondhand shoes to us 'poor-unfortunates'. The shoes were dumped out into a pile on the floor, and on the word 'go', we would scramble to first find one shoe that fit, and then to find its pair. Fights broke out and bullies dominated. If you were lucky, you would find a reasonable pair, and then you'd fight to hold onto what you'd found.

Under these conditions we received what passed for an education. A nun assisted by a 'Coloured' lady teacher gave us lessons, and for standards four and five (now grades six and seven) we were sent to a small Catholic school in Hatfield Street run by two Marist brothers who presided over four classrooms. One of the brothers was a sex predator and we few boys from the children's asylum were easy prey.

The only form of escape I had was the short time when we had to go to prayer or confession in the chapel, and I could just sit and think under the guise of praying. The chapel afforded me a fantasy place – a place to wander through the labyrinth of my life thus far. Important District Six lessons were digested during my sessions in the chapel and served me well for the rest of my life. I was a child who did much brooding; contemplativeness became very important to me. To this day I love the peacefulness of temples and mosques and churches.

* * * *

Another of my jobs was to accompany one of the nuns on the rounds of locking the doors and windows at night, and final inspections of work and bathing areas.

One evening, as we descended the dark stairs to the basement ablution and laundry area, we could hear singing and splashing. We peered into the room and spotted a child, Brian, in the bath, which was about two and a half square metres, cemented and tiled like a pool. As mentioned, only children under seven years could have supervised warm water baths. It had been Brian's job that day to wash all the socks and underpants of the boys, hang them out to dry, then pair them. By the time he'd finished, all had vacated the ablutions room in the basement, so Brian had decided to take the unheard-of liberty of having a warm bath.

The nun crept up on the blissfully unsuspecting boy. 'Brian Hendricks!' she screamed, and Brian got such a fright that he sprang up, stark naked.

The nun, beside herself with outrage, went totally berserk. The hard plastic rod appeared from her sleeve and she beat Brian mercilessly; even when he slipped and fell back into the bath, she continued raining down blows on his body. 'By Jove, you little devil, how dare you stand naked before me?' she shrieked as she wielded the rod. 'I will show you! Jesus, Mary and Joseph, so help me, send this little demon to hell and let him burn!'

I was shaking and petrified at this rage and violence. But the terror wasn't just an occasional incident. It was an everyday affair, and the cruelty and backward thinking of this institution robbed us of our childhood.

Shy and retreating, another boy, Ben, had a combination of features that I came to learn were things that bullies delight in exploiting to inflict terrible pain on their victims: ginger hair and freckles, and an effeminate way of speaking and walking. The nuns started the abusive name-calling and the children followed suit, particularly the bullies: Ben was called Mof-Kop, Moffie, Carrot Kop, Pansy, Girlie, Sissy-Boy and so on.

There was one thing that stood out for me about Ben when he was being brutalised: while other kids would scream and cry loudly, Ben didn't make any noise. His face would go bright red, and tears would run down his cheeks, and his mouth would be open, but no sound would emerge. This would enrage the carers, who would accuse him of insolence and try to beat a noise out of him.

I once watched in horror as Ben's elder brother, Steve, went down on his knees, begging the frenzied nun to stop beating his brother and beat him instead. It was gut-wrenching and it hardened my heart. I found myself clenching my hands into a fist and shaking with suppressed rage. I pulled young Ben aside and told him to stand up for himself. 'Don't allow people to treat you like a doormat!' I said. 'You're their equal! Tell them, "I'm as good as you!" Never be down at heel and fight the mockery with your own fire. You are as God has made you.'

After I left the asylum, I heard that Ben was thrown out after being caught in the toilets with an old man molesting him. The old men, though residing in segregated quarters, often tried to lure the boys with sweets and then sexually abuse them, and Ben was a target of enticement by those who seemed to offer love and care.

There were acts of defiance too. I remember when Georgie, on a dare, went into the confessional and recited one of our basement rhymes: 'Father, father, I confess: in my pants I made a mess! Son, son, what have you done? I took a piece of paper, and I wiped my bum!'

The priest flung open his door with a bang, then yanked open the confessant side, grabbed Georgie off the floor by the ears, and marched him out of the church, screaming while Georgie squealed. From outside we heard many whacks. The story was repeated regularly to much laughter and Georgie became a little hero.

A few of us organised ourselves into small gangs for protection in numbers, particularly against the bullies who operated with the nuns – a couple of hardened brothers from Devon and Dublin streets in Woodstock. Those expected to rat out others were aware that if they spoke out, they would get a thrashing from the organised kids, so they were in a scenario of Hobson's choice.

I saw my mother briefly once every two months, and during the mid-year and year-end school breaks, when I'd be allowed out and accompany her to work in District Six. But for those kids who didn't have a parent with whom to spend those short breaks, they experienced nightmares with unvetted 'foster carers'.

People with ill intent would volunteer to take poor-unfortunates like ourselves for a holiday break in a real 'loving home', and then have their wicked way. Nobody would believe a poor-unfortunate reject child. Georgie, for example, was taken into bed by a man and his wife, who began to molest him; Georgie bit the man on his member and ran away, and the cops found him and brought him back to the asylum.

Being deprived of food, locked away in a basement, deprived of lights at night, deprived of visitors, deprived of outings, forced to endure days of silence, being given extra work details, and all the punishments and humiliations never left us. Many of the children from this place we called the Huis went on into adulthood emotionally crippled and ended up as jail inmates or destitute street people, or met early deaths.

Years later I saw gentle ginger-headed Ben from afar. He saw me too, and I called after him. I caught his expression of pain and embarrassment as he walked quickly away, picking up the pace in that same mincing step I remembered. He probably wanted to leave that awful terror behind.

Another time, this fella came up to me, eyes lowered and hand outstretched, asking if I had some small change to spare. Though he looked down and out and much older than I, there was something about him that made me look more closely, and I recognised him as Phillip, one of the lads who was with me in the children's asylum. He was the younger of the two brothers from Woodstock who'd witnessed their mother's murder. 'Phillip! It's me, Patric, from the Huis long ago,' I said.

Phillip looked up at me with a whisper of a smile on his face. 'I heard that you became a somebody,' he said, and I choked up. As children we'd talked about the future and what we wanted to be, and he'd wanted to be an airman navigator or pilot. He'd wanted to see the world. As a teen, he'd been meticulous about how he dressed and looked, styling his hair overnight with a 'swirl-kous' (a woman's stocking worn on the head while sleeping). But he'd only ever got to navigate the streets, battling to survive one day at a time.

Phillip told me about his brother's death by suicide, and how he'd been living for decades on the streets, since he'd left school. He'd had repeated treatment for mental illness and couldn't hold down a job. I heard later that Phillip had succumbed to illness and died sleeping in a doorway on cardboard, in the dead of winter.

As one female ex-inmate of the asylum, now living in Australia and in her 70s, once pondered in a letter to me, 'Should we petition for restitution? Nah! I don't think that I'll ever be paid for all the floors I polished, the laundry I did, the ironing, the feeding of the aged and cleaning of their rooms, the kitchen duties and the stock-taking exercises, the entertainment I participated in, and the heavenly choir that brought in all the donations on a Sunday, or the constant beatings and emotional abuse.' This same woman once had her hands tied behind her back and wet socks stuffed into her mouth, then was left on her back in a bath with the water running, while a nun ranted in abusive language about

Jezebels. Only when the water covered her mouth and nose and she lost consciousness was she yanked up by the hair.

In the Irish Republic, the state set up a commission into abuses in religious institutions – the Ryan Commission – the report of which was published in 2009 and consisted of twelve volumes of testimonies of psychological and sexual abuse, torture and hidden death that many in Ireland said was comparable only to what had occurred in Nazi concentration camps during the Second World War. It failed to include the overseas missions, including the missions in South Africa.

* * * *

When I was eight, I got seriously sick with jaundice and was bedridden for six weeks. My mother had to care for me until I recovered, and she had no option but to beg her landlady, Mona, for me to be able to stay with her in her rented room until she could make another plan.

The conditions imposed by Mona required that I wasn't seen or heard. This meant that I couldn't leave the room and I maintained strict silence, so for a month and a half I was a mouse, remaining quietly in my bed while my mother went off to work each day. I didn't see a soul – not even the landlady. I learnt to cope with solitude.

My mother let me listen to her little portable wireless through earphones – her most prized possession. I had some Oros orange concentrate, a jug of water and some cracker biscuits to nibble on.

My mother always bought the *Weekend Argus*, late final edition, partly because she sometimes played the gee-gees and the newspaper carried news on the races. She also bought me a picture-magazine called *True Africa*, which had stories about Chunky Charlie, Satana, and Samson and the Leopardmen. I would get totally engrossed in these childhood heroes, who were all black men and women with extraordinary skills.

At one stage, there was a competition in the *Saturday Argus* children's section where you could send in a drawing of your mother, and if it got published, you won R1. I admired the fact that my mother was a kind of tough hero who worked long, hard days for little reward, so I titled the drawing 'Working Mom'. My drawing was published, and I got my R1 prize money, but I remember being angry that they'd renamed it – 'Mom in Boots'. They had interpreted my child's version of her shoes as boots.

There was also a time when the *Weekend Argus* ran a weekly illustrated mini-history featuring profiles of great South African leaders in the form of cartoon strips, which included John Dube, the founding president of the South African Native National Congress, which became the ANC; Sol Plaatje, a founding member and first general-secretary of the South African Native National Congress; Clements Kadalie, South Africa's first black national trade union leader; and politician and physician Dr Abdullah Abdurahman, who was the first 'Coloured' city councillor of Cape Town, and the first ever 'Coloured' South African to win election to a public body. My mother assisted me in collecting the entire series. This also became part of my learning curve as a child.

Shortly after my recovery, we went to stay with May, her husband and her first three kids in Cole Street; May gave birth to two more children while they lived there. This was in a little enclave on the border of Salt River and Observatory. The area, part industrial and part residential for people below the poverty line, ran from Cole Street below Lower Main Road, down to the railway shunting yards and factories, and extended lower down towards Chatham Road and the Palace bioscope. It had its own sub-identity of families who'd confounded apartheid, largely people who had over the previous decades married across what became 'the colour bar'. The families were from the lowest strata of the working class – 'poor white' and 'Coloured'. May was married first to an Afrikaner, who died young, and then to an immigrant seaman from England. They were considered 'poor whites'; May had been registered 'European' at birth and her children were classified 'white'. When her children grew up, the three boys married 'Coloured', Nama and Xhosa women, while one of the girls married an Afrikaner and the other remained single. The grandchildren are Camissa Africans.

The terraced homes in that Salt River/Observatory enclave, owned by a few Jewish landlords, were in a ghastly state of disrepair. (In our time Jewish people owned whole districts of rent-controlled dilapidated properties. In District Six, Woodstock and Salt River, the white people who affected every part of our lives weren't Boers, they were Jewish.) An unwritten understanding prevailed whereby they carried out no repairs but kept the rentals low. Walking down the street, we could see through holes in the yellowed walls into people's homes; the roofs were rusted and leaked huge amounts of water into homes in winter; the floorboards were rotten.

It was an area well known to police and welfare officers whom people feared would steal their children from them; rats were not the only pests with which people wrestled. We lived in limbo, seldom venturing out of the area. Our way of living and thinking was cut off from the bigger South African picture.

My memories of the place are still vivid. Here, children played football and cricket in the streets, often breaking windows; if this happened to one in May's house, she would keep the ball.

Some youngsters belonged to gangs and there would be street fights, sometimes with fatalities. I remember one young lad from the Smee family who was killed when his opponent stabbed him in the eye with a screwdriver. His heart was used in a heart-transplant operation.

There were also rival families: adults, children and even their dogs went for each other. My sister May's husband would shout 'Bioscope!' and we'd run to take up positions at the windows to watch the barney.

In winter when it was rainy and cold, we burnt paraffin heaters for warmth, and piled on jackets, coats and blankets to keep warm. My sister had four dogs, and each bed had a dog to snuggle at our feet. It was a depressing place during winters: for weeks on end, the rain poured down, causing little rivers in the streets because of blocked drains and it washing the rubbish out of the lanes between the houses into the street. The children would be sick with influenza, croup and asthma.

The tiny bathroom had a wood-fired geyser. The children would go to a carpentry factory nearby and wait for wood offcuts to burn for hot water, which was supplemented by heating water in a large empty paraffin tin perched on a primus burner. My mother and I also heated water that way in our room, and had basin-baths using a large metal tub: you would soap up, then stand in the tub and pour water over yourself to rinse off. We had a covered bucket toilet in the room. And Mom also cooked in that room, which was our bedroom, bathroom and kitchen all in one.

There was never enough money, but our elders knew how to stretch money to ensure there was food on the plate. On Friday evenings, when my mother came home from her job at the laundry in District Six, and later at the laundry in Salt River, it was kuite (fish roe) and bread for supper. On Saturday it was walkies (chicken feet) and giblets. On some lucky Sundays it was pot-roast chicken or meat and pot-roast potatoes; later, when my mom was able to afford a paraffin oven, we had the luxury of oven roasts.

During the week we ate tasty bredies (stews) and curries. My mother grew her own chillies as potted plants. She would invoke a common Cape working-class expression, that anything could be made on 'spek 'n boontjies' (literally, bits of fat, animal skins and beans), meaning that a little can go a long way. And offal was a regular part of our diet.

When we fell on hard times, 'waiting for our ship to come in', as Mom would say, we kids would be sent to the kindly butcher nearby to buy five cents' worth of 'dog bones'. The butcher knew they weren't for the dogs and would make sure he gave us particularly meaty bones. With ten cents' worth of 'greens' from the corner store, and some spices, we'd have the tastiest of meals.

The corner shop was run by an Indian family who practised their own form of benevolence. They allowed poor families to buy 'on the book' and pay when they had money. Down on Lower Main Road was Safodien's, a Cape Muslim vegetable and fruit shop, where items were sold according to what you could afford – for example, five cents' worth of tomatoes – rather than by weight and a set price. This is very similar to how spaza shops operate now.

For us kids, the streets were our playground. We'd make go-carts out of boxes and ball-bearings, and we played kerem, a boardgame also made of scrap wood. We'd walk to Woodstock Beach to play and swim in the ice-cold water. When the Cape Town docks were extended from Duncan Docks to a new container dock called Ben Schoeman Docks, Woodstock Beach disappeared – poor Camissa African people were robbed of a playground.

Salt River had originally been an expansive estuary and marshland with two rivers, the Liesbeek and Black, entering it at different ends, and with a narrow shallow crossing called Vaarsche Drift. In the early 1960s our favourite pastime was to make a net with cloth tied to the end of a pole to catch fish that we called guppies in the Liesbeek River.

By the end of that decade, the river had been straightened and canalised where it ran through the wealthier suburbs, and a new terrain created, taking away our natural playground. From 1960 to 1967, over a kilometre of river was cut off in 1968 and replaced by a newly created stretch of canalised waterway going past the Royal Observatory.

The Liesbeek Park Recreation Club had been built in 1939 for white railway workers, and much of the area, which had been wild waterlogged marshland for centuries, was dug out, the soil removed and replaced with waste materials including building rubble from demolitions where people were forced out by the Group Areas Act. This is one of Cape Town's many dirty little secrets.

With the apartheid drive to separate and control people, this enclave where we lived, existing as it did on the border between Salt River, declared a 'Coloured' group area, and Observatory, a 'White' group area, became zoned for industrial development. At first, nobody took the new race demarcation laws seriously. Because of undereducation, most of the residents lived under the radar, working at jobs that nobody else vied for, unemployed or doing odd jobs, or working at sea. There were also women who were 'looked after' by visiting seamen, usually Asians, as regular port-of-call partners; they were known as 'sugar girls' and often had children from such seamen.

I was quite young but remember at least one case of a teen couple in our community who were separated by being declared as 'Coloured' and 'White'. They couldn't cope with the pressures threatening to separate them, so the boy jumped in front of an oncoming train at Salt

River station. His blood merged with the plum-coloured train and the rust-coloured sleepers and rails. His parents' eyes, wet and empty, gazed, staring ahead, when given the news. The tears that rolled down quietly rusted many of our hearts forever.

So that neighbourhood of my childhood just disappeared, a piece of history and heritage wiped from memory. Today those many long rows of dingy dilapidated terraced houses are no more, although May's rented house – the only standalone house in the street – is still there.

3

YOUTH: EARLY LEARNINGS AND PART-TIME WORK

My mother's mainstay, her sister, my Aunty Doll, returned from London with my cousin Louisa and her two grandchildren in 1967. Life had been too tough in London's East End, and they'd decided to rather brave it out in South Africa.

Louisa, who we all called Toekies, was diagnosed with cancer and died, and Aunty Doll then had to work and take care of her grandchildren. She got a job as a toilet attendant for the female facilities in the panhandle at Castle Bridge.

At the bottom of Hanover Street was the area historically known as Castle Bridge, a beautiful triangular oasis shaded by trees, named after the place where a bridge once crossed the Castle moat. Cape Town once had the Camissa river system, which comprised many springs, streams and a forked river which flowed into the sea. From 1660 the colonial authorities started building aqueducts and canals to harness and redirect the water, and in places built the first bridges over the river and streams. By the mid-1800s the Camissa river system was radically reconfigured into a series of canals: Buiten-Singel, Buitenkant, Kasteel Sloot, Kaisergracht and Buitengracht. In those years, to get to District Six, you had to cross several of these canals, hence the suburb's old name, 'Kanaldorp'.

From 1860 the Camissa river system was steadily driven into underground tunnels which still exist today, and water pumps were erected to supply water across the city. An outbreak of the plague, spread by rats living in the remaining waterways, at the beginning of the twentieth century, finally got rid of the last of the openly flowing Camissa waterways, except for the restored moats around the Castle of Good Hope and the pools within.

The public toilets at Castle Bridge, one for females and one for males, weren't segregated by race. The toilets were kept in pristine condition by its two guardians, Doll van Rooy, the 'spook lady', and Abubaker Jaffa, the khalifa. Doll was very pale, like a ghost, while Jaffa was very dark in complexion; both would have given you a fright if they'd jumped out at you in the dark. Both were also very sage and wise, and both could spin a good yarn that had listeners in stitches.

The city council's official grand name for the toilets was 'chalets' and those employed to take care of the toilets were called 'chalet-keepers'. In our local Cape patois, a toilet is called a jamang, related to the Indonesian word jambang, meaning 'pot', so, for us, Aunty Doll was the jamang-keeper.

The jamang chalet of Castle Bridge became a very special place in District Six because of those spiritualist guardians: my Aunty Doll, a smoker with a rasping laugh, was a clairvoyant and gifted spiritual guide, and everyone would come for consultations with her at her chalet on the female side of the jamang, while Mr Jaffa, a khalifa who presided over ratiep ceremonies (a trance-linked art form practised by some Muslims that is rooted in Sufism) was also a deeply spiritual man who led a Sufi group practising the very old Southeast Asian and Indian ratiep in which, in a high state of spiritual trance, devotees can walk on hot coals, pierce themselves with skewers and draw sharp swords over their bodies without bloodshed or harm. Aunty Doll and Mr Jaffa were two of a kind, who enjoyed each other's company and who respected each other and their spiritual gifts, sharing a little oasis in a very cruel and demeaning world.

My Aunty Doll had a welcoming array of African violets, ferns and chilli plants in the doorway and lobby just as you entered the chalet, where she would sit on her chair like a queen on her throne, flanked by vegetation handmaidens. When the company inspectors came around to the laundry shop, I would sometimes go down to sit with Aunty Doll and take in her world, listening to her telling the fortunes of her visitors by reading tea leaves or studying their palms. She often spoke of her excursions in the spirit realm. I loved her world, which gave me a sense of belonging.

Aunty Doll and Mr Jaffa were my angels to balance out the many demons who did me so much harm in my other world of the children's asylum.

The humourist Mr Jaffa would say that the chalet at Castle Bridge was a place of racial harmony under apartheid, because it was a great equaliser, where all men stood shoulder to shoulder at the urinals, regardless of colour, all aiming percy at the porcelain and breathing a sigh of relief and happiness as their waste went down the same drain. And, in fact, the chalets survived apartheid, only having been demolished in 2020 as a result of vandalism, and replaced by a fenced-off mini-park.

* * * *

On 11 February 1966, District Six was declared a whites-only area under the Group Areas Act, and within two years forced removals of all people classified 'Coloured' were in full swing. Sixty thousand people were systematically cleared, street by street, removed to the new 'Coloured' suburbs many kilometres away on the windswept and desolate Cape Flats, as buildings were razed to the ground. District Six was renamed Zonnebloem.

In those years, I remember how people talked in worried tones about the creeping destruction, of the imminent ethnic cleansing under the Group Areas Act and the building of the new freeway, the Eastern Boulevard (today's Nelson Mandela Boulevard). The spectre of destruction and forced removals stifled that happy spirit and slowly the music died. Something inside of me also died when I could no longer go to that world. By the time I entered my teens, large parts of District Six were nothing but rubble, broken bricks, twisted metal and the colours of rust that dominated my childhood. The last of the removals took place as late as 1986.

The same forced removals took place across the city environs, into the Cape Peninsula and countryside towns. Once reasonably integrated southern and northern suburbs were cleansed of people classified as 'Coloured', 'Indian' and 'Native/Bantu/Black'.

People were moved in council trucks or private bakkies. The little muisnes (mouse nests) houses built on the sandy Cape Flats had tiny rooms that couldn't accommodate everything the families brought. If your goods couldn't fit on the trucks or in your new abode, you'd have to sell them to the secondhand dealers or auctioneers, who would hang around waiting for the pickings from those undergoing forced removals. To this day people find their old prize possessions in strange places.

People who owned property were forced to sell for peanuts, and white people moved into the vacated and expropriated homes that weren't demolished, scoring cheap although often very highly valued houses, and sometimes the antique contents of those homes too.

The City of Cape Town has never apologised or taken responsibility for paying reparations. There's never been a land and homes tribunal to deal with this horrific part of the city's history. A half-baked land-restitution process for property owners has been dismally managed. But the real situation was that most of the 60 000 people forcibly removed from District Six were tenants rather than homeowners; there has been no restitution for them.

The displaced now have hundreds of thousands of descendants, many of whom are backyard dwellers, or living in shacks, or are homeless street people. They have not only never received justice, they're also increasingly victimised by the aggression of the City of Cape Town police.

* * * *

I left the Huis for good in 1968, along with a fellow inmate we called Dodger. Dodger was an abandoned kid who'd been at the Huis much longer than me. I at least had a sometimes-mother, but Dodger had nobody. The welfare department and the Catholic St Vincent de Paul Society continued to look after our upkeep until the age of 16.

We were re-institutionalised at an industrial trade school, the Salesian

Institute on the corner of Chiappini Street and Somerset Road in Cape Town, where all the Huis's male children were sent for pre-apprenticeship training in trades such as cabinetmaking, fitting and turning, and printing.

The Salesians of Don Bosco, also known as Bosconians, was established in Valdocco in Turin in 1859 by John 'Don' Bosco to provide a mission to the many youths moving from rural Italy into the city to find work in factories. These youth at risk often were barely eking out an existence, and living rough on the streets. In 1910 the Salesian rector-general sent a group of five pioneers to South Africa to teach printing, bookbinding and joinery, the first of several trades to be taught to poor and needy boys, many of whom were orphans, and all of whom needed a trade skill with which to earn a living.

The time I spent at the trade school was formative. A small group of dedicated men helped to mould me to be the person I am. 'Don Bosco's men' were Paul, Thomas, Peter (Motchie), Victor, Tom, Vincent (Vinny), Daniel, Patrick, Duffy, Brian, Ahern, Melly, Antonio (Bull) and Dominic (Mole), a bunch of religious brothers, priests and laymen who were industrial artisans and teachers.

One of these, Brother Paul, was a quiet and reclusive, gentle soul, although he spoke in a fast and abrupt manner. He'd been part of the institution since the end of the 1920s, in an administrative household services position, and always ensured that everything we had was numbered. He had an incredible memory and could match a face with a number and a year of intake: according to him, all the boys had the same name, Joseph, but were distinguishable by a number and year. I was one of around sixty Josephs; to Paul, I was Joseph number 36 of 1969.

In a chalk-and-cheese comparison with my four hellish years at the Huis, at the Salesian Institute we were treated with deep respect. Coming from the working class and poverty was seen as something to be proud of, as we were survivors of life's hard knocks. And to learn a trade was seen as qualifying yourself to play an important role in society. This lifted a heavy weight from my shoulders.

We followed training courses in various trades, which included trade theory, technical drawing, applied mathematics and science, languages and history. For half of our time we were in overalls at workbenches and machines; these same workshops brought in some income to cover our schooling, along with welfare grants, as well as fees from the very few who had parents who could contribute.

I was also given basic training in political literacy and trade union literacy. We were told that it was our duty to join a trade union once we were in employment, and that it was our duty to fight for non-racial trade unions and workers' rights for all. It was also our duty to fight for social justice in all areas of society, and for an end to pass laws, and for the establishment of a democracy with universal suffrage.

We were shown films from around the world about the struggles of people and introduced to worker leaders like American founder of the Catholic Worker's Movement Dorothy Day and Martin Luther King in the US civil-rights movement.

We were also introduced to what was called 'preparation for a happy death', which was held on the last Friday of every month. It was a mass and a reflection time. It included a homily that was always on the theme of being ready to die at any time and be able to say that because you'd lived, you'd lived for something and left a legacy for future generations. This, we were taught, was the foundation for happiness in death: our social responsibility and social contribution were emphasised as being the contributors to a happy death.

The teaching and mentoring community were known as the 'commies' (community) and we were the 'young men'. The commies spent not just teaching time but also recreational time with us, always engaging with us. There wasn't in-your-face discipline, but rather a quiet mutual-respect kind of order that recognised that we weren't just any kids: we'd become grownups before our years because of social circumstances. We were treated accordingly and instilled with social responsibility towards each other and towards the commies, and indeed towards society. Along with our manual-work trades education, we were encouraged to read and take an interest in social affairs, and we were exposed to a bigger picture in life.

There was no corporal punishment at this institution. If there was a serious clash between boys, or between a boy and a teacher, the rector produced two pairs of boxing gloves, and a time was designated for a refereed boxing match down in one corner of the grounds. I remember once when an altercation got physical in one of our classes between the teacher and one of the boys, the two were rolling on the floor in a scrap that had to be stopped by the rector. They were given the 'shake hands or take up the boxing gloves' option. They took the gloves and although the boy was a bit of a streetfighter, he came up short.

It was the same with smoking. It was deemed unhealthy that it happened in secret in the toilets, so it was encouraged that it be done in the open, but only in a designated spot.

There was one, most important, rule that Don Bosco's men practised as a fundamental to the Bosconian way: if there was one really bad apple in the box, and it was deemed irredeemable, it had to be taken out of the box. It was believed that it took one rotten apple to contaminate the others in the box. This was done on occasion, such as when habitual antisocial or criminal behaviour occurred, and every effort had been made through counselling, but to no avail. Where antisocial behaviours and ill-discipline threatened to spread into the social community of the institute and pose a threat to social cohesion, action was taken to remove the 'bad apple'. But even then, I know of cases where boys ended up in jail, and one of Bosco's men would go bail them out and try again to put them on the right path.

We were all given personal attention and a level of care that I'd never experienced until then. Perhaps surprisingly, both Dodger and I found it difficult to handle the freedom and respect shown to us – that's what institutionalisation does to you. And we were also both unable to complete a full education – the state removed the welfare subsidies of schools that wouldn't do the bidding of the regime and strictly follow apartheid prescripts as to who could and could not attend, and this was to be the fate of the Salesian Institute.

In any case, Dodger just didn't have it in him to adjust. He went on to lead a life of crime and was in and out of prison; institutions remained his home. He died young. Many years have flown by and I still miss him. He always introduced himself by saying, 'Pleased to meet you. I'm a thief.'

For me, my mother had inculcated a self-sufficiency. When she'd had any time on her hands after work, she'd produced things on her sewing machine, and she often made ends meet by knitting and crocheting items that I sold door to door. While I hawked my mom's wares, I wasn't allowed to beg: my mother strictly forbade me from ever asking people for money or from accepting any money from someone for free.

* * * *

Father Vinny O'Gorman cast the official history textbook into the bin on my first day of his history class when I was thirteen years old. He declared it to be rubbish and propaganda, and said that he would teach us about being discerning in navigating different versions of history and to gain what he called perspectives.

In this way, the Salesian brothers dared to teach and mentor in a nonconformist manner to equip youth for the rigours of a very difficult South African environment. They used the ideas of Brazilian educator Paulo Freire, specifically that of seeing education as the ticket to freedom or liberation, and employing 'project-based' education that focused on thinking skills and problem-solving.

The foundational beliefs that emerged from my early adverse life experience were built on in this way, and I was helped to attain an intellectual framework and analytical skills for navigating the future and, in my case, a resistance road. I was strongly influenced by Latin American liberation theology that placed overcoming poverty at its centre. Two personalities that had a profound effect on me at that time were young seminarian Nestor Paz and priest Camilo Torres.

Radical Catholic socialists, both lost their lives following the course of their convictions as guerrilla soldiers in Bolivia and Colombia, respectively – both in their first combat actions. Paz left us his diary as inspiration and Father Camilo left us many sermons. The inspiration of these men and the lives they led would later lead to my joining the liberation struggle and taking up arms against the apartheid state.

At that time, with a poor formal education (I'd attained only a junior certificate – standard eight; today's grade ten), I educated myself by being an avid reader. I discovered a treasure trove of books through the Catholic bookshop at St Mary's Cathedral and the Catholic repository at the Salesian Institute, which had somehow got past the eye of the censors. These books contained lengthy quotations and lessons from leading historical and contemporary socialist figures, and in this way I was also introduced to Peruvian philosopher Gustavo Gutiérrez, one of the founders of Latin American liberation theology; Argentine Methodist theologian José Bonino; Nicaraguan priest, politician and liberation theologian Ernesto Cardenal; Mexican Christian communist militant and theologian José Porfirio Miranda; Brazilian theologian Sister Ivone Gebara; Brazilian archbishop and advocate of liberation theology Hélder Câmara; former Catholic priest Leonardo Boff, known for his support for Latin American liberation theology; Brazilian Catholic theologian Hugo Assmann, who helped develop the ideas surrounding liberation theology; Sister Maura Clarke, who served as a missionary in Nicaragua and El Salvador; Uruguayan theologian Beatriz Melano Couch; Archbishop Óscar Romero of San Salvador; and others. And through studying the Latin American liberation theologians, I also got to know more about the Cuban struggles of José Julián Martí Pérez, Che Guevara and Fidel Castro.

Through these works I learnt a theology of liberation and about the power of the poor in history. I began to explore a different approach to history – the silenced history. This literature acted as a bridge to the world of black theology, as well as African literature and poetry, and I also read about China and Vietnam and its cultures and peoples, and their struggles too.

My vocabulary was limited, and these works had many words I didn't understand: I often consulted a dictionary.

* * * *

During my stint at the Institute, I spent much of my time living on the premises. Most of us lived there, sleeping in a long attic room in the roof of the wonderful old Italian-style building, in rows of metal-framed beds. During the earthquake of 1969 (centred on the rural town of Tulbagh, 120 kilometres north of Cape Town; but felt as far away as Durban, 1 600 kilometres up the coast), I remember all the beds sliding together.

My mother, through her winnings on a horse-racing bet, had managed to buy herself a small semi-detached house in Woodstock, which she soon sold to buy a similar little semi-detached house nearer to May and family. So, on term breaks during the year, I'd spend a few days at a time with her and with May.

On the weekends, Father Vinny would organise jobs for some of us as ushers at Hartleyvale football stadium in Observatory on a Friday night, and at the Institute premises on a Saturday morning. We'd be paid fifty cents for each shift, and with that R1 we could do a lot of things.

I'd also try to get jobs during term breaks, and by the age of thirteen – and with my mother's encouragement – I was working part-time as a shelf-packer at supermarkets or going to sea on fishing trawlers. To get on a boat, all I had to do was get down to the docks before sunrise and queue with the rest of the 'casuals'. Every ship was prepared to take two or three kids, usually as engine-room boys and deckhands. Scrawny and short, I wasn't deck-hand potential, where the work was much more physical, requiring a lot of strength. In a trawler ship's engine room, however, you needed to get into tight spaces and move quickly and efficiently between and under the pipes that crisscross the place, so when the recruiter shouted out for an engine-room boy, I would raise my hand and, in as deep a voice as I could muster, shout, 'Me, boss!'

The engine-room was steamy, hot and reeked of fumes – an unpleasant environment made worse by the vessel constantly being rocked in every direction as it moved across the sea swells. In the first few days everything inside my stomach wanted to come out, with the nausea made worse by rank smells of oil and diesel, and the constant chug-chugging and vibration of the vessel.

The work of an engine-room boy is all menial. He's a 'gopher' ('go for this', and 'go for that' commands were constantly spat at me) but also helps to ensure the healthy working shape of the heart of the ship and therefore everyone's safety on a voyage. Oil-cups and grease-nipples had to be serviced continuously on the ever-running engines.

It wasn't an easy life for a boy and took some getting used to. At sea there's no law but the captain's law, and what he didn't see, he didn't want to know about, which left plenty of latitude for sadists and bullies. But the thinking was that if you were grownup enough to get yourself on board a ship, then you were grownup enough to sort out your own battles.

The trawlers would go out for eight to ten days – perfect for my term-breaks. I worked six hours on, six hours off, throughout a voyage. When a shift ended, I'd try to get a bite to eat and then fall into a bunk to sleep but it always seemed that my head had hardly hit the pillow, and it was time to be back in the engine-room. 'Wakey, wakey, rise and shine, hands off your cocks and onto your socks! Heave ho, heave ho!'

It was a magnificent sight to behold when the nets were drawn up, making a huge bag of fish. Gannets dropping from the skies like kamikaze pilots, accompanied by gulls, albatrosses and the tiny southern storm petrels. Seals and sharks were about. The wide-open blue on a calm day and the fresh sea air after constantly inhaling engine-room fumes became a piece of heaven. Then the deckhands got to work – hard and dangerous work – as the fish were sorted and packed as soon as they hit the deck.

When the ship got back after a trip, usually at night, taxis were waiting, along with some skimpily dressed 'sugar girls', ready to get their cut of the mariners' earnings. We earned what we called decent money (but was just a pittance, really) and could take home as much fish as we could carry. We youngsters were sharp enough to align with a few of the older hands who just wanted to get home to their families, and we'd club together to pay the negotiated taxi fare. This would get us safely out of the docks, with our money and fish intact, as there were many dangers to negotiate there.

I would go to May's house down on the corner of Cole and Nansen streets on the border of Salt River and Observatory – and what a great feeling it was to be welcomed home as a breadwinner and to put fish on the table and have your mom brag to others about how resourceful you'd been! It was short-lived, however, as soon I'd be away from my family and back at the Institute. But a plus was that I'd also have a few yarns with which to entertain the other lads.

Through my working at sea, I came to have respect for two priests who did work at the Mission to Seamen near the docks, one a Catholic, Father Brian Curren, and the other an Anglican, Father Bernard Wrankmore. Father Bernie became known as 'The Man on the Hill' when he fasted on Signal Hill for 67 days in 1971, protesting the death in detention of Imam Abdullah Haron, who'd been arrested by the security police because of his opposition to apartheid. A post-mortem inquest into his death showed he had a broken rib, 24 bruises and a blood clot as a result of trauma, but the security police attributed his death to a fall down a flight of stairs.

This was how I took my first faltering step into the arena of political resistance. One of my first overt political actions was to organise a protest fast in solidarity with Father Wrankmore. After three days I collapsed and woke up in a clinic bed. It was through this that I learnt that you can go without food for a long time, but not without water.

I went on to organise solidarity activities at school to protest group areas legislation, forced removals, population registration legislation, prohibition of mixed marriages legislation, the immorality act and separate amenities act, the pass laws, migrant labour conditions and the denial of trade union rights to those labelled 'Bantu'.

This all culminated in an event in June 1972 when university student protesters converged in a mass protest outside St George's Cathedral in Cape Town and I joined them. The police arrived in large numbers to break up the protest and we fled in all directions, some into the cathedral. The police followed them inside and beat them. It was my first clash with the police.

I asked a student for a bunch of their pamphlets, which I took back to school and handed out.

* * * *

In my last months at school, I got caught up in what was called the Jesus Movement, a counter-culture religious trend that had been imported from the USA. They called themselves the Jesus People; other people called them the Jesus Freaks.

A youth movement among the hippies who were rebelling against the mainline religious establishment, it was initially a vibrant nonconformist movement centred around an indoor fleamarket, surfer shops and a nightclub. However, it soon was taken over by the conservative evangelical and pentecostalist Assemblies of God (AOG) church.

The AOG developed out of the African American working class. Its roots were in the pan-African movement that had emerged from Africans studying abroad, and the African diaspora who'd formed the Pan African Association in London in 1897 – a Camissa African woman from Kimberley, Alice Alexander Kinloch, together with advocate Henry Sylvester Williams from Trinidad and Ghanaian Francis Zacharius Peregrino.

In South Africa, it was Nicholas Bhengu who embraced the AOG in the 1920s. In his youth, Bhengu had been a key figure in the struggle for African advancement as a member of the Industrial and Commercial Workers' Union Yase Natal under AWG Champion, of the Communist Party of South Africa, and of the ANC. Bhengu, a Zulu, was imbued with African nationalism, and he expressed a deeply held belief that capitalism was a negative system for Africa. He also strongly voiced the importance of accountability to the people among pastors – a unique liberationist theology, long before its time. By the 1950s he was considered by many to be the Billy Graham of Africa.

Unlike most of the other evangelical and pentecostal churches in South Africa, which were white churches with missions to black people, the AOG started among black people and spread to white people. Its black leaders thus had a lot more influence, even though the AOG quickly became controlled by whites with a conservative leaning.

So initially when the AOG homed in on the Jesus People movement in Cape Town, for me it seemed to fit with the nonconformist culture of this new movement and gelled with some of my ideas. The strength of the Jesus People movement lay in the entrepreneurial figure of Brian O'Donnell and a spiritual father figure, an artist by the name of Chrisman Stander, who had a long nonconformist history including an attraction to Islam. I too had been influenced by Islam and Sufism, and this endeared me to Chrisman, who became my mentorship figure and guide.

Brian took the Jesus People movement into a new orbit of success when he organised a first ever pop-rally of the Jesus People called 'Give God a Chance' at the old Green Point Stadium, the home of Hellenic Football Club. Within a short while after the AOG took over, I became disillusioned with the movement as it's character changed entirely.

4

MANHOOD:
TYRANNY AND PROTEST

I left the Salesian Institute in 1972, at the age of sixteen, to face first unemployment and then working life as a teenager. It was a frightening and daunting experience after years of institutionalisation, finding myself all alone in a much bigger world than I'd thus far known. I was challenged to sustain myself and survive without anyone to turn to.

I initially went to live with my mother, who had moved from her little semi in Woodstock to Lower Main Road in Observatory. She wasn't accustomed to sharing her space, however, and led an insular existence. Also, we were two very different characters, with different beliefs and practices, having grown apart for most of the previous years. She'd retired and, as a pensioner, she wasn't the same person of my childhood. She'd fallen in line with the system, living as a 'European', but wrestling with all the ramifications it threw up, as she still lovingly embraced and regularly engaged with her black family. In-betweenness had her leading a furtive life under apartheid, a lifestyle that I couldn't embrace.

I confronted the ambiguity of identity head-on, rather than simply ignoring the world of apartheid around us. I had a political consciousness about poor-white status and its relationship to multi-ethnic integration in our areas and families, which my mother, because of lack of education, age and being set in her ways, couldn't understand. For me, there was a strong co-relationship between class and colour.

For my mother everything, including suffering poverty and race classification, became the will of God, against which we could not rebel. This led to many arguments. She believed that God was punishing us for our family's 'sin' of race-mixing, because this was what the government and churches were brainwashing people to believe. To her, we had become 'poor-buggers' affected by the order of the day and should just get used to it. To me, that was like accepting being a second-class 'white' rather than a first-class 'black' and I got very angry hearing this.

It was very sore to see my mother, whose closest family and friends, our people, were classified 'Coloured', no longer fighting for who we were, and becoming lonely and reclusive as a result. But at the same time, I could see that she was trying to protect me by attempting to cultivate fear in me: 'Boetie, don't think you are more clever than the government; they will put a rope around your neck and you will swing,' she would say.

It was a very difficult arrangement, and I felt like an intruder.

My mother, from the first day, was constantly telling me to get a job and reminding me that she couldn't support me, and that I should be bringing in money to help her. I had no skills or qualifications except for my pre-apprenticeship training, and I was finding it difficult to get an apprenticeship.

I remember walking in cheap sandals – I had no shoes – from Salt River to Vasco, some nine kilometres, to follow up on a job advertisement for an apprentice welder job. I had no fare for a train or bus, and the only clothes I had were inappropriate for an interview. I did well in the interview nonetheless. When the boss asked me where I lived, and how I'd got to the interview, I told him I'd walked. On hearing this he said that I had determination and pluck, but that was unfortunately not a sustainable way to get to work, and I lived too far away.

One after the other, the available job opportunities I pursued hit dead ends. As time progressed, I became increasingly frustrated and downhearted, and found surviving more and more difficult. I'd hang out on the streets or with mates because my mom would just keep nagging about the obvious need for me to find a job.

I worried that I'd become like my older half-brother, Henri, who for a long time since his release from a reformatory had been living on his wits, on the streets and on the mountain. His face was lined and his skin weathered; his whole persona was that of a man battered by life and I didn't want to suffer the same. And it really scared me that I might end up on the streets like others who'd been in institutions during their childhood. I knew lots of homeless street people, many having come from around where I grew up.

Eventually, I managed to get an apprenticeship as a precious-metalworker in a small Jewish family-run jewellery sweatshop factory in Rhoodehek Street in Cape Town – M Obler & Son. I joined a trade union, the Jewellery and Goldsmith Workers' Union, a former affiliate of the banned South African Congress of Trade Unions (SACTU). My wages after deductions were R9.40 per week for a ten-hour day, six days a week, with a half-hour lunch break and two ten-minute tea breaks. My annual increases as an apprentice would be R1 per year over five years.

One day I was walking down the road to catch the train to work, and I became aware of a car coasting slowly down the road alongside me. The driver caught my attention. Thinking it was someone who needed directions, I went over to the window to ask if I could assist. To my astonishment, the driver said, 'I'm your father.'

'Mister you're making a mistake,' I said. 'My father is dead.'

'Don't you be funny with me, you little skollie,' the man shouted. Then, pointing aggressively at me, he yelled, 'You've been stealing my money!'

'You're mistaken, mister,' I said. 'Leave me alone! I have to go to work!'

I turned and ran, and he tooted his car horn at me in anger.

When I got home that evening, I was met by my mother wailing and pulling her hair and beating her chest. 'Why were you rude to your father?' she shouted at me.

If I'd been shocked and upset that morning, it was nothing compared to what I was feeling now at my mother's question. 'But you told me he was dead!' I said.

'Don't you be funny with me, mastermind,' my mother snapped. 'You're acting just like that bladdy rubbish father of yours!'

I was absolutely gobsmacked but the shocks weren't over. 'So when are you going away with mister?' my mother demanded to know.

'I'm not going anywhere with him,' I assured her. 'Ma, I'm a big man now, earning my own living. I don't need a father any more.' I didn't bother to add that I had, after all, largely brought myself up.

It transpired that the 'stolen' money my father had referred to was the R5 per month papgeld (maintenance) that he'd been paying my mother that I knew nothing about.

Immediately following this traumatising experience, my mother went back to insisting that my father had died in a motorcar accident and that she was a widow. And for the next 28 years none of this was ever discussed again.

I could do nothing but entertain my mother's fictional world.

* * * *

At the jewellery factory, we produced gold and silver rings, bracelets, earrings, bangles, and other precious-metal goods for jewellery shops. The value of just one of these items was much greater than a week's wages, and each worker could churn out over fifty items in a day.

We worked at a row of benches. Each seating place had a cut-out semicircle with a leather catch-all attached to it that covered one's lap to catch the gold or silver filings. The foreman would brush this off into a bottle before we could get up, and it would be smelted so that there was no wastage.

It wasn't an easy place to work – the foreman constantly hit me on the head with his knuckles or a piece of wood, to make me work faster – and I ended up running away. Luckily, I hadn't signed the apprenticeship papers, but they still sent the police to my mother's house with an order that I should return and work in a period of notice. I did, and during that time they tried to make me sign the apprenticeship papers, but I refused. So once more I found myself unemployed.

I found part-time work at the hippie market in Loop Street, Cape Town, with the Jesus Freaks. The people in this fringe movement were my first post-school friends and prevented me from going to the dogs on the street. The hippie market became a home from home for me, and it was there that I managed to find my legs.

The indoor flea market was the first of its kind in South Africa. Each stallholder ran an independent business, but of course it bound them to their stalls six days a week. That gave me a gap for a survival strategy – they all needed someone to stand in and give them a break from time to time. I charged them fifty cents to a rand to look after their stalls for an hour, for lunch breaks or any other time that they needed to be away.

My mother hated the people at the hippie market – she always referred to them as 'those bladdy hippies' or skollies. But she was happy that I now had some money coming in, to pay my way at home.

It soon became clear to me, however, that none of the leaders of the Jesus People movement or the white AOG, which had become the guiding church of this non-conformist religious movement, had any real knowledge or understanding of the black roots, pan-Africanism or African nationalism and anti-capitalist roots of Nicholas Bhengu, and the African history of the AOG in South Africa. These white leaders, including Brian O'Donnell, were naked apologists for apartheid and the status quo. They called my beliefs the 'social gospel', which was a false gospel of the devil in their eyes. I quickly became disenchanted with my newfound religious friends.

Still, my occasional work at the hippie market gave me the opportunity to meet people and network to try and get a permanent job with some prospect for advancement. Someone told me about an opening for a junior warehouseman or storeman at the Epping fresh-produce market, so I tried my luck there. I didn't get the job, but through that contact I was given a reference for possible employment at the regional hospital stores in Chiappini Street in Cape Town – and that's how I became a junior storeman in the hospital service at R25 per five-day week for an eight-hour day.

I worked with a great bunch of people there and will always remember them and their idiosyncratic behaviours: Zackie; Hiema; Eddie; John the boxing trainer; Ware and Watson, two alcoholic old men; the one-eyed Anglophile Steenkamp and the Boer Orantjies still fighting the Boer War; Hoppy, Curly, Tiny and Pietie; and one time Berlin Olympic boxer Alec Hannan, who during Hitler's Games witnessed African American athlete Jesse Owens's feat of scooping four golds and single-handedly crushing Hitler's myth of Aryan supremacy. We all got on at a superficial level, but there was a definite divide between the black warehousemen and the conservative white warehousemen.

It didn't take long for me to run into problems with the superintendent and his deputies. I had joined the Public Servants' Association union and organised protests at the Regional Hospital Stores that were not supported by the then conservative union. My outspokenness about working conditions and apartheid practices at the stores put a target on my back. One of the conservative storemen, Curly, who passed for white, was the piemp (snitch) who ran to the superintendent with stories that would get us into trouble. And things got worse later when I was up against security police surveillance, where they had a person at my workplace keeping tabs on me and reporting my every move.

My increasingly vocal left-wing stance on apartheid and class politics was also a source of friction at home, with my mother telling me to tone it down because I was heading in the direction of arrest and having them 'put a rope around my neck'. 'Mark my words, you're going to swing for that cleverness, mastermind,' she'd say.

Saying that I was being influenced by skollies and that she couldn't handle me, my mother took the astonishing step of approaching child welfare to 'take me in hand'. I was summoned to their offices in Cape Town and interviewed by an official, who told me that my mother had requested that I be placed in a reformatory. The welfare officer had consulted with the police and found that I hadn't been involved in any criminal activity, and that because I was already over sixteen, they could make no intervention.

He asked me several questions, and we talked for about an hour, at the end of which he said, 'I must admit, I'm surprised, given your history, that you're such a well-balanced individual. I'd like to give you a word of advice. Now that you're working, perhaps you should seek accommodation away from your mother, as clearly it's not working for both of you. Perhaps with some distance between you, a new relationship will develop.'

* * * *

I was proud that I'd made the transition from unemployed to employed, and was now able to contribute at home and to have some money in my pocket. Nonetheless, the relationship between my mother and I remained uneasy. This was made more difficult when the ghost of my long-dead father was resurrected when, as a sixteen-year-old, I applied for an identity document.

At the department of interior affairs, I immediately complicated matters by telling the official that 'De Goede' wasn't my real name. I had no birth certificate, so could only produce a baptism certificate – on which my mother had put the name of her former husband, not my father.

'My surname is Mellet, not De Goede,' I said. 'I want my real name on my documents.'

The official taunted me about this, saying I should desist from trying to confuse her, and that she could only go on what the paperwork before her said. 'The baptism certificate is your only proof of who you are, if you can't show any affidavit from your mother saying otherwise.'

The next issue was the vexed one of what colour I was. Race classification was, of course, a central component of the Population Registration Act. I rejected 'race' classification but – under protest – registered as 'Coloured' and thus started a war of words with the official, who said that I should be classified as 'White', based on what I looked like. I refused to change what I'd written on the form, and in the margin the official wrote 'Other'. It was an explosive confrontation and compromise.

The official then made a sneering remark. She said, 'I know what your game is, boetie. You just don't want to go to the army.'

In 1967, military conscription had become compulsory for all white men in South Africa over the age of sixteen, who would join the South African Defence Force to uphold the apartheid regime, fighting against liberation movements in Angola, Namibia and Mozambique, and often deployed to townships to quell anti-apartheid action. Some allowance was made for religious objectors, but it only allowed for non-combatant service such as the medical corps where all other military protocols except for bearing arms had to be observed.

I lost my cool and told the official, 'Of course I don't want to serve in your army, madam, but this application form is about my identity, and you don't get to tell me who I am or what I am.' I said that I chose to be part of those in my family whom she called 'Coloured', and that that was my birthright, even though the terms 'White', 'Coloured', 'Bantu' and 'Asian' were useless because my family had a bit of each of these in us, and I would not be me if I were to cut off 'Coloured' from 'poor White' or 'Indian' or 'African'.

Again, she sneered. 'Go tell that to the race classification board,' she said.

She struck a nerve with that remark. My Aunty Doll's son, Herbie van Rooy, whom we called Busy, had already gone through what I was experiencing with the internal affairs department, and had subjected himself to the indignity of the race classification board. The reclassification process was fraught, and the board used the mixed criteria of 'appearance and general acceptance and repute' and nineteenth-century 'ethnography' to decide to what race group a person belonged. Complexion, eye colour, hair texture, genitalia, facial features and bone structure were examined by board officials, and they could summon any relative and examine them in the same way. For Afrikaans speakers, there was a distinction made between 'white' and 'black' Afrikaans dialects, expressions and pronunciation, for example, 'bobbejaan' versus 'bobjan' or 'jakkals' versus 'jakalas'. It was a humiliating and Nazi-type process in which ignorant officials molested people in the name of pseudo-science.

Herbie had an ID card that said he was 'European', but, unlike me, he was very dark in complexion and had strong Asian features. When he was a youngster, pre-apartheid, there were many 'Coloured' people who had some European ancestry who were called 'European'. He was the only one of my Aunty Doll's children who'd remained in South Africa, and he was having a difficult time with his ID card because it was seen as fraudulent. So he went to the race classification board, to have his race classification changed from 'European' to 'Coloured'. As he would say, 'I told them that they can go stuff their "European" up their arse.'

Herbie and I became very close in later years, when I returned from exile. He also spent much time out of South Africa by choosing a seamanship career, but came home to Grassy Park regularly, and had a family with his wife Daisy Falken, who bore him four children, Edgar, Clint, Russel and Vanessa.

So I said to the internal affairs official, 'You don't get to tell me what I should do. I'm not asking anyone's permission to express my identity. I am who I am.'

She had the last word, saying, 'You little smart-arse communist, whether you like it or not, you will go to the army. We'll see who wins in this little game of yours. They'll knock this shit out of you.'

So I was an identity-less person at the mercy of apartheid officials who could decide whatever they wished about who or what I was.

* * * *

Today, I have a strong and proud sense of my African Camissa sub-identity as a South African and I'm constantly involved in the promotion of the understanding of Cape slavery and indigene heritage. Today, the younger generation of my family, as their ancestors did in the past, still cross the bloodlines of Camissa, European, Southeast Asian, Indian, Chinese, amaXhosa, Cape Khoe, Griqua, Korana and Nama, and I have a strong pride in this heritage.

The term 'Coloured' was first introduced by the British in the mid-nineteenth century but it originally meant all people who weren't Europeans or white; in other words, all considered to be African or Afro-Asian – 'non-whites'. Official documentation referred to the 'British Coloured' people of the Colony of the Cape of Good Hope.

'Coloured' people have their roots in seven different tributaries, starting with the first Khoe //*Ammaqua* traders, 'water people' (watermans) who lived in a small community on the banks of the Camissa River in Cape Town, at the shoreline, and traded with European ships. This settlement was seized by the Dutch in 1652, and over the next eight years the *//Ammaqua* people were forced out of the area. At the same time enslaved peoples from other parts of Africa and from Asia were forcibly brought in chains into the Camissa embrace.

The Khoe, the enslaved, and other diverse black migrants became the cornerstones of a new creole African population – which colonial officialdom came to label as 'Coloureds'. Today some of us refer to ourselves as Camissa Africans. We are defined not by colour, features, ethnicity or race, but by a common experience of facing and rising above systemic adversity and a range of crimes against humanity – colonialism, slavery, ethnocide and genocide, forced removals, de-Africanisation and apartheid.

In 1904, a census committee met in Pretoria to prepare a race-classification matrix for the Union of South Africa. Guided by the work of the father of race classification, German-born Wilhelm Bleek, an ethnographer, linguist and anthropologist, Africans were divided into two groups. The first, labelled 'Natives', were all those who spoke any of the Bantu family of languages, which numbered more than 700 across Africa. (It was Bleek who created the linguistic term 'Bantu' and migrated the term to denote a race labelled 'Bantu'.) All other Africans who spoke any other language, including San, Khoekhoegowab/Kora, Afrikaans and English, were labelled 'Coloured'.

In 1911 a formalised race-classification system with no scientific basis was introduced under which all South Africans were categorised into one of three silos – 'Natives', 'Coloureds' and 'Europeans'. But the system wasn't watertight, and many considered 'Coloured' were still referred to on birth, death and marriage documentation as 'mixed-other' or even as 'Europeans'. Likewise, many with family ties to those called 'Natives' had documentation saying 'mixed-other', and vice versa.

In 1950 the system was further finessed when 'Coloureds' was split into seven subcategories; and from 1959 this was reduced to four ('Cape Coloured', 'Malay', 'Griqua' and 'Other Coloured'), with the other three subcategories put into a fourth race silo, 'Asians' ('Indian', 'Chinese' and 'Other Asiatics'). The new system was much more efficiently enforced than the 1911 system.

Both my grandmothers were referred to as 'Coloured' and my grandfathers were Afrikaner and English, seen as 'European'. My mother's family contradicted the official segregationist paradigm, as they were made up of people who would under apartheid be classified as 'Coloured', 'Indian' and 'European', and just didn't neatly fit under the apartheid labels. In fact, all the folks in my world of growing up were people having roots in all four of the official race silos; we were people whom race classification couldn't neatly define. It seemed that by our very existence, we were a threat to the apartheid state, which was absolutely oriented around the concept of race. We were the embodiment of the antithesis of apartheid, and living proof that segregation and race theories were absolute nonsense.

My paternal grandfather, Pieter Francois Mellet, was from a small village called Lemoenshoek near Barrydale in the Kannaland area of the Western Cape. His father, Petrus Francois Mellet, had married Susanna Catherina Francina Steyn, an Afrikaner whose heritage was a mix of European, Khoe and enslaved people from Africa and Asia. A direct family descendant tested for matriarchal mitochondrial DNA showed that Susanna carried the haplogroup L0d, found among San and Khoe and in South Africans classified as 'Coloured', illustrating the significant maternal contribution of Khoe and San people to the 'Coloured' population of South Africa.

At the age of eighteen, after my grandfather was run out of town for impregnating a younger girl, he came to the city of Cape Town and worked as a telegraph linesman. Grandpa Mellet married my grandmother, Elsie Petronella le Cordier, who was from District Six. Grandma Elsie's family heritage was Khoe, enslaved African and Asian, and European.

The new couple lived at 6 Sterling Street, District Six, for about ten years. Four children were born there, including my father, also named Pieter Francois Mellet, who made his appearance in 1922. In the 1930s the family moved to Bokmakierie near Athlone, then to Doornhoogte (today's Rylands). Grandma Elsie, a traditional healer, passed away at an early age in 1939. My grandfather then moved his family to Crawford, where he remarried and had three more sons.

My father's family were mainly Afrikaans speakers. My paternal grandpa and grandma, between them, had a long history in the Cape tracing back in verified lineage over almost four centuries. Their ancestors in our family tree included twenty-six enslaved people from Angola, Madagascar and Ethiopia, as well as from India, Sri Lanka, Myanmar-Thailand and parts of Indonesia, and Japan and China. The enslaved ancestors also included locally born African 'creoles', or 'new creations' (as distinct from first-generation enforced migrant enslaved).

There were also five Khoe ancestors in my paternal grandparents' lineage, and several European non-conformists from six different European countries, including Britain, Denmark and Holland, but of which France was most prominent. These Europeans had relationships and marriages across the colour line. Some assimilated into black societies and others had their offspring assimilate into the Afro-European or 'white' society.

Among my ancestors are Krotoa of the Cape indigenous ǁAmmaqua trader community and her daughter Petronella, as well as a woman whose baptism records record her as 'Caatje Hottentottin Voortman', most likely of the Cochoqua people in Tulbagh, and her two daughters, Susanna and Anna Maria, who married two French brothers, Johannes and Jurgen le Cordier.

My maternal great-grandfather was an Englishman, William Hadden, born in 1808, who came to South Africa as a British soldier in the years just before the War of the Axe in 1846, after which he was demobilised. My maternal great-grandmother, Francina Jagers, was a black woman of mixed local African and enslaved lineage who'd been born in 1830 to a freed slave woman, Dela, from the Kat River valley in the Eastern Cape.

William and Francina went to live on a farm in Thembuland in the Eastern Cape, somewhere along the Tsomo River near what would become the town of Cala. (This was before the territory of the Thembu kingdom was annexed in 1876 into the Cape Colony.) They had six children. The family were part of the Catholic mission parishioners who increasingly were referred to as 'mixed' or 'Coloured', and separate from the European or 'white' parishioners. The family were bilingual English and isiXhosa speakers, though the isiXhosa was lost as a home language within one generation.

My grandmother was the Haddens' daughter Mary-Anne, who was a nurse's aide at a hospital in Mthatha. It was there that she met my grandfather, William Huntley, an Englishman who at the age of eighteen came to the Cape to fight in the Anglo-Boer War of 1899-1902. Mary-Anne and William were married in the Roman Catholic Church in Mthatha.

After my great-grandfather died in 1908, my grandmother, Mary-Anne, who'd been nursing her elderly parents, stayed on in Cala until Francina, too, passed away, in 1914. She and my grandfather, William, then moved, first to Port Elizabeth (now Gqeberha), then to the poor area of Onderdorp, Wynberg in Cape Town, which was an enclave of mainly those who were classified 'Coloured' after 1911. There were also some in the area who were classified as 'Native' and even a few poor white 'Europeans'. This is where my mother, Annie Gladys Frances Huntley, and some of her siblings were born, in a house in Kent Street. My mother was born in 1917. Mary ('Doll'), Bill and Charlie were her older siblings, and Bob and Mabel were her younger siblings.

* * * *

The letter promised by the department of interior affairs confirming my identity never came; resolution of the dispute did not materialise; and a proper ID document was not forthcoming. Instead, I received conscription papers for the apartheid military. This thrust me into a headlong conflict with the state at a time when there were no political or human rights support structures, and the church refused to help me.

After seeking and being refused support by a Catholic priest and an AOG pastor, I sought the assistance of a lay preacher, whom we knew as Uncle Eddie, a white English-speaking man. Uncle Eddie declared that he didn't support my position of challenging the state on race classification or refusing to be conscripted, but he helped me to draft a letter which I immediately sent to the military and to interior affairs. In it,

I stated that I did not consider myself 'white' and was not prepared to take up arms against my people by serving in the apartheid armed forces. I declared myself a conscientious objector prepared to engage in civil disobedience.

I also once again requested the department of interior affairs to classify me as 'Coloured', the same as many of my family members. There was no response.

The defence ministry did respond: I was instructed to report for duty and then put my case before the military authorities.

I refused to reply and was forcibly taken into military custody in 1974.

5

REPRESSION:
THE FIRST CLASHES

I was taken under arrest by train to Upington where the 8th SA Infantry was based in a large tent-camp on the edge of an arid area. There, without any support, I made my lonely stand. I clearly stated my opposition to race classification, and to apartheid and what it had done to my family, as well as my opposition to being classified 'white' and called up as a conscript. I refused to cooperate, to salute, to show respect.

In retaliation, they shaved half my hair off and left the other half intact, to humiliate me. I was forcibly unclothed and then dressed in an overall. When they tried to issue me with a weapon by thrusting it at me, I threw my arms up in the air and let it fall onto the ground. Soldiers crowded around me, barking orders and pushing me around. 'I am a conscientious objector, and I am not one of you,' I repeated, endlessly. 'I have made my position known in writing. I will not serve under arms nor accept your classification.'

At one stage PW Botha, then minister of defence, visited the camp. I was pointed out to him. While he kept his distance from me, he stared in my direction, then waved a finger at me while instructing military officers. He then addressed the troops with a patriotic nationalist speech which included some railings about 'betogers' (protestors) and 'kommuniste' (communists) in our midst, and he urged them to deal harshly with such elements. It was clear that he was referring to me and everyone stared in my direction. They were being given instruction to use mob coercion on me, and from that point I was addressed as 'Kommunis'.

Over the next few weeks, the South African Defence Force tried to break me using a variety of methods, from beatings to psychological abuse and violent mob pressure. I refused to bend. Finally, after I was admitted to the military clinic coughing up blood, having collapsed and lost my voice, they tried something new.

A military chaplain of the Dutch Reformed Church, a dominee, was called in to 'reason with' me. He told me that I was being influenced by satan and should stop this foolishness; if I did, they were prepared to give me another chance. Bizarrely, he then proceeded to attempt to do an exorcism on me to cast out the demons that supposedly had possessed me. Here was a church man, 'laying hands' on me and ranting for the demons to come out, and I was the one who supposedly had lost his mind!

I was sent under military-police escort to Pretoria, where I was left under the pretext of having been a 'misplaced conscript'; nothing was said about my protestations to my racial classification and objection to doing military service. I realised that they thought they were giving me an opportunity to start again with a blank slate. But I was not going to play their game.

In Pretoria, I was issued with a light automatic rifle, which I again declined to accept. I held my ground, refusing to fall in with military discipline or to salute. The military police wanted to know where I'd picked up my politics and learnt my defiance; they were convinced that I'd been put up to it by unnamed communist instigators. I was interrogated about my political beliefs and affiliations, and whether I intended to leave the country. I had nothing to tell them.

Finally, I was released, under constant supervision, within the confines of the services school military camp at Voortrekkerhoogte (now Thaba Tshwane). A few days later I was taken by the military police and handed over to officials at the security police headquarters in the notorious Compol building in Pretoria. The security police, or 'special branch', which wielded great influence as the 'elite' service of the South African police, were known for the systematic use of torture in their detention facilities.

It was now the fourth month since I'd first been taken in, and the interrogations became much more intense. Following their remit of collecting and evaluating intelligence, the special branch began trying to find out what I knew about the ANC, the SACP and 'communism'. I was only eighteen years old and my politics were largely self-taught; at that point, I had not yet had any direct contact with the ANC. I had left-wing ideas gleaned from literature, so I wasn't ignorant as to what was going on, but I had no experience in fielding the kinds of questions they asked repetitively and aggressively.

My storyline was simple and also repetitive: I was not one of them, I did not accept the 'white' classification, and I would not conform to the requirements of conscription into which I'd been drafted under duress. I also stated that their conduct was outside of the law, and that, having been arrested, I should be charged if I had done something illegal.

Increasingly impatient with me and frustrated with my answers, the questioning grew progressively sharper and more intense, with up to three people often asking questions at the same time. I was psychologically and verbally abused. I was subjected to sessions where I was forced to stand in one spot for long durations of time. I was physically shaken, manhandled and shouted at. I felt I'd been through this before: some of what was happening resonated with my childhood experiences in the children's asylum.

I was not, however, struck. I think they realised they were on shaky ground, as the legality of my call-up remained in question: I still had no formal ID, and my 'white' classification was still in dispute. So they couldn't charge me with anything, nor could they connect me to any organisation or any subversive activities.

Also, the security police left any physical attacks to the military conscripts so it could be argued that these were just private scraps between boys. The conscripts were constantly told that I was contaminating their intake and unless they put me – 'their maatjie', or 'little friend' – right, they wouldn't get an unblemished inspection record. Fault would be found in them collectively because in the army if one man is a bad egg, it reflects on all of them. So, as a result, I would be called all sorts of names, get pushed around, and in cases aggressive Boer conscripts would beat me up and tell me that it was their patriotic duty to do so. Frequently I was told that they would find a way to kill me. But sometimes some of the English liberal conscripts would step in to protect me.

Very few other people, if any at all, were taking a political stand against conscription in those years – this was well before the 1983 formation of the End Conscription Campaign in protest against compulsory military service – and I could see that the South African Defence Force didn't know how to handle me. Lots of consulting up the chain of command happened, and it became clear to me that both the military police and the security police were convinced that somebody or some organisation had put me up to it. How otherwise would an uneducated working-class boy from a poor background come up with these stupid ideas?

Naturally, they wanted to know why I, a 'poor-white halfnaatjie' as they saw it, was mad enough to want to be classified 'Coloured' when there were programmes to help 'poor whites' to advance and do well in life. 'No sane person would want to be a Hotnot Coloured,' they told me. They took me to see a doctor for mental evaluation; I don't know what transpired or what was in his report, but I don't think that the doctor was prepared to have me committed or declared mentally unfit.

At one stage I was taken into a lecture room at the Compol building and made to watch an anti-communist propaganda film, and shown various exhibits of equipment and photos of terrorist handiwork. A black sergeant, a former ANC operative who supposedly had seen the light, was brought in to question me and tell me his story. Later in life I came to know such people as askaris, originating from the Persian word for 'soldier'. In East Africa it was a term used for Africans who served in colonial police and armed forces; in South Africa it was a term that described former members of the liberation movement who were turned to work for the security police.

This sergeant tried to be convincing and told me that, as had once been the situation with him, I was being brainwashed by communist and satanist propaganda. The emphasis again was on who could have possibly influenced me to take this path.

I had no backing from the church. I had approached both the Catholic church and the AOG for support; both had refused to help, and had indeed told me that I must be inspired by the devil to do what I was doing. I was told that, according to the bible, God wanted me to obey the authority placed over me, because all authority was ordained by God; it followed, then, that the 'communist authorities' to whom I apparently was giving my allegiance must have been ordained by the devil. A liberal Anglican priest brought into the fray for an opinion, told them that he believed I was genuine in my objections but this never went any further.

Finally, I was sent back to Voortrekkerhoogte services school and, a few weeks later, under military escort, back to Cape Town, to the Wynberg 11 Supply and Transport camp. Here, I was given another 'opportunity' to change my mind. When I kept up my resolve, I was goaded into a fight and ended up assaulting a corporal who just happened to be the nephew of the regimental search major.

Again, I was arrested and interrogated. I was asked why, if I were prepared to be violent and assault a fellow soldier, I was not prepared to fight the enemies of the state? If I was a pacifist, why was I now showing a capacity for violence? It proved, they seemed to think, that some sinister anti-government communist force was using me.

Additional contorted arguments came hard and fast. I was supposedly associated with a drug-addicted soldier involved with drug dealing, and who had been arrested – a bald attempt to get rid of the inconvenience of dealing with a political case by turning it into a much more straightforward criminal case.

Repeatedly, I again asserted my simple positions that I was not one of them and did not support the apartheid system or government, nor was I prepared to serve in, take up arms for or show respect towards the apartheid armed forces.

My next stop was Rundu military base on the Namibian/Angolan border. Rundu was in the Kavango region, situated halfway between Oshakati to its west and Kasane at the eastern end of the Caprivi Strip of Namibia. Calai was the nearest Angolan town, nine kilometres away across the border in Cuando Cubango province.

At the time, South Africa was illegally occupying Namibia and were opposed by the People's Liberation Army (PLAN), the military wing of the South West African People's Organisation (Swapo), in a war conducted largely in the border region of Namibia and Angola, and deep inside Angolan territory. Some of Swapo's leaders, like Herman Toivo ja Toivo, were imprisoned on Robben Island along with Nelson Mandela and other South African leaders and activists opposed to apartheid and colonialism.

From 1975 the South African Defence Force had also invaded Angola and allied with the National Union for the Total Independence of Angola (Unita), which was engaging in a civil war to overthrow the People's Movement for the Liberation of Angola – Workers Party (MPLA) government of Angola.

In Rundu camp, which was in the thick of the war zone, I was made to load and unload provisions onto and off of trucks. I was given a green jacket that made me stand out from the rest of the conscripts in their khaki, and was instructed to carry a wooden broomstick as a symbolic weapon, and so that I could be taunted and humiliated, but I refused.

I was told by the NCOs who were tormenting me that being on the border of Angola would give them the opportunity to get rid of me by saying that I'd been killed in the operational area as a conscript. They told me that nobody knew about me refusing to serve or being arrested – I could just disappear, and nobody would be the wiser and nobody would miss me.

A prisoner without being in prison, I was constantly in a state of fear. I was so scared that I sometimes trembled and felt like I was going to have a breakdown. I had no option but to bear with the situation. There was no escape.

I was made a servant of Sergeant Major James, an English-speaking officer who served with the South African Special Forces Brigade – the Recces – in cross-border raids. He spoke Afrikaans smoothly and would speak English only to his closest friends. He called me his Hotnot batman and ordered me to call him 'Baas James'. This brute was the state's most intense weapon used against me in its psychological war.

I was constantly pushed and shoved around, and demeaned at every turn: I had to hand-wash his clothes, including his filthy socks and shitty underpants, clean his kit and tent, carry his kitbag, and do any other menial task he assigned me. 'Jy wil mos 'n bont Hotnot wees, nou werk soes 'n Hotnot, jou kommunis bastard, fokken rooi Rus.' (You want to be a pied Hottentot, now work like a Hottentot, you communist bastard, fucking red Russian.) James continuously bragged about how many terrorists he'd killed in Recce operations and suggested that I would be one of his stories soon.

Regularly I was surrounded by James's buddies for taunting and roughing up. I was told that the only way that I would ever be released or go home again was as a sensational story in the newspapers – they would tell the public, they said, that I'd been killed by a terrorist ('jou Kommunis maatjies' – your Communist friends).

They took me on trips to show me truckloads of Portuguese refugees from Angola, and told me that it was 'my kind' – my terrorist friends – who'd made these innocent people homeless. They also showed me caged people who were brought into Rundu camp and who'd obviously been assaulted, and said that these were my Swapo friends. I was told that they were lucky to be alive, for now, but that I would not be so lucky.

At one stage I was taken to a casualty area where wounded soldiers were being brought in by helicopter from a combat clash. They allowed these soldiers who had just come from that firefight, injured and angry, to take out their fury on me. Things were allowed to escalate to near-deadly assault before I was dragged away. They laughed and said, 'Amper jou beurt, Kommunis. Maar môre is 'n nogge dag.' (Your turn will come, Communist. Tomorrow is another day.)

Despite being under strict custodial observation day and night, even while performing my ablutions, I was accused of transmitting information to the enemy, Swapo. They wanted to know how I'd got my hands on radio-transmitting equipment, where it was, and what my relationship to Swapo, the ANC and the Angolan liberation movement was. It was a ludicrous charge, done just to keep up the pressure on me.

Once I was asked by some of the liberal English-speaking soldiers to explain my situation, and when I did, they also said they thought I was mad. 'The Boers are going to kill you,' one of them warned me.

A sergeant by the name of Rabie, a thickset Boer, overheard this interchange. He came rushing over and grabbed me by the neck, lifting me off my feet, and shoved me up against a stack of maize-meal sacks. Holding me in place with one meaty hand, he took out his weapon with the other. He put the gun to my temple, then into my mouth. Red-faced, spraying saliva, he screamed at me, 'Vandag gaan jy hel toe! Vandag, Kommunis! Ons het vir jou gewaarsku en jy wil nie luister nie jou kont!' (Today you're going to hell! Today, Kommunis! We've warned you and you don't want to listen, you cunt!)

Another staff sergeant came running, yanking Rabie away and disarming him before pinning him down.

This was part of the almost daily gauntlet I ran.

* * * *

In May 1976 I was released from the army, having never cooperated, and remained true to my refusal to take up arms since early 1974. Before my release I was threatened that they would always be watching me, and that in time I would get what was coming to me.

Around the same time, the department of interior affairs formalised my classification. In those days, the thirteen-digit-long number was made up of the birthdate of the holder, a number signifying gender, another to indicate whether the holder was a South African citizen or not, and a number to signify race, running from 0 for 'White', through the racial classifications of 'Cape Coloured', 'Malay', 'Griqua', 'Chinese', 'Indian' and 'Other Asian', up to 7 for 'Other Coloured' – my classification. ('Bantu' people were considered citizens not of South Africa, but of one of the ten 'independent homelands' artificially created by the apartheid government for 'designated ethnic groups', and therefore didn't qualify for a South African ID number.)

Interior affairs never gave me any explanation for this classification. To me it wasn't important, however, because I went back into my small marginal mixed community of poor white and 'Coloured' where classifications were irrelevant.

REPRESSION

I also went back to working as a hospital warehouseman at the stores in Chiappini Street, Cape Town. True to their promise before I'd left the army, however, the security police kept an eye on me, visiting my workplace regularly to check up on me, speaking to my workmates, tapping my calls and following me around. The whites at work never lost an opportunity to badger me about being a 'Kommunis' under observation of the security police. My life at work was made miserable because of this, and eventually I was forced to change jobs.

I began training as a maintenance fitter at Herzburg & Mulne printing and packaging factory in Epping Industria. I joined the South African Typographical Union, which had separate branches for 'Coloured', 'Bantu' and 'White' workers. It also had a system of a full vote for 'White' members, half-vote for members classified as 'Coloured' and quarter vote for those classified as 'Bantu'. (Later, in the 1980s, when in exile, I led a protest against these racist policies, as a SACTU activist and a member of the British trade union the National Graphical Association, and succeeded in getting the South African Typographical Union suspended from the International Graphical Federation, a global union federation that brought together unions of printing workers around the world.)

But I couldn't shake myself free of the security police, and in no time a person at my new workplace – a British right-wing immigrant – had been recruited to watch and report on me. In an argument with me, he let slip that he was reporting to a Major Lourens.

My long periods of enforced military custody, interrogations and abuse had hardened me and made me even more resolute; I was only twenty years old but felt much older. I started listening to the ANC's Radio Freedom, which broadcast from Tanzania, Zambia, Angola, Ethiopia and Madagascar; being caught listening to it was a crime carrying a penalty of up to eight years in prison. I decided to answer the call by president Oliver Tambo appealing to young people to join Umkhonto we Sizwe (MK), the ANC's military wing, and to use every means at their disposal to get training and fight the apartheid regime.

In a twist, it was all the interrogation that I'd been forced to endure and the attempts by my tormentors to pin ANC and SACP labels on me that endeared me to those organisations and made me seek them out.

Around this time I made a new friend, James 'Jimmy' Dryja, who was a member of the Young Christian Workers, and invited me to join the organisation. This global left outfit in the Catholic church was originally called the Association of Factory Workers and was first started because the church was losing a lot of working-class youth to socialist and communist parties in Europe. The emergence of liberation theology deepened the political character of the movement.

Our cell consisted of myself and Jimmy, who was an office worker; a railway worker, Teddy Dosson; three shop-workers, Barbara Dryja, Helen Saad and Maria Farelo; and three domestic workers, Maggie Oewies, Lydia McMaster and Suzie Swart. Maggie used our branch as her base to build the first Domestic Workers' Union.

The Young Christian Workers used a method in our activism called 'see, judge, act, report and reflect', whereby we took in all that happened around us at work and in our neighbourhoods, and identified strategic tasks, came together to analyse what we'd seen and decide on action to take; then acted, and reported back to the cell, where we reflected on the actions. It was also a support system aimed at building confidence in young workers.

Jimmy and I would hire a 16 mm projector and reels of movies, and take them to church youth gatherings all over the Cape Flats, regardless of the 'Coloured' and 'Bantu' area demarcations. The first movie would always be of the 'skop-skiet-en-donner' (action movies) or 'kung fu and car chase' varieties but the second would carry a social message, such as the 1940 *Grapes of Wrath* based on John Steinbeck's novel set during the Great Depression of the 1930s and focusing on a family's fight against economic hardship, agricultural industry changes, and being forced out of work. Through this we could introduce what we called conscientisation – consciousness-building to develop greater social awareness and preparation for resistance.

James and Barbara, and Maria and I, were two couples who met through Young Christian Workers activism, and we got married on the same day in 1976. We were inseparable as friends for a while.

Jimmy worked for the Automobile Association, and he also did their Friday road-report on Springbok Radio. He owned a car, and taught me to drive by the simple expedient of taking me as a passenger into the centre of town and there, in the middle of the traffic, getting out and telling me to shift over into the driver's seat, with cars hooting all around us!

* * * *

On 16 June 1976 Soweto, the huge black township on Johannesburg's southwestern border, exploded in a youth rebellion that would become known as the Soweto Uprising. Acting as a fuse that lit a national youth uprising the likes of which had never been seen in South Africa, it continued for eighteen months and engulfed the whole country – it should more correctly be called the National Youth Uprising of 1976-77. Cape Town, Durban, East London and (then) Port Elizabeth all saw similar youth uprisings and angry anti-apartheid demonstrations – and all from communities classified as 'Coloured', 'Bantu' and 'Indian', in cross-community political cooperation also never seen in the country before. Hundreds of youths were killed and maimed, and thousands were arrested, with thousands more being forced to seek refuge across the borders in neighbouring countries.

From August, and particularly in what many of us saw as 'Black September', the youth of Cape Town swung into action, and this uprising continued for over a year, into late 1977. In 1976 alone, 128 young people were killed and over 400 seriously wounded in Cape Town.

I vividly remember a clash in Adderley Street on 3 September 1976 in which I was involved as a young worker who joined the school students in protest. Police had been brought down from what was then the Transvaal (now Gauteng, North West, Limpopo and Mpumalanga provinces) to supplement the Cape Town cops. They were ruthless racists and enjoyed terrorising and shooting protesting kids.

The police had fired a volley of teargas into the air after one of the workers on the Golden Acre building site standing next to me had thrown a brick at a stationary cop van. We began to run in all directions as the police reloaded and began to give chase, now shooting the teargas canisters directly at us. In the fracas, I stumbled over a lone toddler, screaming and overcome by teargas. As I picked up the child, a comrade stopped a canister that was hurtling across the ground towards us with his foot, then picked it up and hurled it back at the cop who'd shot it. This gave me a chance to dash with the child in my arms to seek safety.

I rounded the corner where the flower sellers usually peacefully hawked their wares, between the OK Bazaars and the bank, and began banging on the glass doors of OK Bazaars' side entrance. Those huddled inside pulled us in. I quickly explained about the child and left him with a flower-seller, who said she would sort out finding what must have been a very worried mother.

I exited again to rejoin the fray and to look for my pregnant wife. I only found her back at home much later in the day, following the leads of people who'd seen her taking refuge in one of the buildings.

For over a decade I kept many news photographs and dramatic newspaper clippings of what had happened to us on the streets of Cape Town that day. In my constant moves during fifteen years of exile, these were lost. Today, few of the thousands of photographs capturing the involvement of Camissa African youth can be found. It's almost as if the 'Coloured' schoolchildren and workers' resistance has been erased from memory.

* * * *

As a result of the national youth uprising, there developed a need to keep momentum and to have some coordination across the country, and the Comrades Movement emerged in townships across Cape Town. It was a pragmatic, organically formed organisation rather than a formal political movement; everyone had their own affiliations. It was also a school-students-driven form of organisation to communicate between schools, as well as a means to talk to workers who went on a general strike for three days in mid-September. I teamed up with a small Comrades Movement group in Gugulethu.

At this time two main forms of action were being carried out. The first was taking to the streets in protest marches against 'Bantu education' and 'Christian national education', and the separate education systems imposed for different races. The protest was also about building black unity and black consciousness, and thus was an attack on apartheid and its inferior offerings for all black people.

The second form of action was the organisation of stayaways from school, work and shops. All of these required communications, networking and logistics. My development as a liberation printer began around this time, when I started using a children's printing set with rubber lettering to compose block text. We understood that use of typewriters, photocopiers and some printing methods could result in track and tracing that could ultimately be used in court. Thus, we studied methods of secret operations by reading old French Resistance stories from the Second World War.

I had learnt the basics of lead compositing in the printing press at trade school, and I used that knowledge to print out notices from our Comrades Movement group. On the days before stayaways occurred, we would print the ultimatums of Gugulethu school students to their school principals to shut down schools – 'or else we will take action against the school'.

In order to get the info that would be included in these flyers, my wife Maria and I would, without a permit, cross into Gugulethu on foot to attend the Catholic church where, after holy mass, we would meet with our Comrades Movement at the church under the pretext of church work. (Just as people then classified as 'Bantu/Native' had to have a pass to enter 'Coloured' and 'White' areas, so too was it necessary for 'Coloured' and 'White' people to have a permit to enter 'Bantu/Native' areas. It was all part of apartheid separation laws. Of course, we did not cooperate with these oppressive laws, which would have meant going to the dreaded Bantu affairs administration board offices, which connected to the security police, to apply for a permit.)

At our meeting we would then draft a short ultimatum letter, which I would take away with me to typeset with the rubber letters, and print.

Later, I would get copies back to our comrades for distribution to the school principals, teachers and students.

On one of these occasions, as we crossed back from Gugulethu to the 'Coloured' side of the bridge, which separates the 'Bantu/Native' township from the 'Coloured' Cape Flats areas, a police sedan cruised up to us and the driver told us to get in. We obeyed. The driver, a police sergeant, did a U-turn on the bridge and started driving in silence away from the police station near the bridge. Next to him sat a police lieutenant. They drove past schools with broken windows, and some other burnt-out buildings, while talking about 'betogers' (instigators) and the destruction they cause.

I was shit-scared. If I was searched, they would find the draft letter we'd drawn up that evening, and that would immediately serve as evidence to hand me a long prison sentence. It was very likely that I would also face torture, in order for them to get the names of others from me. I had to think very quickly.

The two policemen addressed us roughly, asking what we were doing in a township and where our permits were to be in the area. Instinctively, I adopted my polite-but-dumb persona, speaking apologetically and addressing the officer by a higher rank while repeatedly calling him 'sir'. So I said, 'Sorry, Captain, we don't know about permits, sir. We have come from church. The priest at this Catholic church used to be a parish priest at our church and now he is in Gugulethu, and we like his sermons. He makes a lot of jokes, sir, and he knows us well.'

Then they wanted to know whether we were university students. Again, we knew this type of reasoning: the police hated students, who they considered troublemakers. My response wasn't entirely put on, because at that time I too had a disliking for university students, thinking them to be spoiled rich brats playing at trendy politics. 'No, never, sir!' I said. 'We are not students, sir. We work for a living. I'm a hospital storeman and my wife is a shop assistant in town, sir.'

This changed the tone of the whole conversation, and I capitalised on this by asking whether the 'Captain' knew of a certain Catholic police captain who was a cricket player, whose family were known to me. That completely broke the ice, and the policemen generously informed us that we were a bit stupid to be walking into a 'Bantu' area, as it was dangerous. They added that if we wanted to go to church there, we had to get permits. I continued playing dumb and asked them where we could get the permits. After telling us about the Bantu affairs administration board offices, which of course we already knew about, they offered to drive us to the nearest railway station to get a train back home.

Back in our dilapidated rent-controlled cottage below Lower Main Road in Salt River, we hid the draft letter until we were certain that we weren't going to get a surprise visit. The dismal condition of the little house was useful to us for this: the roof had many leaks and the floorboards were rotten in places from the rain. Under one of these rotten floorboards, right at the furthest reach of an arm, was a nail, and onto this was hooked a rope tied to a waterproof plastic bag containing the printing sets, and later other printing equipment, paper, inks and other compromising papers and literature. This was lowered into the deep pit in the house foundations below.

That incident with the police shook me and caused me to think. In January 1977 Maria and I had had our first son, Dylan Mtshali (named for Dylan Thomas, Bob Dylan and Oswald Mtshali), and the stakes had become much higher for me. I was conscious that I was leading my revolutionary existence in an amateurish way, but that at the same time, life-or-death decisions were being made and I was getting deeper and deeper into serious activities for which I needed much mental preparation as well as skills that I did not have.

* * * *

It was while attending holy mass at the Catholic church in Gugulethu that I made contact with the older generation of the ANC inside South Africa, through Bernard Matthews Huna. One of his sons, Lumko Huna, had been influential in the Young Christian Workers movement.

Bernard Huna and his wife Emily had six children, and lived in Nyanga East, having been forcibly removed from Kraaifontein. He had worked at a petrol filling station in Observatory at the height of his activism, and rose to a leadership position in the ANC and served on the district committee of the SACP. In the late 1950s and early 1960s, Bernard was a key figure in the distribution network of communist publications. When the repression rolled out in the 1960s, Bernard Huna did not leave the country and kept his head down, but also gave guidance to the new generations, and in the mid-1970s he was there again to guide us. Bernard was a close comrade of one of my later SACTU mentors, Zola Zembe (Archie Sibeko), who headed SACTU's office in London. Bernard passed away in 1990.

At that time, in the mid-1970s, things were just coming together again in Cape Town after many years of the ANC being fairly dormant as a result of its banning. I was only four years old when, in April 1960, the ANC had been declared illegal, after which the liberation movement had formed Umkhonto we Sizwe (MK), Spear of the Nation, to fight against apartheid utilising guerrilla warfare and sabotage. The mid-1970s was an era of few activists, and we often worked absolutely on our own or with just a few others. The need-to-know principle was strictly kept, for everyone's safety.

During 1976 and 1977, I was deeply involved in planning and carrying out activities of political education and of practical actions that built confidence and involved shutting down some institutions in protest action, as well as developing action by organised labour. I quickly improved my own political education to a level where I was being invited to small meetings to share my knowledge, and I found myself taking a leading role among other youth.

Early in 1977 I developed an ambitious plan for a single-day coordinated bombing attack on road and rail bridges on the main arteries into and out of Cape Town. These were at the Settlers Way railway bridge in Mowbray, the Voortrekker Road road-rail bridge in Salt River, on De Waal Drive and on the N1, together with a small hit on Wynberg military base 11 Supply and Transport, of which I had intimate knowledge.

One of our group, Vuyani, was asked to leave the country to see the ANC in Lesotho, to apprise the movement of our plan and get instructions on whether it was feasible, as well as whether we needed additional direction and training. In the event, Vuyani chickened out at the border and returned to Cape Town, and we broke off any further contact with him.

It then fell to me to convey the plan to the ANC, which I did much later, when I fled across the border to Botswana. The ANC chose not to implement my plan because it couldn't guarantee that no civilian lives would be lost, and the liberation movement's approach had always been to avoid any civilian casualties. President OR Tambo had considered the doctrine of the 'just war' and also the Geneva Protocols on the conduct of war. As such, he constantly reminded young people that recklessness would undermine our struggle, and the huge goodwill and solidarity we had garnered around the world as one of the pillars of our strategic approach to the struggle.

At the time, I was a bit frustrated, as the operation had been planned for the early hours, before the trains were running and when there was little traffic on the roads. I am now, of course, appreciative of the sensible and responsible older leaders who'd employed much deeper and more careful consideration than my naïve self.

The murder of Steve Biko in 1977 and the events that followed pushed us onto the road of no return. In August 1977, Biko was arrested by the security police. While in custody in Port Elizabeth, on 11 September he was brutally beaten and then driven over a thousand kilometres to Pretoria. The next day he died alone, his head battered, naked and shackled.

Biko's brutal murder – the twentieth death of a prisoner in detention over the preceding eighteen months – sent shockwaves through the ranks of activists. But at the same time it caused the apartheid regime to crack down on newspapers and newspaper editors and people known to be friendly to Biko, as well as all the organisations in the family of the black consciousness movement, banned organisations, left-wing religious organisations and the emergent trade unions. From 19 October 1977, the apartheid government unleashed a wave of terror against a range of media, oppositional organisations and individual activists.

By this time, I felt that I had outgrown the Young Christian Workers and I broke with them, taking some members with me to form an independent organisation, the Peninsula Workers Forum, which then became known as the Southern Socialist Working Youth. I also started two free newspapers, produced using an old untraceable Remington portable typewriter and printing equipment bought from secondhand stalls on the Grand Parade. Over a few months I set up a small illegal printing outfit, with the paper and inks paid for out of my wages.

Young Voice was a free underground anti-apartheid newspaper that carried bits of news, cultural pieces, and excerpts on liberation theology and black theology. It also highlighted the repression happening in the country, and called for the release of detainees and the unbanning of organisations. We targeted church services for 'hit-and-run' distribution, as people left holy mass on a Sunday – we would quickly hand out the paper as people came out of church, then disappear, and the next week we'd target another church, and especially the youth.

Young Voice was banned within weeks. Immediately, I started another, similar newspaper called *New Voice*. It was also banned.

* * * *

In 1978, in answer to global expressions of outrage, the apartheid regime admitted that it had more than 450 people in detention without trial. The true figure was much larger. Particularly singled out were journalists and editors, black consciousness movement organisations, trade unions and left-oriented church organisations. The Young Christian Workers movement, in which I had cut my political teeth, was being harassed by the security police, and between May and June that year, fourteen leaders of the movement were taken into detention.

It was during this time that I first met Kallie Hanekom, the Catholic lay chaplain in the Young Christian Student Movement for university students. He lived in Oak Street in Observatory, and gave us access to his extensive library. Maria and I and our child Dylan would later move onto a farm in Kuils River with Kallie's brother Derek and his wife Trish. Derek, who would go on to serve in the cabinets of Nelson

Mandela, Jacob Zuma and Cyril Ramaphosa, had travelled abroad working for various organisations including on farms, and when he returned to South Africa, he continued farming dairy, poultry and vegetables.

At the time, nobody who frequented the Oak Street house and the farm knew anything of my background or struggles – we were just working-class youth interested in politics and seen as a bit odd. Those engaging with Kallie were mainly from the white student left, who we were sceptical about in terms of their political explorations. I also didn't like the way white students or academics, when communicating with those they deemed to be inferiors, talked down.

I became a close friend to Heather Garner, who was working with the Churches Urban Planning Commission, a non-governmental organisation (NGO) formed in 1968 as a response ministry to the disruption to people's lives caused by the Group Areas Act and mass forced removals. The Churches Urban Planning Commission provided a network for radical voices, regardless of religion, at a time when activism was hardly able to function except clandestinely.

Heather and I immediately struck up a rapport because not only was she a down-to-earth person who spoke to us as equals, she came from a working-class background and was also steeped in a theology of liberation. From the beginning I had a good feeling about her, and she became like an older, wiser sister to me, and has remained so for 45 years. Over time I came to know that Heather was also a clandestine operative for the liberation movement working on the religious front.

Because of the political climate of repression, confiding in anybody was dangerous, and at the time I couldn't tell Heather everything I'd previously been through or about my childhood history, history of activism, South African Defence Force experiences, arrests and abuses. But I was able to trust her enough to share some of these things, and over the years she came to know me sometimes better than myself. Nonetheless, Heather understood that although I was more or less the same age as the university students with whom we came into contact, I'd been working for a long time, while they were fresh out of school and had never had real jobs. They lived on allowances from their parents, which were often way more than the meagre wages on which we had to survive. They had a verbal form of radical politics, but I'd already been arrested and gone through hell for standing up against the authorities all on my own.

Also, Maria and I had a child, and with parenting came extra responsibilities for us as activists; we had another life to think of. This didn't stop us from contributing to the full, however.

Another comrade in the Churches Urban Planning Commission was Michael Sedgewick, who had originally lived in Claremont before the Group Areas Act had made it the trendy white area of Harfield Road. His family had been forcibly removed to Hanover Park on the Cape Flats. Michael initiated some of the seasonal holiday schools for high-school students where they were exposed to conscientisation programmes at the Dora Valke Centre, a community centre in Strandfontein. Some of the facilitators of these programmes were people like the poet James Matthews and me.

Youth through these sessions were taught the fundamentals of socialist history and theory, and introduced to resistance praxis under South African conditions, as well as the full anatomy of the apartheid system and why it was important for our generation to give our all in opposing it. These classes at Dora Valke became the final straw for the security police, who were closely monitoring our activities, and we suspected that we'd been infiltrated by two police informers, both of whom had been observed at different times working with police.

We were asked to try and get confirmatory information about the first suspected informer, so when he came to visit us at the Kuils River farm, we managed to steal his bag in which we found conclusive evidence that he was lying to us and was connected to the security police. This included a letter from the union he claimed to have been working for, responding to a job application he'd made to them and turning him down for the job – so he couldn't have been working for the union, as he'd presented to comrades. We confirmed this with the union, then confronted him, and he broke down. We chased him off and we never heard from him or the second informer again. I heard the second informer tried to pass as an exile, but all structures in the liberation movement had been alerted to the danger he posed. Years later, his name surfaced in a speculative newspaper report about his alleged involvement in the assassination of apartheid activist Dulcie September in Paris, France, in 1988. The story went dead, however, and nothing further was heard about this connection.

By the end of 1978, in the continued wave of repression, more church organisation activists were detained, Heather among them. Word reached me that I was about to suffer the same fate and that I should leave the country immediately. (I learnt much later that my name appeared on the 'wanted ANC terrorist' lists distributed to all police stations, on the 'Coloured' list, the 'Bantu' list and the 'White' list, because officialdom did not know how to deal with the ambiguity of my identity.)

My wife, eighteen-month-old son and I were forced to leave South Africa in a hurry, driving through the night to cross the Botswana border. We left everything behind, taking just the essentials with us. We left on pay day and I had to forfeit my wages; we had a little money saved but that wouldn't last a week.

I never got to say goodbye to my family and friends, and I wouldn't see most of them, or South Africa, again for the next thirteen years.

6

EXILE:
INTO BOTSWANA

On a Sunday in September 1978, my wife, my son Dylan and I crossed the border into Botswana and arrived in a sleepy Gaborone not knowing what would happen next. Our little grey 1966 VW Beetle was as exhausted as we were. We had no money for accommodation, and it slowly sank in that we were now refugees and would have to beg for help.

We made our way to the Catholic church by asking for directions. We were looking for Drake Koka, a trade unionist and formerly an activist in the Catholic Justice and Peace Commission. Drake would be able to put us in contact with Isaac Mokopo, aka Kopsie, the head of the ANC mission in Botswana.

There was nobody around at the church other than the gardener-caretaker. I struck up a conversation with him and he suggested that we would find the priest at a convent on the outskirts of town, and should go there. He could see that we were desperate.

It was late afternoon by the time we found the convent but the priest wasn't there. We were tired and hungry, and Dylan was irritable and hot. The mother superior listened to our story, and by a stroke of luck it turned out that she knew Drake Koka. She said that she could arrange for him to come and see us the next day, and in the meantime we could stay overnight at the convent and they would give us a meal.

The following day Drake Koka came to see us. After confirming our bone fides through much questioning, he said that Isaac Mokopo would send someone to fetch us and take us to a safe house. Thus began our life in our first country of exile – Botswana.

The next few weeks were intense. We were taken to Isaac Mokopo's

Bontleng office-residence and Maria and I were separately debriefed. Then we were moved to a safe flat and supplied with basic provisions. We were told to keep a low profile and not venture out of the flat until being given the okay to do so.

A few days later we were taken first to the Botswana police to register as refugees seeking political asylum under the auspices of the ANC, a lengthy process that involved extensive questioning and both of us writing up our biographies. We were then given asylum documents, with restrictions on travel within Botswana – if we did need to travel, we would first have to get permission from the police station in Gaborone, and then report on arrival to any other police station in the town to which we were going.

Next, we had to register with the United Nations High Commission for Refugees. The United Nations provided each refugee with a small stipend per month, but to receive it each month, you had to queue up and submit to an interview. Maria, Dylan and I would arrive early in the morning on the appointed day each month, and queue with other asylum seekers in the burning sun in a dusty courtyard without shade.

The United Nations stipend was thirty pula for the head of household, twenty pula for a wife and six pula for each child – the equivalent of about R56 per month for our family of three. This was our only cash income, but the ANC supplemented it with meat, vegetables, canned foods, rice, sugar, salt, tea and coffee.

We were provided with political education books, the Cuban newspaper *Granma*, and Soviet reading materials from Novosti Press, the state-owned news agency, including the periodical *Sputnik*. We also got a chess board and book to teach ourselves to play the game. After a few weeks of being cooped up in the flat, we were given permission to walk to the Gaborone Mall and back.

We were looked after by four cadres, including Henry 'Squire' Makgothi; occasionally we would see Isaac Mokopo too. Some time later, Ray Alexander Simons of SACTU and the SACP leadership, John Gaetsewe, the general-secretary of SACTU, Ruth Mompati from the ANC leadership and women's section, and Reg September from the ANC and SACP leadership (also a trade unionist, and founder of the South African Coloured People's Congress), all came to Botswana to do debriefings with us. Henry Makgothi, Jeanette Curtis Schoon, Marius Schoon, Lauren Vlotman and Pete Richer became the group of people who handled all affairs relating to us during 1978–79. Dan Tloome handled my induction into the SACP structures.

Marius Schoon had been arrested for sabotage in 1964, and sentenced to twelve years' imprisonment, after which, in 1976, he'd been placed under house arrest and banning orders. In 1977 he and Jeanette Curtis, who'd been banned for trade union and National Union of South African Students activities, broke their banning orders, got married and escaped to Botswana. While we were in Botswana, their little daughter Katryn and our son Dylan were playmates on the occasions we got together.

The ANC leaders showed special interest in the 'Coloured' and the mixed 'poor white' communities in Cape Town, and their level of organisation in trade unions. They were particularly keen to make a breakthrough in organising within these communities because to that point this had proven difficult. There was also fascination with my story, because we came out of a very different background to most that the ANC was encountering at the time, and we had taken great risks and left as a family.

* * * *

Our abode changed frequently. From the safe flat, we were moved to another house in Bontleng with some journalists who ran the Southern African News Agency. I felt very uncomfortable and out of place living there, and had misgivings about some of the people from the South African white student left who were coming and going. The house was the most open secret in Gaborone as a contact between the white student left and the ANC, and it had become a dangerous crossroads of intrigue. I requested that we be moved. A couple of years later we learnt that the South African security police were monitoring the place closely, and had had a hand in setting it up, infiltrating agents and manipulating others.

We went to live in Mahalapye in rural Botswana with Pete Richer and Lauren Vlotman, where we underwent some political education and training. Pete and Lauren were ANC/SACP/MK operatives working under the cover of being teachers at a local school. Pete was originally from Rhodesia (today's Zimbabwe), where he'd started his working life as a chef. He was a patient and able teacher who put us through the basics of the history of the liberation movement, political theory and what would be expected of us. He helped us to see what it was that we could do in the movement in the future. He introduced us to broader political books than we'd thus far been exposed to.

While Maria and I really warmed to this couple, by this time, we were going a bit crazy. It was a life of isolation. Together with Pete Richer and the Schoons, we looked at the feasibility of returning to South Africa, as operatives in a different area, but this was quickly ruled out unless we were prepared to separate as a family and I assumed a new identity. We decided against that option.

I indicated that we'd like to build on the liberation path that I'd started on in South Africa – printing and publishing liberation materials for the underground work of SACTU and the SACP, ANC and MK. We would preferably like to do this from the frontline states, possibly Mozambique, we said. So this became our focus, and a training course was arranged for us at the Brigades Development Trust in Serowe over the whole of 1979.

The founder of the Brigades was a former Union of South Africa diplomat and Liberal Party man by the name of Patrick van Rensburg. He had first founded Swaneng Hill School secondary school in Serowe in 1963. A second project, the Serowe Brigades Development Trust, was his next contribution to Botswana.

At the Brigades Centre for skills development and learning, the curriculum included skills training in agriculture, building, carpentry, metalwork and printing. Each of these areas became a cooperative business in its own right, thereby creating employment opportunities. Along with the skills development, his trainers taught applied mathematics, applied science, technical drawing, typing, darkroom photography, history, English and African literature. In many ways, the education-in-production approach was similar to the industrial trades school that I'd attended, the Salesian Institute.

When he established the Builders' Brigade in 1970, Van Rensburg's aim was that it should be a vehicle to build more schools. Parallel to this, he launched the Serowe Youth Development Association. Soon there were other brigades in Serowe, and not long after, brigades and brigade trusts all around Botswana.

Along with seventeen other ANC and Zimbabwe African National Union (Zanu) students, at Serowe we would learn a range of technical skills alongside an education programme involving English, African literature, Southern African history, maths, science, and artisan theory and practice. Five cadres from the Zimbabwe African National Liberation Army (Zanla), the military wing of the Zanu, would be sent to train with us, and two of these would join the printing brigade with us. (Although the Zimbabwe war of liberation would come to an end shortly, in December 1979, at that time it was still ongoing.)

The rest of the ANC cadres were mainly early Kongwa MK training camp cadres associated with the Wankie/Sipolilo campaign generation who had originally been among the first MK soldiers to train outside of South Africa. The primary aim of the unsuccessful Wankie/Sipolilo campaign was to move through the then Rhodesia into South Africa to open up a guerrilla war front. MK soldiers in the Wankie/Sipolilo campaign were all trained in the only camp that the ANC had at the time in Africa – Kongwa in central Tanzania. It was a privilege to have been assigned to this contingent and the training programme.

Patrick van Rensburg was hoping that the ANC would appoint him as principal of what would become the Solomon Mahlangu Freedom College at Morogoro in Tanzania, an educational institution established by the exiled ANC in 1977 at Mazimbu, Tanzania, with the purpose to give the youth who'd fled South Africa after the 1976 Soweto Uprising and the children of exiles a good primary and secondary education. The training programme for liberation-movement cadres at the Serowe Brigades was a kind of trial run to see how the ANC and Van Rensburg would work together. As it turned out, the answer was not very well.

When we arrived in Serowe we found that no organisation of living quarters had been done. My family and I were driven up a steep rocky hillside to two dilapidated stone cottages. When we entered one, the stench of goats' excrement hit the nostrils – and indeed goats were living in the place which was piled high with goat droppings. There was no water and no electricity, although Van Rensburg provided paraffin lamps, utensils and bedding – as well as spades and buckets to clean out the cottages. He said that when the others arrived, we would have to dig a trench to lay a pipe for us to get water from around 200 metres away, downhill. We looked at him incredulously.

I was intensely annoyed that he had misled the ANC and that he expected us to bed down with our child, with no basic amenities in what was basically a goats' shed. I demanded that he accommodate us elsewhere until the other comrades arrived, whereupon we would collectively come to a solution on accommodation. So we stayed in Van Rensburg's comfortable home that night.

When the others arrived the following day, they took one look at what was on offer and simply refused to live like that. We were all used to a spartan lifestyle with just the basics, but this was just not acceptable.

We also pointed out that the isolated location near the top of the koppies, with just two cottages for nineteen people, was an easy target for an attack and posed a great danger to us. The day after my birthday in March 1979, our premier camp in Angola, Nova Katenga, was the subject of a South African Air Force attack. In our isolated spot on the side of a hill just outside of Serowe, we were jittery in the aftermath of this attack and wondered whether this entire scenario was possibly a setup. We had reason to be paranoid when we saw how disorganised our host was about the programme, and that there was frequent engagement between the Serowe Brigades and white South Africans.

We brought the security threat to the attention of Pete Richer and the Schoons, to whom we were still reporting, and demanded that we be spread out among the villagers in the sprawling rural town of Serowe, and that we split into units of no more than three per dwelling. Van Rensburg thus arranged for us to be tenants among the population.

Each group of three was also taken to a large trading store and given basic equipment and supplies, and we all got a regular monthly stipend for food and other items.

The other major problem was that no structured courses had been planned. Our group began to work with the largely expatriate European instructors to give the programme a structure and discipline, with desired outcomes.

At the Serowe Brigades in Botswana my training in basic agitational propaganda ('agitprop') journalism, graphic layout and design, photographic darkroom work, and lithographic printing took place under a Danish man called Peter Jensen and a Dutch Surinamese man, Bram Dilrosen. The Serowe Brigades Printing Press, known as Mmegi wa Dikgang, also had a small newspaper of the same name. It combined commercial work (such as printing labels for canned goods) with creating periodicals, posters, pamphlets, certificates and display buttons.

We worked on producing underground agitprop materials, which prepared me directly for running a liberation press, hopefully under the SACP and SACTU in Mozambique. Our ANC seniors on the training programme were two ngwenyas, or 'old crocodiles', Brenda Ndlovu and Alfred Gaza from the earliest MK intakes at Kongwa camp in Tanzania in the 1960s.

In the end the training was of high quality, and we achieved what we'd set out to do. Alas, our success had little to do with Patrick van Rensburg. To his credit, though, the Brigades and the Swaneng Hill School that he had established could structurally accommodate nineteen mature adults with military-political skills, to make a success of the programme.

Resolving both the accommodation and the course programme, with the sparse foundation provided by our host, was an exercise in collective determination by MK and Zanla soldiers.

* * *

Serowe was traditional town largely made up of mud huts alongside small single-storey cement breezeblock buildings with corrugated-iron roofs.

A few of the European development agencies had built fancier homes for their volunteers. Many of these male volunteers lived with local women in concubine relationships. It was a lesson in twentieth-century colonial behaviour.

We still lived very basic lives. We had no electricity and had to walk to the water source to fetch water in plastic containers. Laundry was done in a large metal bath, which we'd also carry to the water source, and the clothes would be scattered over bushes to dry.

It wasn't easy on Maria and Dylan (everyone called our toddler Mtshali, and Maria was maMtshali). I'd grown up nomadically, and largely homeless and in poverty, whereas Maria had led a relatively stable life. But she was strong and never complained, and she put up with much difficulty. Dylan was still in nappies, and he constantly had diarrhoea. In time he just walked around half naked, wearing only a shirt.

We ate meagre meals. A local butcher knew that we were freedom fighters, and he would sell us small portions of meat for twenty thebe (about twenty cents) and throw in an extra piece saying, 'For the young one.'

The constant threat of enemy attack created much anxiety among us. We knew that the South African Defence Force and the Rhodesian forces didn't distinguish between military and civilian targets, and certainly wouldn't consider us to be students on a civil programme. For the first time post-1976, many ANC personnel had come southwards, closer to South Africa, rather than moving northwards, which made our group one of interest to the security establishments of both countries. On top of these factors, ours was a mixed ANC/MK-Zanu/Zanla group. Up until then the ANC had been strongly associated with the Soviet Union-aligned Zimbabwe African People's Union (Zapu) and Zimbabwe People's Revolutionary Army (Zipra). With a Zimbabwean settlement on the horizon, this action would have had intelligence analysts worried.

In Botswana we found that our life of dodging the security police in South Africa had been swapped for a life of insecurity and low-key war in exile, rather than one of finding refuge in the frontline states. Telephone tapping, stalking, assassinations, disappearances of activists and cross-border raids became the order of the day. The entire region was gripped by low-intensity war. In all respects it was no different from what was happening within South Africa and at some levels it was worse.

We lived near Bessie Head, another South African exile of Camissa African roots, although she was very reclusive. She was the author of several books, including *Serowe: Village of the Rain Wind*, which later gave us a better understanding of the place that we had lived in for a year. Bessie's life and her life's work was and still is an inspiration. She too had had a very difficult upbringing and early adulthood; in some ways she reminded me of myself, and in many other ways of my mom, and the breakdowns and turmoil that she'd gone through. Bessie, like my mom, was one of the saddest people to cross my path.

Assisted by Patrick van Rensburg, Bessie had taught at Swaneng Hill School, and had also worked for a while at the Cooperative Farming Brigade and food-processing unit on the other side of the koppie from where our 'goats' cottages' were perched. She died relatively young, aged 48, from hepatitis, six years after we left Serowe.

The dry, desolate sprawling town of Serowe will always have a place in my heart. We integrated ourselves into the town, and its people opened their hearts to us. For the first time rural life and African indigenous history and heritage came alive for me.

I was introduced to the history textbook on Southern Africa used throughout the region for Cambridge high-school exams, written by Neil Parsons. It was completely different from the colonial and racist rubbish that was being taught in schools in South Africa; indeed, even what was taught at universities. For the first time, African social history free of stereotypical and racist anthropological and archaeological pigeonholing came to the fore for me. I learnt about social formations and cultures rather than about the stone-age and iron-age hominins that were South African history staples.

During our time in Serowe, I tried my hand at writing a book, by candlelight while listening to the radio. It was an illustrated history of South Africa, and it helped to while away the evening hours. It was never published and would have required a lot of work to do so. I still have the tatty old copy as a keepsake.

I learnt about the role of traditional leaders in settling disputes when one day I found two newborn goats in the compound where we lived. I could see that they were hungry and there was no nanny-goat around. My neighbours said that I had to go seek counsel from our local traditional leader, and took me to him. He pronounced that it was my duty to ensure that the kids were nourished and cared for, because if they died in my care and an owner came forth, I would have to pay compensation. However, if the owner did not come forth in the period that the traditional leader ruled on, then the goats would be mine. I was blessed for seeking the advice and sent on my way.

I bent over backwards feeding those two kids, and two days later I encountered a noisy nanny-goat with a sore udder in my compound. I quickly got the kids out to her, and all three out of our compound, with plenty of laughing spectators looking on.

On another occasion I rescued a dog from some children who were hanging it from a tree and pelting it with stones. When I asked the children why they were hanging the dog, they said that it had committed the crime of eating chickens and must die. I then asked why they were stoning the dog as it was already going to die. They answered that the dog had to be taught a lesson before it died. So we argued, and I managed to save the dog by offering another solution. I suggested that the dog be taken away into the sorghum and millet fields out of town, where there were no chickens, and there the dog could be used to chase away birds or mice that destroyed the crops. The children were a bit peeved because they'd been stopped from perfecting their throwing skills and the boys from impressing the girls, but it was accepted as a workable solution.

As a city boy, not brought up with African traditions, but with some of my grandmother's rural etiquette from her birthplace in Cala in the Eastern Cape instilled in me, Serowe added depth to my understanding and respect for Africa's rural soul. Wherever you walked in the expansive village, time wasn't a factor. If you passed an elder, you stopped to greet them, and greetings were never just hello and goodbye. You expected to be asked how your parents were, and the family, and the answers had to be considered. Likewise, you had to ask the same, and this could take some time with each person you encountered. It taught thoughtfulness and respect.

Then there was respect that had to be shown to the dead. If a funeral hearse and cars passed, you stopped alongside the road and bowed your head. These were important community protocols to be observed.

I left Serowe a better person than when I'd arrived.

* * * *

By the time we'd completed the programme at the end of 1979, the ANC was still not ready to deploy us. The SACP/SACTU press to be established in Mozambique had for some unknown reason fallen through, and they were now discussing establishing a combined press in Zambia in Lusaka. But the ANC was having problems in Zambia, where the Zambian government was facing its own internal problems, and was being highly prescriptive of the ANC about how many personnel it was allowed to have in the country.

From the late 1960s an Africa Liberation Centre had been established in Lusaka's Kamwala township, where the various liberation movements of Southern Africa had offices, and by 1977 the ANC effectively had its headquarters there. But the Zambians also blew hot and cold as to whether they had really agreed to allow the ANC to have its headquarters in Lusaka. It didn't help that Ian Smith's Rhodesian forces had carried out a series of relentless attacks on targets in Zambia from October 1978, including on Joshua Nkomo's house and Zapu camps – and, in April 1979, an overland attack which came through to Lusaka and destroyed the Liberation Centre, including the ANC official offices.

Also, at times it was relatively easy to clear ANC cadres through Lusaka International Airport, and at other times it was very difficult. Zambia particularly refused entry clearance to several known senior communists. By the time we went to Lusaka at the end of 1979, ANC personnel from the headquarters were doing the clearances.

Towards the end of our year in Serowe, two of our ANC cadres defected back to South Africa. It came as a shock to us that the two would rather hand themselves over to the South African police than return to Tanzania. From listening to the conversations between the other Kongwa camp veterans on the course, a bleak picture emerged of hardships and disgruntlement in Tanzania and Lusaka during their long years of exile there. At the time, I really didn't understand much of what this was about, but through my own experiences, I finally realised that most of the cadres, who clearly had undergone many difficulties, were disciplined nonetheless, and proud to be in the ANC and MK.

Inevitably, the defectors would become askaris, a constant threat that we had to live with, and this made it very hard to trust our own comrades at times, and even some leaders. This was part of a difficult learning curve.

At the end of 1979 the Lancaster House Agreement saw the end of the Ian Smith Rhodesian regime, and independence for Zimbabwe in 1980. From December 1979 to March 1980 the refugee camps for Zimbabweans in Botswana began to empty – the first phase of the United Nations High Commission for Refugees repatriation operations, during which over 18 000 Zimbabweans were repatriated from Botswana. Those refugee camps were touted as the new home of South African refugees in Botswana; we South African refugees resisted this idea.

At the end of our course, we moved down to the village of Palapye, and then to Mochudi, and thereafter back to Gaborone. To help make ends meet, I managed to get a gardening job with an expatriate Mennonite family twice a week, earning an additional ten pula. These Quaker and Mennonite missionaries also provided us with shoes, clothes and blankets, and gave us a domestic workers' quarters to live in.

My mother and my nephew Anton, one of May's sons, came up to Botswana from Cape Town to see us in 1979. They travelled to Gaborone by train, and my mother was able to chat to Reg September and Henry Makgothi, who assured her that her grandchild and I were being well looked after and there was nothing to worry about. Because we had left without a goodbye, this trip for my mother was the goodbye, as we explained to her that for a long time there would be no more communication. Once we left Botswana for Mozambique or Zambia, and were involved in operational work, we wouldn't be able to communicate from those countries, as it was too difficult and dangerous. Communications with family also put them at risk.

Jimmy Dryja and his wife Barbara also came up to meet with us and the ANC. That was my goodbye to James.

I was getting impatient. I was always enquiring of Dan Tloome and Henry Makgothi as to when we would be going north, so that I could get on with printing.

They said that it was much better working from Botswana, away from all the silly competitiveness and bickering, and the messy style of working and intrigues that dominated up north and further afield. 'You will miss Botswana one day, just wait and see,' they told me. 'Life is much simpler here and the struggle will always be stronger in your nostrils. You can serve our people in a deeper way here than there. You will curse your impatience.'

In time I would learn that Uncle Dan and Uncle Henry were right. They knew through experience what I was yet to learn about the realpolitik of the liberation struggle.

* * * *

In the 1970s, the many who arrived on the ANC's doorstep had been attracted by a political call formulated in the 1969 post-Morogoro conference framework and a predominance of a guerrilla warfare strategy. (The Morogoro Conference was an inaugural consultative ANC conference held in Morogoro, Tanzania, in April 1969.) The training people wanted was still based on the old guerrilla-warfare model where after a short military training stint they would form platoons and units, go back into South Africa, and engage in classic guerrilla warfare and create liberated zones.

By then a new, more complex strategy had emerged in the ANC, requiring more sophisticated insurgency skills than the old guerrilla-warfare model of the 1950s and 1960s. Revolutionary guerrillero-romanticism and trendy intellectual-acrobatics of the left intelligentsia had now given way to a well-conceived programme to take South Africa on a path away from white minority rule and empower the majority of the population to take their future into their own hands.

The movement looked east to Vietnam, which had successful practical experience to share not only on military matters but also on mobilising and organising their population – and this made all the difference. It became abundantly clear that as part of creating a climate conducive to popular insurrection and a people's war, the immediate purpose of armed actions was to support mass political defiance and activity. This required building new organisational formations, clandestine political activity, and strikes – where armed action was oriented towards confidence-building, rather than old-fashioned guerrilla warfare aimed at a military victory. Work inside South Africa had to have an open mass organisational face complemented by a clandestine face which linked to the liberation movement and was coordinated to move in the same direction rather than pulling in different directions.

From the time of our flight from South Africa in September 1978 until December 1979 when we left Botswana for Zambia, MK had carried out over 30 operations, according to press reports. Our generation of politically and militarily trained personnel were beginning to make an impact, and that in turn boosted morale where more open political activity and trade union activity was taking place in South Africa. Whereas in the 1960s a wave of repression had forced everything underground and resulted in a more subdued climate of political activism, the post-1976–77 wave of repression resulted in the complete opposite. It emboldened people to stand up and fight like never before.

The ANC, a relatively small organisation with manageable numbers, grew into something much bigger as a result of the 1976–77 uprising in South Africa, followed by the turbulence caused by increased repression in the country during the 1980s. It has been estimated that between 1976 and 1978 over 12 000 people left South Africa, and of these 9 000 joined MK, with more joining other structures of the ANC: some wanted to be soldiers, others wanted a place in the ANC leadership structures, and others wanted bursaries or simply to live a new life abroad.

The apartheid security police were at the same time making use of this pressure of influx into the ANC to build their structures within the movement. The worst assumption would be to think all were motivated by some sort of revolutionary zeal and the fight for freedom. Opportunism abounded.

What had been South African resistance to repression in our country had quickly grown into a regional war across Southern Africa, combining conventional warfare and unconventional terror attacks carried out through surrogate special transnational forces like Koevoet (the counterinsurgency branch of the South West African police, which included white South African police officers, usually seconded from the South African security branch, and black volunteers from Namibia), Renamo (a right-wing Mozambican political party and militant group), Unita (a large Angolan political party that received military aid from apartheid South Africa), the Mashula gang (allied to the South African Defence Force and aimed at creating instability in Zambia) and askaris. ANC residences were regularly attacked in frontline states, in Lesotho, Swaziland, Mozambique, Botswana and Zambia, with much loss of life and destruction of property.

False flag operations, committed with the intent of disguising the actual source of responsibility and pinning blame on another party, were carried out by the security police, the South African Police and the South African Defence Force, where blame was apportioned to MK in attempts to discredit the ANC. Inside South Africa there was a rising death toll in this war involving massacres by the apartheid security forces, not to mention abductions by ghostly hit squads and deaths in detention.

At the Truth and Reconciliation Commission, the ANC submission on MK operations showed that throughout the 1960s there had been 190 MK operations against economic targets, the South African Police, the Rhodesian military and the South African Defence Force. From 1970 to 1984 there were 227 operations. But in 1985 alone there were 136 operations; in 1986 there were 230 operations; in 1987 there were 234 operations; and in 1988-1990, when the armed struggle was suspended, there were at least another 140 operations. This was a total of over a thousand recorded military operations, and there were likely many more laissez-faire military actions by informally established MK self-defence units.

Through our collective of comrades in the Serowe Brigades, I learnt that while most of them had trained at Kongwa and in Eastern Europe and the USSR before the Wankie and Sipolilo campaigns, there were now many more ANC camps in Angola – Benguela, Nova Katengue, Gabela, Fazenda, Quibaxe, Pango, Malanje, Caxito, Quattro, Funda, and Viana transit camp near Luanda. MK was also active in the conventional war in Angola and is said to have lost over a hundred combatants in the Battle of Cuito Cuanavale.

Whatever critique there may be about the nature, successes and failures of MK, only the most ignorant would say that no war was fought. There are those who still deny that a war happened in South Africa and Southern Africa but those of us who experienced this war know exactly what we went through and remember many faces who didn't make it. We went through a struggle, but we also went through a very dirty war.

7

LUSAKA:
CUTTING MY ANC TEETH

Right up to just before we left Botswana at the end of 1979, Maria and I were still expecting to go to Mozambique to establish a printing press in Maputo. Finally, just as pressure was mounting for us to go to the vacated Dukwe Zimbabwean refugee camp, my family and I were airlifted to Zambia to go and work at the ANC headquarters. My deployment orders were to start a liberation press just outside of Lusaka.

We used United Nations travel documents issued by the High Commission for Refugees in Botswana. We boarded an old airplane, on which we were seated next to the Russian ambassador's wife, who made small talk all the way to Lusaka International Airport.

The Lusaka we arrived in was not the Lusaka of the mid or late 1980s, when frequent trips were being made by delegations from South Africa to meet the ANC. The ANC population then was less than a third of the size it later became. There were fewer than 400 of us at that time, scattered around Lusaka and further afield.

The ANC was still battling to develop itself as an organisation appropriate to its mission. Its office-bearers were political leaders but not adept in the huge amount of administration required to run a rapidly expanding organisation with a complex mission that included a military wing. Along with this was the need to isolate the apartheid regime internationally by building a global anti-apartheid movement that would move towards blockading South Africa and disrupting its economic lifeblood. The ANC was thus challenged to engage in organisational development, skills development and infrastructure development to create a formidable machine to accomplish this.

I arrived in Lusaka just as the pioneering of this new approach was taking place and was experiencing pushback by old ways of thinking on the one hand, and counterinsurgency operations of the apartheid regime on the other hand.

The necessary logistical support lines for a new approach weren't in place, and neither was the mass of the population geared towards providing full cover for guerrilla military units. The new strategy required several components and not simply a military solution, and so the ANC's four-pillar strategy (armed struggle, building a mass civic movement, building an underground resistance, sanctions and isolating the apartheid regime internationally) emerged and got refined as a counter to the apartheid regime's total strategy.

The change in approach and the lack of conscientisation of MK soldiers to the changes led to frustration and disgruntlement. The apartheid counterinsurgency exploited this with mischief on a grand scale. It didn't help that to most of the soldiers in camps it seemed that they may never be deployed and would remain there for a lifetime. The ANC didn't handle this entire problem well, but in time things would change for the better.

By 1979, the ANC had at last developed the appropriate theory required to take the struggle forward but it had yet to develop the necessary organisational capacity. It was a steep learning curve for all of us, and in this context skills development and education were placed much higher in prioritisation than before, leading to much greater mobility and skills acquisition for comrades who had previously been stuck in an extremely uncomfortable rut.

The period 1979–1981 was the make or break of the ANC, and the apartheid regime did everything in its power to destroy the movement. The ANC, under the steady and skilled hand of president OR Tambo, survived this assault and went on to develop a formidable machinery for a new era. It was a period of 'trial and error' organisational development.

It was against this backdrop that I was asked to set up a liberation printing press from scratch. It was to be based about eight kilometres outside of Lusaka at a rural place called Makeni. From Makeni you could see the city skyline in the distance.

Back in 1965 Dr Shaik Ahmod Goolam Randeree, a veteran of the South African Indian Congress, and his family had moved from South Africa to Zambia and set up a medical practice. He had a house at Makeni as well as a large plot of land, and it was here in 1967 that he started producing the ANC newspaper *Mayibuye*. Makeni was at the coalface of pioneering the ANC's new approach through print and radio agit-prop, and I was part of the new generation, led by Peter Mayibuye (Joel Netshitenzhe). Our mission was to revive *Mayibuye* and extend the insurgency literature that would mobilise people power and take us forward to create a climate in South Africa that was conducive to insurrection and collapsing apartheid.

The ANC's department of publicity and information, headed by Thabo Mbeki, was strategically linked to fall under the office of the president, and it linked to both international relations and to the newly emergent political military council. Under Thabo and based at Makeni heading the communications section was Sizakele Sigxashe, with Peter Mayibuye heading publications and radio.

It was humid and rainy on the day we arrived at our new base in Makeni, which then consisted of a cluster of four buildings with a fence around it, sheltered by large mango trees. Two of the original houses were joined by a modern research centre and an office, plus a second office for president OR Tambo. Next door, on the other side of the fence, was another house, occupied by Reg September and his wife, Gwen Miller, an Englishwoman. Between their house and the Makeni base fence was a plot of groundnuts in neat rows.

Maria, Dylan and I were shown to a house that had been prepared for us, from which we could see Reg September's place, with a fence separating us. Soon we were visited by a short, dapper man with spectacles and a Clark Gable-style moustache, followed by another man with a beaming smile. These were Wolfie Kodesh and Benny 'Natho' de Bruyn, the latter the husband of Sophie Williams who was a big heroine of ours, and who'd been in the leadership group of women who'd marched on the Union Buildings back in 1956, the year of my birth.

Wolfie was a through-and-through socialist and anti-fascist who'd cut his political teeth during the Second World War as a serviceman activist in the left-wing Springbok Legion. In December 1961 when the ANC and SACP formed MK, many of the Springbok Legion's leaders were founding members. Wolfie Kodesh was one of them.

Wolfie was full of jokes and said, 'You know, you are very important people. OR personally gave me a mission to look after you and get you well settled and make sure that your every need is looked after. I'm not sure what makes you so important, but the old man has said that for more than eighteen months, since you escaped from South Africa, you guys have been going through hell, so we must make you feel at home. You are very important to the movement.'

Apparently, Ruth Mompati, Dan Tloome, Ray Alexander, John Gaetsewe, Mac Maharaj, John Nkadimeng, Reg September and others had all long been talking to Oliver Tambo about this young working-class family from a poor mixed community in Cape Town, who'd escaped South Africa after having defied the apartheid regime since our teens. Wolfie with his characteristic chuckle continued, 'Now I can see you are just hoi polloi like me.' The perceptive Kodesh could see that I didn't understand the phrase and explained, 'It means common people, the working-class public, just like me.'

Benny, who'd been a logistics man in the Wankie campaign, and did all the movement's building work as well as serving on the regional political committee (and who would later be ANC chief representative, first in Lusaka and later in Rome), and Wolfie, who headed logistics, made sure that there was a proper home for us, which we shared with Ace Megwe.

After my first day at Makeni, Ace called me aside and said that he'd been told by Wolfie and Benny that I had to be trained to handle military weapons, as everyone staying at and working from the Makeni site had to be part of the defence protocol. This meant that I had to be part of guard duty and all other defence duties of the centre. (This wasn't just for show: some years later, in the mid-1980s, when I was in London, the Makeni centre was an identified target and was jet-strafed by the South African Air Force.)

Ace had been briefed about my political training and work in Botswana and South Africa, and he knew about my ordeal within the South African Defence Force. He recognised that it took a soldier's mind to handle the action in the heart of the beast, as I had done. It was the first time that I received recognition for what I'd been through. I was also told that what I'd witnessed on the inside of the beast would be invaluable to share.

Ace asked whether I had any objection to taking the MK oath and committing to the discipline of MK, which was a prerequisite to receiving small-arms training and being issued with weapons. I understood its meaning and the obligations it set out, and agreed to take the oath. I said it sentence for sentence, aloud, after Ace.

'I, comrade Patric, do solemnly declare that I am a soldier of the revolution. I pledge myself in the service of the people, the liberation movement, and its allies. I promise to serve, with discipline and dedication at all times, maintaining the integrity and solidarity of MK, the People's Army.' It went on, 'Should I violate any of these promises . . .' followed by the penalty for breaking any aspect of the oath, and concluded, 'Till victory or death! We shall win!' It was a revolutionary oath that bound us until the formal demobilisation of MK.

Ace then issued me with a Kalashnikov assault rifle, two magazines of ammunition and two defensive grenades. My first training experience with Ace, in dismantling and cleaning the weapon, was nearly disastrous. We sat closely side by side, and he went through each step, with the rifle barrel pointed upwards between our heads. In the firearm handling process, you remove the magazine, then cock the weapon, barrel up and away from anyone, and pull the trigger in case there's a round in the chamber. Ace had neglected to carry this out in a safe manner, and with the rifle barrel between us, luckily pointed upwards, he pulled the trigger and *Blam!* There was indeed a bullet in the chamber. What a fright we both got, jumping to our feet, shouting, 'Yoh, yoh, yoh!'

I'd noticed that Ace had a piece of thumb missing – an old wound that had healed. Apparently, he'd nodded off during guard duty one night in Angola, with a finger on the trigger of his rifle and the thumb of his other hand on the top of the barrel. He'd despatched his thumb by accident to another dimension. He'd also alarmed his comrades into action, thinking that they were under attack.

He related this tale with a mixture of humour and embarrassment: it was all part of his learning curve and it inadvertently had become part of mine.

We went through many rounds of loading and unloading of magazines, dismantling and reassembling of rifles, and grenade training, until I had it right.

After my training in small arms, I was taken through an exercise of familiarisation with the entire property to look at defence points, escape routes and possible enemy assault route combinations. Then I was put on the guard-duty roster with everyone else. Guard duty, particularly the graveyard shifts into the early-morning hours, was the unglamorous and tedious part of the struggle. So was the cooking, where twice a month one of us would have to prepare food for all sixteen people working at the centre. (Of the sixteen, nine of us lived there permanently.)

Around this time I wrote a poem 'Frontline Noise in the Night' in my journal, which creatively reflected the tension that we constantly lived with in Zambia.

Death stalks us every night
when putting head to pillow
bag of essentials
and rifle within reach
settling into a fitful sleep
waking in the dark
at the slightest of sounds
breaking out in a cold sweat
numbed by that paralysing fright
hands operating automatically
grab for AK and grenade
only to discover it's the creak of
Comrade Newsflash's bed . . .

and we all relax
back into our pillows
all six of us in that stuffy
mosquito-filled room
thank God it wasn't the Boers.

* * * *

Over the years the ANC had used all sorts of technologies for disseminating information. Bibles containing tipped-in false pages were used to get illegal literature into South Africa; and printing on the metal inside of tins of baked beans, ricepaper printing, floppy thin vinyl records, comics like 'The Story of Simon and Jane' contained instructions on making gunpowder and Molotov cocktails, and training for target shooting.

So I was excited to see what building space there was in Makeni for the press and what equipment had arrived – we had, after all, been talking about developing this press for over a year while still in Botswana. All my hopes were dashed when I was taken out into the rain and shown a roofless and windowless shell of a building, with no piped water or electricity. Under plastic sheeting was a guillotine and a small printing press. There was no process camera or darkroom equipment, no plate-making equipment, no inks, chemicals, solvents or paper. There was a golfball typewriter that had been donated for typesetting – over in the research library, in another building. The modest rural press Mmegi wa Dikgang in Serowe had been so much more advanced!

This was my first taste of what Dan Tloome and Henry Makgothi had warned me about when I was so keen to go to Lusaka. I was being asked to conjure up miracles and wonders. I was expected to do the layout and design and to print the materials with what was provided – but the key equipment was deficient, and the supplies needed to print were just not there.

The ANC treasurer-general, Thomas Nkobi, said that he wasn't prepared to make any further purchases until he saw us using what had already been acquired but not yet used. He just could not get his head around what it took to produce print on paper. To be fair, he wasn't a print technician, but he should have been more receptive to the chain of very experienced voices imploring him to get the full set of equipment and supplies.

Try as I might, it was impossible to obtain what was required to get the press up and running. When I explained to Thomas Nkobi that printing processes required darkroom materials, plate-making equipment, chemicals, ink and paper, not to mention a building with water and electricity, I found myself up against a brick wall. The otherwise jovial Thomas Nkobi remained unmoved. I would come to learn that people in political organisations, particularly office bearers, are stubborn and hard-headed – and 'always right'.

Benny de Bruyn was most sympathetic and within a few months had fitted a roof, doors and windows in the old building, and created a separate darkroom with piped water. He also connected us up to three-phase electricity. We still lacked chemicals, paper and ink, but in the meanwhile, the work had to go on, so I focused on the typesetting, layout and design of the periodicals *Mayibuye*, *Voice of Women* (*Vow*) and various pamphlets.

Mayibuye, *Dawn*, the January 8th Statement, and campaign pamphlets for the underground fell under Peter Mayibuye and Victor Matlou. Joan Brickhill worked on *Mayibuye* and Radio Freedom, and was married to a guy who was a cadre in Zapu, Jeremy Brickhill. *Vow* was edited by Rebecca Matlou (Sankie Mthembi-Mahanyele), Mavivi Myakayaka-Manzini and Mavis Nlapho (Dr Thandi Ndlovu). Also working with us were David Nkadimeng (son of SACTU leader John Nkadimeng), and Manala Manzini. *Mayibuye* was a single-sheet publication that concertina folded, thus producing a six-page layout when printed on both sides on newsprint. It was a unique layout designed not to be cumbersome, and it obviated the need for metal stitching or binding glue. It was easy to transport in large quantities and for distribution.

Radio Freedom was headed by Victor Moche, with Max Molweni assisting him. I also carried out broadcasts for Radio Freedom on Radio Zambia's external service that I'd once listened to at home.

In December 1979, ANC and MK activists Tim Jenkin, Stephen Lee and Alex Moumbaris dramatically broke out of Pretoria Central Prison. The difficult feat had been masterminded by Jenkin, who'd spent months making keys for all the doors from their cell to freedom. The event was a huge morale booster throughout South Africa and the frontline states. After their escape from South Africa, they came to Lusaka on 2 January 1980, where they appeared at a press conference with president OR Tambo to tell their stories, before going on to London. They were photographed in full uniform, with their AK47 rifles. This was the first story I worked on, together with the ANC's department of publicity and information, for the first edition of *Mayibuye* that year.

Our team got underground literature out and back into South Africa through the different units in the various frontline states. Working with some of the best cadres in the liberation movement, I learnt a lot about geopolitics and internationalism, and improved my ability to speak and to write. At the same time, our team attended regular political education classes under political commissar Professor Jack Simons.

While working at the department of information and publicity centre at Makeni, I would find a ride into Lusaka twice a week and go to the official ANC headquarters building off Cha Cha Cha Road. There, I would try to make the case for the rest of the equipment to whomever would listen and had any power of communication with the treasurer-general. Despite my best efforts, after a year, the press was still not running.

My first encounter with president OR Tambo was at headquarters – while I was on a steep learning curve around issues of protocol. The building had a large walled-in courtyard and a large foyer with seats around the wall. From the foyer, there was a doorway into a passage from which the various offices could be accessed. Joe Nhlanhla presided over the foyer area, assisted by a handful of MK security personnel who regularly changed shifts. (Wolfie Kodesh had, apparently, been appalled at the lack of security when he first came to Lusaka, and had pointed out that here was a place where the top ANC leadership were often under one roof but with little regard to security; he'd drafted a high-level security plan and, together with Joe Nhlanhla, ensured it was implemented.)

One day, while I was waiting in the foyer, president OR Tambo came in and walked straight through into the offices. All rose from their seats and stood to attention – except me. I was day-dreaming and not paying attention, and the president had passed through the room so quickly that I'd barely registered his presence.

After about twenty minutes Joe Nhlanhla came over to me and asked me to take a walk with him. Very gently, with his arm around my shoulders, he explained that I was now among soldiers and had taken the oath, and that I had to conform to military discipline and ANC protocols. In future, he said, whenever the president entered the room, I should smartly stand to attention with my arms at my sides until he'd passed. Joe told me that he hadn't wanted to make an issue of this in front of the others, as he didn't want to embarrass me. He was always very gentlemanly and a stickler for discipline, and was to provide me with many lessons in my time in Zambia.

Joe Nhlanhla also assisted me in making my case for getting the printing press going, but pressed me to understand that patience was necessary, and that the completion of the press may be a long time coming, as the movement had a major shortage of funds and was reliant on solidarity funding. He also intimated that there were many difficult things happening at that point in Lusaka, and that I should bite my tongue lest it looked like I was grumbling and undisciplined.

Joe explained how Thomas Nkobi was facing his own real problems as treasurer-general, and that putting together a printing press was just a small element of a much bigger task before him. Parallel to this he needed vehicles, food for over 400 people in Lusaka alone, medical supplies, support of all types for about 8 000 cadres in Angola and another 2 000 in Tanzania, and then around another 800 scattered throughout Botswana, Lesotho, Swaziland, Zimbabwe and Mozambique, as well as the upkeep of twenty other missions abroad, and so on. My little logistical problem was only one of many.

Wolfie Kodesh, in his patient and comprehensive manner, also explained the culture and the lines that I should avoid crossing within the ANC, particularly in exile. In the SACP and SACTU you could spread your wings and contribute fully, but the ANC was a different creature into which I needed to grow slowly, to find the space to contribute without pissing people off. It was very easy to become a threat to someone's ambitions, and intrigues were a dime a dozen. There were also different political tendencies living uncomfortably in the same skin, and vindictiveness could quickly come to the fore. The narrow nationalists within the ANC didn't have the same approach as the left liberationists, and were only in degree different to the bantustan elite who all were once in the ANC.

Wolfie explained the ANC had been infiltrated over the years and that nobody really knew how pervasive the infiltration was or how high up in the leadership chain enemy agents had risen. At that time he was already aware of a huge destabilisation attempt that was unfolding in the movement in Lusaka, but was bound by the need-to-know ethos. His cautions were restricted in terms of spelling out to me that we were all in danger. It was better to be circumspect in behaviour and not simply give trust to everyone just because they were fellow comrades, he advised. Everyone had to earn each other's respect. We were at war and the rules of war applied.

Wolfie sometimes took me to visit Ray Alexander Simons and her husband Jack Simons at their home in Roma in Lusaka. I'd previously met Aunty Ray for long debriefings in Botswana but this was the first time I met Uncle Jack, an exiled communist academic, then teaching at the university in Lusaka, who welcomed me heartily. He also introduced me to Uriah Mokeba and Captain Lerole, who in turn introduced me to my SACP cell, which included Kay Moonsamy and Doreen Motshabi. The term that was generally used for the SACP was 'the family', and within the party my nom de guerre was Oscar.

Rochelle 'Ray' Alexander was a legend in Cape Town – the godmother and midwife of political industrial unions in South Africa. All young left-wing workers knew her by reputation, and it was a dream fulfilled to have teamed up with her in exile.

She was sixteen years old when she arrived from Latvia as a young communist in 1929. When she set foot on land after her ship docked, she immediately started engaging stevedores at the Cape Town docks to enquire whether they were unionised. At the age of 23 she became a member of the central committee of the Communist Party of South Africa. It was she who drew a line between syndicalist unionism and politically conscious industrial trade unions. Syndicalist unions most often were general workers' unions or associations, or with a craftsmanship orientation, which strictly stayed out of political alignment and were ambiguous to broader social issues in South Africa. The Industrial and Commercial Workers' Union of Africa was an example of a syndicalist union, whereas the Food and Canning Workers' Union, started by Ray Alexander, was a union in a specific industry and it aligned itself to socialist politics and tackled broader social issues and not just workplace issues.

Wolfie, Jack, Ray, Uriah and Kay were all unanimous in saying that whatever shape a socialist future may have in South Africa, it would require African characteristics, and this wasn't to be found in gospel European left politics, slogans and literature – it had to be homegrown. The role of national liberation from imperialism, colonialism and apartheid was integral to the class struggle for socialism in Africa. They explained that it was all a process of what Bertolt Brecht called 'the persistent tying and spreading of the party's net'.

After a few months in Lusaka, Wolfie introduced me to an old, retired trade unionist from South Africa who lived there, Isabel Jordan. She was an eccentric but interesting character who personally knew all the Zambian politicians, with much history in her head, and was totally up to date with all the gossip of Zambian high society. She lived alone in a big house off Cairo Road, with an almost hairless old dog that was wracked with arthritis and in much pain, and over which she fussed. Her home and every need were catered for by a male domestic worker by the name of Cholozi.

Isabel Jordan brought in an income by giving slimming classes to overweight upper-class Zambian women. These classes basically comprised of having the women stand on a contraption leaning into a vibrator belt for half an hour, during which their excess weight was supposed to be shed through the vibration of their bellies.

She also ran the Zambian Consumers' Association and produced a monthly magazine on consumer protection. All her advice pages started with big bold-type letters declaring 'Isa says', followed by snippets she'd lifted from a range of British and South African publications. Wolfie organised for her to pay me a few kwachas per month to do her magazine layout and design. It wasn't much but it was better than nothing.

* * * *

Once a month, we each received an allowance of seven kwacha (roughly R5), and the women were given an additional sanitary-supplies allowance. We called this our 'arbeit' (labour). Sometimes we would club our arbeit together and buy a case of Mosi lager; at other times we would try our hand at making fermented drinks. If any comrade was sent to a conference or mission abroad, they were under strict instruction to bring back a duty-free bottle or two of whisky or vodka. Everyone got just a tot, but it was great for camaraderie.

In our difficult financial circumstances, we got handouts of clothes from abroad, often from Eastern Europe and the Soviet Union. Most times these clothes were impractical for the hot weather and came in really large sizes. There were also lots of suits. But we needed jeans or light cloth trousers, underwear and shoes, so comrades would take these swanky donated clothes and find Zambians who were needing costly suits for weddings, and swap them for what we needed or for cash. This shadow economy was called phanda (literally meaning 'to go investigate', but slang for bartering). Although it was discouraged, it flourished.

We received weekly supplies of meat and pap, sometimes with a few vegetables from the ANC farm, delivered by a comrade by the name of Awolowo Mogau. There were two ANC farms at Chongela and a third near Makeni. One week the meat was chickens slaughtered at the farms, and the next week it was pigs. (I didn't eat pork.) Pap was the staple starch, but sometimes we got potatoes too. There was a shortage of salt and little or no spice.

Cleaners' Boy: Me in 1956, the year I was born, and (second from left) in 1963.

Top: Sketch & photo: Great-grandma Francina Jagers Hadden.

Below: Great-grandpa William Hadden (1808–1908) and grandfather Willie Huntley.

Cleaner's: Annie Gladys Frances Huntley in 1952, 1957 and 1989.

Left to right: Van Rooy cousins Louise 'Toekies' with babe-in-arms and Maureen, with Grandma Mary-Anne Hadden Huntley, 1957.

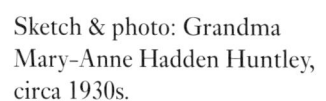

Sketch & photo: Grandma Mary-Anne Hadden Huntley, circa 1930s.

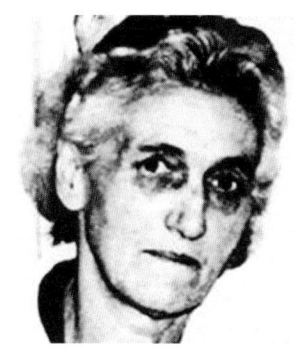

Mary 'Doll' Huntley van Rooy and Christian Clarke van Rooy, circa late 1920s.

Aunty Doll van Rooy, 1967.

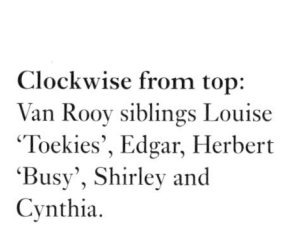

Clockwise from top: Van Rooy siblings Louise 'Toekies', Edgar, Herbert 'Busy', Shirley and Cynthia.

Cousin Herbie and Daisy van Rooy's children:
Back row: Vanessa and Russell 'Toffy'.
Front row: Clint, Jamie (Russell's son), and Edgar jnr.

Cousins: Surrounded by Van Rooys and Stores.

Left to right: Some of my sister May's children and grandchildren: Anton du Plessis and partner Nozi; Sharon du Plessis and Nozi's son Zozo; my grandniece Melanie September and great-grandnephew Christian with Dad and Mom, May's son Ian and late wife Anna Elsegood.

Father: Pieter Francois Mellet (WW 2) 1943 and in the 1970s.

Returnee exile: Me with my mother, Annie Huntley.

Painting: Nannucci laundry, District Six (Douglas Treasure 1917–1995).

Clockwise from top: Me when I was involved with the Young Christian Workers/All African Socialist Youth; Comrades Movement with Vuyani and Mafay 1977; Masthead of *Young Voice* newspaper.

Makeni, Lusaka: Address by president OR Tambo under the trees, with members of the regional political council (left to right) Benny 'Natho' de Bruyn, King Sabata Dalyindebo, John Gaetsewe, Captain Lerole and Hector Nkula.

My dear mentor: Wolfie Kodesh.

Comrade Pat, aka 'Zinto'.

At the liberation media hub and press in London, with Mafa Ngeleza, Zodwa and Mandla Maseko.

'Mzala' Jabulani Nxumalo or just 'Mzi'. Friend, comrade and outstanding thinker and writer on political theory and praxis.

Class of 1982: With African and Asian fellow students at the London College of Printing.

Liberation movement media hub and press at Mackenzie Street in London.

Mayibuye, my first design and printing job in Zambia; my last production, the first ANC publication after the leadership group returned to SA.

The team under director Horst Kleinschmidt at the International Defence and Aid (IDAF) in London.

My son Dylan playing with Katryn Schoon while her father Marius looks on. Katryn and her mother Jenny Schoon lost their lives in Angola in 1984, blown up on receipt of a parcel bomb.

Inseparable: With cousins Herbie and Edgar van Rooy at parliament.

Heritage whisperer: Engaging with children on history and heritage.

Above left: With speaker Dr Frene Ginwala, presenting President Mandela and constitutional court chief justice Arthur Chaskalson with a flag that flew over parliament during a State of the Nation (SONA) address by Madiba.

Above right: OR Tambo, Wolfie Kodesh and Nelson Mandela soon after Madiba's release from prison.

Above left: With the late Reg September shortly before his passing in 2013.

Above right: Thembi 'Eva' Makona my mainstay on returning from exile. She passed away a year after this photo was taken.

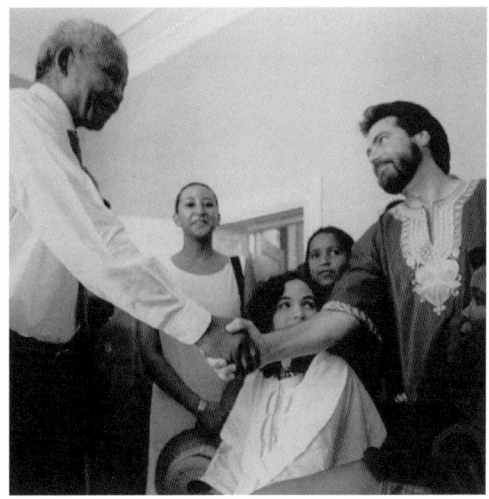

Above left: Accompanying Cuban President Fidel Castro on his visit to Tuynhuis and parliament – to meet with President Nelson Mandela and to address parliament.

Above right: With President Nelson Mandela at Tuynhuis, accompanying Shelley Barry and other persons with disabilities after they provided a guard of honour at the president's SONA address.

Above left: Accompanying former president of Tanzania, Mwalimu Julius Nyerere, father of African Socialism theory, hosted at parliament by speaker Dr Frene Ginwala.

Above right: Leading the hosting and protection detail with President Fidel Castro after leaving the National Council of Provinces chamber.

On completion of my service in the Immigration Services Inspectorate – Maritime and Aviation Ports. Last day in uniform.

With my counterparts in the Cuban Naval Guard while on a mission to inspect our coastal and Mozambique borderline.

With my Grassroots colleagues and friends at a rite of passage ceremony for Raymond Schuller, together with Harold Coetzee, Philip Balie and Vernon Weitz.

With my best brothers and fellow fishermen Clive Newman and the late Stephen Smith.

With my spirit daughter Samantha Castle. We adopted each other 25 years ago.

Son Dylan (middle) flanked by his sons Caleb (left) and Celeo and Tyler (right).

Son Manuel.

With Manuel on Table Mountain.

Nazli and Vuyo.

Son Vuyo and wife Nazli Jugbaran.

With my sister May's children, grandchildren and spouses.

With Celeo and my wife Leenah.

My wife Asirawan 'Leenah' Deeying.

Daughter Watsana Thanomputsa; son Cheyttha in foreground with Watsana and Leenah at the back.

Awolowo always tried to get something extra for those of us who had children. For Dylan's sake, he managed at one time to get a bag of flour although it was filled with weevils. I sifted it to get rid of the weevils and made bread, a very scarce treat in Lusaka. On the positive side, I was never overweight, nor did I have a belly while based in Zambia!

Having a very young child in our home lent an awkward existence contextual to the unconventional war conditions under which we lived – our ability to protect ourselves in a hurry had to be weighed against the potential for Dylan to get hurt. Because he was very inquisitive, I would always remove the charges from the grenades and keep the two parts in separate places, out of his reach. I also had to ensure that there were no rounds in the rifle and that the magazines were kept separate and well hidden.

One day, Dylan didn't arrive home from his preschool in Lusaka as usual, and we began to panic. In the morning, Max Molweni would drive our son to his school eight kilometres away, on his way in to work at Radio Freedom; and in the afternoons, an ANC driver was supposed to bring him back.

When it grew dark and Dylan was still not home, we were beside ourselves with worry. At around 9 pm I noticed that Reg September's car was parked next to his place, so I went and knocked on his door and asked him if he could drive me into Lusaka to look for Dylan. Reg and Gwen, who were already in bed, immediately understood the gravity of the situation, and Reg got up, and he and I drove into Lusaka. There, we found Dylan with the Zambian nightwatchman of the school, in his small office. The ANC driver had been smoking dagga and forgotten to pick up Dylan. The nightwatchman was, understandably, furious, and asked me what kind of parent I was to abandon my child in this manner.

A few days later, I was sitting on the edge of the stoep of the research building at Makeni, my thoughts on the Dylan incident, when somebody gently put his arm around my shoulder. Looking up, I was startled to see OR Tambo. Recalling Joe Nhlanhla's tutelage, I immediately jumped to attention.

'At ease, son,' the president said. 'I can see that something is troubling you. Come into the office with me and sit a while and tell me what's on your mind.'

He was such a caring and wise man who had a pastoral way about him (I would later learn that he was a man of deep faith), and I found myself opening up. He was my mother's age and for those few moments he was my father; I realised why everyone called him 'Papa'. From that time on, OR Tambo and Adelaide Tambo were 'Papa' and 'Mama' to me, too, and they both always addressed me as 'son'.

OR Tambo was really annoyed to hear what had happened to Dylan, and I had the president of the ANC apologising to me as a parent that because of indiscipline, we'd been put through such an ordeal.

I then told him about my frustrations regarding the equipment for the press. Although I didn't articulate this to him at the time, it seemed to me that there was some competitiveness between those wanting London to be the centre for ANC printing, those who wanted the press in the frontline states closer to home, and those who wanted the main liberation press to be in Lusaka. I found myself in the middle, with little chance of breaking the impasse. There was always a degree of competitiveness between different structures in which there were an array of ambitions and egos to be massaged.

Of course, Wolfie had helped me to make the case for the printing press, as had Kay, who worked in the treasury close to Thomas Nkobi. Dulcie September worked in secretary-general Alfred Nzo's office, and she would tip me off when Thomas Nkobi was due to arrive so that I could try and get his ear between his many trips abroad. Still, we ended up having to take our designed and composited work to a commercial press in Lusaka to have it printed.

Papa OR Tambo explained how much patience it had taken for all, over the preceding two decades since 1960, for the ANC to get to where it was. He said that he could fully understand how younger people got frustrated and how alien the situation must be for someone like me, from a city like Cape Town, and how we must feel in a rural area in a new faraway country, when all we wanted was to get on with the fight. He said that this was why he'd taken the trouble to ask Wolfie, Benny,

Reg, Captain Lerole, Jack and Uriah Mokeba to help me adjust and cope with these rigours. It was a beautiful and encouraging moment that I'll never forget.

I would later learn that there was much going on in terms of destabilisation of the ANC in Lusaka. I was initially oblivious of this and how it was impacting on everything within the organisational infrastructure of the ANC, including the completion of the press project.

* * * *

I arrived in Lusaka as a raw, hot-headed, angry young man. I was just a youngster, and outside of all the intrigues and great political dynasties and those they gave patronage to within each of the three powerful communities – African, white and Indian – which dominated in different regions. Camissa Africans were just a small fringe within the structures and, being so few, posed no real threat to others. The ANC community were scattered across a very large Lusaka and the 'need-to-know' principle was strictly practised.

It was Wolfie Kodesh who patiently moulded me over the years, and I became a more whole person because of his intervention. He was one of that small band of special Jewish socialist activists who played a larger-than-life role in the liberation movement over his entire life.

Wolfie was Oliver Tambo's greatest gift to me. They all knew that I had never had a father, and he became a teacher, mentor, guide, father, comrade, brother and friend, all rolled into one. Benny de Bruyn and Reg September likewise became my uncle figures, always giving me careful advice and showing care. The trio helped me greatly to become the person that I am.

8

SHISHITA: THE CLEANSING

While living in Lusaka, I got to see and experience everyday Zambian life, which was quite different to life in South Africa. For example, the only time that I ever attended a cinema in Lusaka, I experienced how before the movie, everyone stood at attention while the national anthem played – a relic of colonial life that also existed under British colonial rule in South Africa.

I experienced the sparse shopping at informal shops and the sprawling market in Lusaka. And we went on a few excursions organised by the ANC women's section for parents and children, such as a visit to the zoo. These were all rare bits of normal life.

On May Day, SACTU and the ANC Youth, including myself, dressed in uniform and marched in a parade through Lusaka to be addressed by President Kenneth Kaunda, who entertained us with a rendition of 'Tiende Pamodzi ndim'tima umo' (Let's walk together), his favourite Zambian song. Kaunda always fiddled with a handkerchief and often shed a tear. My mom had a similar habit and he reminded me of her.

* * * *

Over the first nine months of 1980, there was a series of murders by the notorious Lusaka Strangler. Milton Sipalo was finally arrested, suspected of having killed 29 women. A Zambian Defence Force soldier, he managed to escape onto the roof of the police headquarters building, where there was a standoff as he threatened to jump. I was in the crowd that gathered below, and I witnessed him taking his own life by diving off the building.

An unsettling series of incidents then unfolded, mirroring the difficult climate of destabilisation that had begun to manifest in Lusaka about ten months into our time in Zambia. The apartheid regime was putting much energy into smashing the ANC, and was extending its war to all the frontline states that were supporting the ANC, and using unconventional means to do so.

There was a climate of suspicion, with comrades accusing other comrades left, right and centre. Arrests were being made in the movement and people were disappearing, with rumours about 'panel-beating', a euphemism for violent interrogations. It was said that the ANC security mechanism itself had been infiltrated, and that old grudges and vendettas were playing out. I likened this period to the time of the 'crucible' – the 1690s Salem witch hunts captured by Arthur Miller's eponymous play.

Early in January 1981, president OR Tambo had been called in by President Kaunda, who'd complained about a wave of indiscipline among some ANC cadres. This included dagga smoking and abuse of alcohol, but also some shooting incidents: a Zambian policeman had been killed by an armed ANC man. The Zambians had also complained that ANC people were involved in drug rackets, stolen goods and stolen vehicle rings, and had caches of illegal weapons, and were abusing the conditions of our stay in Zambia.

President OR Tambo had been mortified.

At a general meeting of all the ANC members in Lusaka in the same month, where we were seated on chairs arranged under the mango trees in the open area at Makeni, president OR Tambo was a disappointed commander-in-chief of MK. At the podium table, the officials of the regional political council, Benny de Bruyn, Captain Lerole and Hector Nkula, King Sabata Dalindyebo, the king of the Thembu kingdom in exile in Zambia, and John Gaetsewe, the general-secretary of SACTU, were seated with the president.

President Tambo was frank with us at that meeting, saying that the behaviour of elements within our ranks had endangered our status as a movement in Zambia and could lead to our expulsion from the country.

Most of us who were just getting on with our jobs were oblivious to how deep a crisis we were in.

There also was a threat being posed in Zambia by surrogates of the South African Defence Force, the Mashula gang.

As a result of these things, the president of Zambia was ordering the ANC to give over all our weapons to the Zambian Defence Force. We were to be disarmed, then issued with Zambian Defence Force identity cards, which were always to be carried along with our ANC identity cards, and if we came under attack, we were to make our way to the Zambian Defence Force camps, where we would be armed.

It was a crazy imposition, because effectively we were being disarmed in the face of armed aggression from South Africa.

President Tambo told us that he was in no position to argue our case because we'd brought this upon ourselves due to indiscipline among our own. He was visibly upset, and gave us all a severe tongue-lashing.

And the wave of mischief was not, it appeared, confined to Zambia, but extended to Botswana and Angola. This crisis was also much bigger than criminal behaviours, and came to be known as the time of shishita, or 'the cleansing'. It had started with a foiled coup plot in Zambia to get rid of President Kaunda, orchestrated by the apartheid regime, with the roll-on intention of overthrowing the ANC leadership and creating a scenario of chaos in the organisation.

It was said that up to 40 infiltrators were operating in Lusaka at that time, and that they came very close to achieving their objectives. They created such toxicity between people that everyone was beginning to accuse everyone else of mischief. As a result of this dangerous climate, we all shrank back from mixing with each other, and when we did socialise, people hardly said anything to each other, as we didn't know whom to trust. In this scenario, I stuck to the older-generation comrades and my trusted SACTU and SACP network in Lusaka.

A character called Oshkosh was working for the apartheid regime and had been seen with suspected agents at a hotel. We heard that Oshkosh had fled to Botswana with another askari, using tickets supplied by a third agent, who was also said to be an infiltrator in the compromised

ANC security who had been abusing the position to accuse good people of being enemies while he was the actual agent.

This news in particular horrified me: from the time we'd arrived in Zambia, we'd come to know of two characters who ran a minibus shuttle for ANC cadres – one of whom was Oshkosh. Their minibus service was, of course, the perfect cover for productive spying.

These two were outed during the time of shishita as being central to the destabilisation of the ANC and the assassinations of comrades. Oshkosh was also the ANC liaison and clearance officer at Lusaka International Airport who'd cleared us and all other comrades and visitors. He turned out to be giving all our information to the enemy, including where we were all living.

Dylan liked the sound of the name Oshkosh, and associated it with travelling in the minibus. Oshkosh was always offering to take Dylan on short excursions with him in the vehicle, and it later struck us that he was likely grooming the child towards ultimately kidnapping him. However, after the terrible experience of Dylan being left alone in Lusaka at night when the ANC driver had forgotten to fetch him from school, we no longer trusted our little son alone with any of the guys driving vehicles – so that painful incident may well have saved us from something worse.

Still, the realisation of how close danger was to our family made us very afraid, as we realised the risks that our child had been exposed to.

A few weeks later, on 30 January 1981, South African special forces attacked three residences at Matola in Mozambique, where we were going to initially have the printing press. Twelve MK cadres were killed, including SACTU leader William Khanyile, husband of Eleanor. Comrade William's death was a blow to all SACTU cadres: as a union federation, our slogan was 'An injury to one is an injury to all'.

It was a shocking time for all us. I wrote a piece of poetry in my journal to capture what that experience was like, called 'No Music':

It was absolutely quiet
there was no music
when those trucks pulled up

soldiers spilled out, moving swiftly
against the bewildered
awaking from slumber
steel hit bodies, blood flowed
sporadic blasts, amidst shouts of abuse
women and children screamed
people gurgling their own blood
it was absolute horror, terror
no revolutionary romanticism
this is what real war is like
there's no cheap slogan
there were no dramatic refrains
no action music, to cushion the terror
just tears and dirt and blood . . .
and degradation . . . and then they were gone
the quiet of disbelief, whimpers, and sobs
the smell of flares and gunpowder
there was no music, just silence, and anonymity
the price paid for standing up against apartheid
the blood price of FREEDOM.

President Kaunda had his security ratcheted up, with a helicopter flying over his vehicle when he travelled around in Lusaka. Everyone was jumpy.

As a result of the new conditions imposed on us by our Zambian hosts, many of us were moved around in Lusaka, and even out of ANC properties, to be billeted with Zambian supporters.

Everyone vacated Makeni and we were scattered across Lusaka. My family and I were moved into what was called the Revolutionary Council House. This was a large premises split into two. We occupied two rooms and a kitchen with a separate entrance, while the other half of the house was an ANC detention centre run by the security department of the ANC. The detention centre had a bad reputation, and it wasn't the most pleasant place to be accommodated. It would have also been a prime target for South African special forces.

There was a black-and-white television set on which we were able to watch Zambian TV. On a Thursday night, comrades would come from all over to watch our favourite wrestling matches. The star at the time was a masked wrestler known as Kendo Nagasaki, who was actually an English professional wrestler whose character was a Japanese samurai with a mysterious past and reputed powers of healing and hypnosis. At one stage there was huge excitement in Lusaka at the news that Kendo Nagasaki had flown in from London for a large wrestling tournament but the masked man turned out to be a fraud, part of a scam to fleece money from the public.

One day, a comrade with advanced computer skills arrived and began setting up a computer technology workshop in a small building on the premises of the Revolutionary Council House. This was Govan 'Chips' Chiba, the younger brother of the veteran South African Indian Congress and SACP leader Laloo Chiba. Chips had studied aeronautical engineering at London University, and when he graduated, he headed a team at Rolls Royce that developed computer programs for the design of jet engines and helicopters. He'd given up his job to come to work in Lusaka for the ANC.

In an era that predated this tech age, where everyone has personal computers, tablets and cellphones, Comrade Chips established a secret communication network between the ANC in exile and the ANC underground in South Africa. He was a welcome addition at the house, too, just for fresh conversation, as he'd widely travelled, and we had yet to leave Southern Africa. The ANC had so many talented people.

There was another dear man who stayed with us at the Revolutionary Council House, an old fella by the name of Maru, a former prisoner on Robben Island. He was a good conversationalist but there was such an aura of sadness about him, and he seemed to live a rather solitary existence. I sometimes caught a glimpse in him of what was once a vibrant young man, but now what came across was that old saying, 'Old soldiers never die; they merely fade away'.

His pride and joy was a little ginger cat. One day when he came to me and said, 'Comrade Pat, come see what they did to my cat.' I was horrified to see that the cat had gone to rest under the shade of a vehicle right next to the tyre, and the driver had jumped into the bakkie, started it up quickly, put it in reverse and driven over the animal. Maru was terribly upset as I tried to give him a word of comfort.

We lived a spartan life and there was little by way of distraction in this climate of war. The silence of the night was shattered frequently by automatic gunfire. On a railway line near to where we stayed, there was an explosion one night when a fuel-tanker wagon went up in flames.

As the days wore on, life became more difficult, with a combination of food shortages and the need to vacate where we were staying at night at a moment's notice due to warnings of impending attacks. We might just be bedding down when the warning to move would come, and we'd have to grab an always-packed bag of essentials and move out into the night, not knowing where to go. By this time our arms had been confiscated, and we'd be expected to make our way to the Zambian Defence Force camps on foot from the outskirts of the city through the streets and bush.

Bringing up a child in these circumstances was extremely trying. I was never able to give my child anything as I too was entirely dependent on the fortunes of the movement. It was the environment of war and austerity. Moving around at night after vacating premises at a few minutes' notice with a child in your arms wasn't easy.

On one occasion my family and I were attacked under these circumstances on a dark road. Maria, pregnant with our second child, was carrying Dylan. I had a sling bag over my shoulder with a few necessities in it, and a knife in my hand. It was around midnight, and we were making our way on foot up the road from the Revolutionary Council House which we'd just left, heading for a home once pointed out to us as occupied by people who originally were South Africans from Cape Town who had long settled in Zambia. We'd been told that they might be sympathetic and we were going to ask these strangers for temporary refuge for the night.

We'd almost reached the house when a camouflaged attacker jumped out of the bushes behind us and grabbed me around the neck in a choke hold. Maria screamed and Dylan cried, while a dog started barking, all in a split second.

I let out as much of a bellow as I could, and lunged behind me with the knife.

The lights of the house came on as people emerged. The assailant released his grip and vanished back into the bush.

If it hadn't been for the kindness of those strangers, who also let us stay with them for the night, we might have been killed.

* * * *

One day, during all the shishita troubles, Moses Mabhida, the general-secretary of the SACP and a member of the ANC's national executive committee, who also was an old SACTU unionist, went out of his way to come and visit us at the house, to enquire how we were coping under the strain. He explained that it was a difficult time for everyone, and that it was unlikely under the present circumstances and the financial stresses being experienced by the ANC that the printing press was going to be completed any time soon.

Mabhida said that he'd had discussions with Sizakele Sigxashe, Wolfie, Captain Lerole, Uriah Mokeba, Jack Simons and Ray Alexander Simons, who'd suggested that Maria and Dylan be sent to the UK, where she could have the baby in more conducive circumstances. I would then be able to join her later, to work at the SACTU external mission office in London, and improve my qualifications through study at the London College of Printing.

The plan was that on my arrival at Gatwick Airport, I would say that I was visiting London on holiday and would be staying with my cousins, my Aunty Doll's children. The main thing was to gain entry; that done, the ANC would provide legal assistance to get me refugee status in the UK. It wasn't going to be easy, but they believed that once I'd been admitted by the immigration authorities, they'd be able to ensure that I wasn't expelled. But I was warned that as I already had asylum status in Botswana, UK immigration might immediately deport me to Botswana.

Sending Maria and Dylan ahead of me, also entering the UK on visitors' visas, would test whether we could get away with this approach. The ANC lawyers were already preparing our case for 'second country of asylum' for us as a family, and once I arrived, they would proceed with a family application, using 'maternity complications' to press for 'second country of asylum' status. (In the event, it would take almost two years to get conditional political asylum status for us in the UK.)

Aunty Ray and Uncle Jack Simons had me over for a few briefings. I joined Ray in preparing left-wing literature packs that I had to send to a list of people in South Africa from different postboxes across London once I arrived. These were writings of Marx, Engels and Lenin that had been broken up into quarters of the books, printed on micro-thin ricepaper, the weight of each pack being nowhere near that of parcels that were more highly scrutinised. Ray factored in that some of these letters would be intercepted, so she calculated that by duplicating or triplicating those sent, the chances of being able to put together one full copy of a book were improved. Of course, there was no correspondence accompanying the letters – Ray was an old hand at secret work.

Uncle Jack gave me a hundred pounds, saying, 'You're going to need something in your pocket. I'll be writing to you from time to time. Once you have an address, send me a letter.'

In mid-1981, Maria and Dylan left Lusaka for London. I remained behind for a month, then flew out to join them. After three years of exile in the frontline states, I left Africa for the first time at 25 years old. I had ten years of post-school experience behind me, and had been through a great deal. But, for me, going to London was almost as traumatic as leaving South Africa.

I got through immigration at Gatwick, then called Gill Marcus at the ANC office. She directed me on how to use the underground to get into the City of London, where she would meet me at a station, and she informed me that Maria and Dylan were staying with a friend of Wolfie, an activist in the British Anti-Apartheid Movement called Margaret Ling. Her flat was in Endymion Road, with a great view of Finsbury Park.

The ANC would provide minimum support until we could get through the various legal processes. It was like our first arrival in Botswana three years earlier. First, we had to go to the immigration authorities with the ANC lawyers to declare ourselves as asylum seekers. It was quite a daunting experience in which I spent the entire day once again writing biographies, and arguing that if we were sent back to Botswana, it would be like going back to South Africa, because it was now so dangerous there that several people had had to be pulled out. We couldn't return to Zambia, I pointed out, because we'd been there on temporary special residence visas and the Zambian government had called on the ANC to cut down on its numbers.

After an interview by a special officer who was clearly from British intelligence – and which was more like an interrogation and went on for the better part of a day – we were given a six-month visa, with the possibility of renewal. We weren't allowed to work until our asylum-seeking status concluded through granting us refugee status. This took over a year. We were, however, given a small asylum-seeker allowance of around £7 per person per week – a pittance if you considered that a one-way daily ticket for public transport across London cost 60 pence, bread was 37 pence and milk 20 pence. British citizens' unemployment benefit was £28.50 per week at the time.

A range of British left-wing movements interlinked to our communities and struggles. The Anti-Apartheid Movement, the Mozambique, Angola, & Guinea Information Centre, the International Defence and Aid Fund (IDAF), and the Africa Education Trust were powerful solidarity movements that assisted us in finding accommodation, plugging into social-service benefits (after a year), and organising informal work and study bursaries (there was no restriction on studying). But none of this came easy.

Soon we made friends across the asylum-seeker refugee community of Africans, Latin-Americans, Asians, Kurds and Palestinians, as well as the many different émigré communities. It was a broad cross-cultural experience; the commonality being that we were all 'suitcase' people. As the Palestinian poet Mahmoud Darwish wrote, 'We travel like other people, but we return to nowhere, as if travelling is the way of the clouds.'

In Endymion Road, there was an Egyptian man, Farooq, married to an Englishwoman, with a Spanish couple from Gibraltar as tenants who befriended us – Eli Gomez and Miguel Netto would become the godparents of our second son, Manuel, and that was the start of a long friendship. Miguel was a nurse and trade-union activist in Gibraltar and his father was the leader of the opposition in their legislature.

* * * *

Margaret Ling had committed to allowing us to live with her until our child was born, and our son Manuel made his arrival within weeks, delivered by a midwife. But we immediately had to handle a medical crisis when our new baby began projectile vomiting, and not keeping any food down. He had pyloric stenosis, a rare condition in infants that blocks food from entering the small intestine, and which required surgery to remedy. If we'd still been in Zambia when Manuel had suffered this problem, he would almost certainly have died.

Finally, with Manuel's condition under control, we could look for a place of our own – a process that would prove to be quite complicated.

We'd discovered that staying in Margaret's flat made us 'not homeless', so we had to ask her to turf us out so that we were literally on the streets before the council would consider us as their problem. The council then put us up in a terrible bed and breakfast with seven other homeless families from various countries, mainly Asian and Latin American. This was at the time when a major race riot had broken out in Finsbury Park and the entire area was tense. We were all fearful of going out because police were targeting foreigners.

The place was also bang in the middle of the Finsbury Park red-light district, and rented rooms to sex workers and their clients on an hourly basis. We could hear the continuous clip-clop of high heels on the pavement outside, and the women repeatedly saying, 'Hello, love. Business, love?' This went on all night, with the doorbell ringing constantly.

The breakfast was in a basement common-room and consisted of two slices of bread, two eggs and tea. There was a stove to make lunch and supper that was shared by all.

Ruth Mompati and Frene Ginwala came to see us there and brought us some supplies. They were quite shocked.

The council housing department then threw another curve ball at us. There was a rule that the council had no obligation to assist anyone who had purposefully made themselves homeless, and they argued that as we were refugees, seeking political asylum, by leaving our home country we had purposefully made ourselves homeless. We couldn't believe our ears.

Again, the ANC had to get us legal assistance – at which point the council said that we were not their problem because the ANC offices were in another area, Islington, and we were therefore the problem of Islington council. In the end Islington said that they would offer us emergency temporary accommodation if the other council, Haringey, used the time afforded to find suitable permanent housing for us. So we landed up in a condemned dump of a building in Clerkenwell, in a tiny fourth-floor flat. The previous tenants had set it on fire to force the council to move them out.

It was a horrific scenario. We slept on a foam mattress on the floor. One night, when bedding down, I saw a man trying to get through our fourth-floor window, having edged his way along a fifteen-centimetre crumbling ledge from the flat next door, which was occupied by a gang of youngsters who would regularly burgle the other flats. He scarpered as I approached the closed window. On another night, there was a knock on the door, and I opened it to a guy who lunged at me with a knife. Luckily, we were able to shut the door on him.

After about eight weeks of this, we were offered a council house in Tower Gardens Road in Tottenham. We were so relieved. Life as refugees was tough enough but much worse with a five-year-old and a newborn baby in what were basically squatter conditions. Our allowance didn't stretch to cover all we needed, and friends would bring us parcels of nappies and other baby products. Our threadbare clothes weren't appropriate for the winter weather in the UK. Without the network of comrades, I really don't know how we would have coped.

Getting the council house in Tottenham with its rent rebate, plus a council rebate for electricity, made a major change to our circumstances. For the first time in three and a half years, and sixteen moves since leaving Cape Town, we had a proper home and some semblance of normality.

9

DISPLACEMENT:
BEGINNING AGAIN IN THE UK

In London we engaged in the local British political activities, attending many protest marches on major issues like anti-fascism, anti-war and nuclear disarmament, and the marathon miners' strike of 1984/85, led by Arthur Scargill of the National Union of Mineworkers, which attempted to prevent colliery closures.

Once, Miguel Netto and I joined a protest when the British racist National Front party wanted to use a school hall in Tottenham, a strong black area, for a political meeting. I learnt just how nasty the British police could be behind the 'nice guy' image they try so hard to project when I was isolated from the other protestors by a circle of police and two of them bent me over a car bonnet and worked me over with hard blows to my sides. I had sore kidneys for a long time afterwards.

Maria and I were also being integrated into the political life of the ANC and SACTU in London. I was doing service within the SACTU office, which was then still under John Gaetsewe, although this soon changed when Gaetsewe passed away and John Nkadimeng took the reins as general-secretary.

I was also integrated into the Islington ANC unit of the London branch of the ANC, which had around twenty members. They were a great bunch of people. We met at the home of Maud and James Phillips – James was an amazing Camissa African singer and choir master with strong shades of American singer-activist Paul Robeson to his persona. He was also an old trade unionist and communist, an officer-bearer of the African Political Organisation (made up predominantly, but not exclusively, of those who were classified as 'Coloured', founded in Cape

Town in 1902), and a founding member of the South African Coloured People's Congress (which dissolved in 1967). We buried him from that house in October 1987. (Another whose burial I attended, and which drew huge crowds, was that of Dr Yusuf Dadoo. Doc was buried opposite Karl Marx's grave at Highgate Cemetery in September 1983.)

The old ANC exile community in London felt distant from those of us who came to London in the 1980s. We had somewhat different political, class and social cultures. For a long time in the UK, the ANC exile membership was mainly from those groups classified as 'White', 'Coloured' and 'Indian', with much fewer people who were classified as 'Black'. In a reflection of South African colonial society, those classified as 'Black' were also not as well off. It was a different scenario and the opposite of what I'd experienced in Zambia and Tanzania, where most ANC people were those classified in South Africa as 'Black'.

But by the mid-1980s this scenario began to change in London as more and more young people arrived to study at colleges and universities. The older exiles would use the term 'the comrades' almost as a simile for 'Black' when referring to those newly arriving. There was little socialising across the demarcation lines within the ANC, even though we all attended the same branch meetings. There were no real antagonisms either, simply a class, age and experiential divide.

There were a few personalities among the exile community for whom I had the utmost respect and they fully engaged all cadres equally. These were Wolfie Kodesh, Fred and Sarah Carneson, Norman Levy, Barry Feinberg, Harold and AnnMarie Wolpe, Mannie Brown, Ronnie and Eleanor Kasrils, Joe Slovo, Horst Kleinschmidt, Stephanie Kemp, and Norman and Bronwyn Kaplan. These guys always had time for the younger cadres who were sent to study in the UK.

While the small group of economically self-sufficient exile-émigrés led relatively comfortable lives and enjoyed all that was the best of living in an international capital city, most exiled cadres lived very simple lives in humble shared accommodation with few pleasures, barely having the ability to keep our heads above water. Although we were in London, we couldn't enjoy the theatre, museums, art galleries, libraries and all those wonderful things that the city had to offer. There was little social interaction between the more affluent exiles and émigrés, and those cadres in survivalist mode, except at branch meetings or in the hurly burly of dedicated liberation work.

One exception for Maria and me was Colin Belton and Maria Nobrega, South African friends who offered much support. I first met them as a result of going to see them perform in an avant-garde play in a community hall in a part of London called White City. We had a good laugh at the name – White City is a district of London in the northern part of Shepherd's Bush.

Three years after my arrival in London, I was finally issued with a UK-based United Nations High Commission for Refugees travel document that allowed me to come and go from the UK, and I was also allowed to work. We would refer to the travel documents as the 'blue mamba' because often it bit you rather than helped you.

On one occasion Colin and Maria looked after our children so that Maria and I could go on holiday to Spain to visit Miguel Netto and Eli Gomez. Andalucia became like a home from home for us after we were allowed to travel. (I volunteered to always do ANC or SACTU public meetings in Spain and Greece.) Andalucia is the land of one of my favourite poets – Federico García Lorca, who was murdered by the fascist Falangists during the Spanish Civil War.

* * * *

The ANC, through Ruth Mompati, had managed to get me a bursary from the Africa Education Trust to attend the London College of Printing, now the College of Communications under the University of the Arts – London (UAL). It covered my course fees, books, travel and a modest living allowance. It was a two-year technical higher diploma in lithographic printing and publishing, specially designed for foreign students. It was my first and only opportunity in my life for full-time tertiary study.

I really enjoyed being on this printing and publishing studies programme, using the best equipment in the world at the most prestigious technical institution for printing globally. The community of foreign students on the course also afforded me much opportunity for engagement with other global cultures and international politics – we were from Malaysia, Japan, India, Nigeria, Ghana, Tanzania, Kenya and South Africa. I felt more at home among non-British people in the UK under similar circumstances to mine.

After I graduated, as a former South African Typographical Union member and SACTU member, I was awarded membership of the leading print workers' union in the UK, the National Graphical Association. It was then, and over the next few years, that I spearheaded the international effort to have the South African Typographical Union, with its apartheid membership voting practices, expelled from the International Graphical Federation, the global printworkers' union federation.

On the morning of 14 March 1982, a bomb went off at the ANC office in Penton Street in London, blasting the back of the building apart and shattering windows in many of the adjacent buildings. General Johann Coetzee, head of the security police, and eight other security police operatives admitted to the attack in 1998 at the Truth and Reconciliation Commission. The components of the bomb were said to have been smuggled into the UK in diplomatic bags.

The ANC had a small printing press in the building that was run by Gill Marcus and volunteers. The press was damaged in the blast and one of our cadres, Vernet Mbatha, who slept in a room above the printing press, was injured. (Only a few days before the explosion, Vernet had been at our home for dinner.) The property was renovated and the press repaired, and a decision was taken to move the press and some of the logistics functions to a temporary premises in Islington, until secure premises could be found. I was called on to assist with the printing there.

I also got a job at a left-wing printing press, Spiderweb Press, which focused on printing for the Labour Party, the British left, trade unions, solidarity movements and liberation movements in Africa, Asia and Latin America. So for the first time I was getting a decent salary, had a home and our children were more settled. But it wasn't long before I was called back to fulltime service in the ANC.

In 1982 our third son, Vuyo, was born at home, with a midwife in attendance. It was a wonderfully happy occasion, with friends around. Vuyo's name is a tribute to that great trade unionist and songwriter Vuyisile Mini. It means 'one who brings happiness.'

Some time later, Maria got a job at the International Defence and Aid Fund (IDAF), and within some months I had joined her there. Our colleagues were Horst Kleinschmidt, Tony Trew, Barry Feinberg, Nick Feinberg, Ethel de Keyser, Eleanor Khanyile (whose husband William had been killed in the 1981 South African raids in Mozambique), Zodwa Dabengwa, Shanti and Ramni Naidoo, May Brutus, Peggy Stevenson, Al Cook, Ian Robertson, Norman Kaplan, Tim Jenkin, and a great bunch of British and Caribbean activists.

The IDAF had built up an international network of individual and organisational donors who were supporting the families of political prisoners and exiles back in South Africa, as well as legal teams and non-governmental organisations (NGOs). I'd appealed to IDAF to help support my mother, who was just getting by on her measly state pension. They went to great lengths to pair her up with a British benefactor who would then regularly send money to her, but it needed my mom's cooperation – and what my mother did was send the money back, saying that she did not take charity from anyone.

I heard a story after returning from exile that my mom was at the supermarket one day, and she was looking at products and their prices, and then putting the items back on the shelf as she couldn't afford them. A young black man saw this and got into conversation with her, offering to buy the tin of coffee for her. She assumed that he was an ANC man and told him that her son was 'one of yours', and that her son knew that she never accepted charity from anyone. So the young man took the tin of coffee without my mom seeing and went to the teller. 'When the old lady comes, just put the coffee in her bag without her seeing you do so,' he told her, and he paid for it. When my mother got home and found the coffee, she took it back to the shop and told them that she hadn't bought it. The shop explained that a young man had bought it for her. Mom told them to tell him, 'Thank you, but no thank you. I don't accept charity from anyone. I have always worked for what is put on the table.' Mom was as difficult as ever!

The IDAF had a research centre looking at a range of subject areas in South Africa, from the economy to the political situation; and it developed a photographic and video library on South African affairs second to none. Working at IDAF gave me flexible time off as needed, for me to represent SACTU and the ANC throughout the UK and Europe as a speaker to trade unions, churches, schools, universities and Anti-Apartheid Movement branches, to promote the building of social solidarity, raise material support and strengthen the campaign to isolate the apartheid regime.

I was deeply involved in the work of the ANC and SACTU, and doing quite a bit of travelling too – during my time in London, I travelled to Tanzania, Zambia, Ethiopia, France, Netherlands and the USSR, doing public speaking, and radio and television interviews. I also frequently went to Spain, Greece and Cyprus for trade union work and as an ANC representative to the UN Youth organisation meetings.

In the UK my friendship circles included Greek and Turkish Cypriots, Spanish and Latin Americans, Palestinians, Southeast Asians, West Asians and Caribbean people. These interactions deeply influenced my eating culture, music, faith and belief system. When opportunities arose to carry out missions in some of these countries, I took them with both hands.

Many of those experiences moulded what I have become and played a huge part in bringing nuance into my political outlook. The doctrinaire, mechanistic and rigid, became less of a feature in my political outlook as new dimensions and different interpretations created an interplay of ideas, and new ways of interpreting the world. It fashioned the praxis of my political consciousness. For instance, I got a much better understanding of the meaning of Gramsci's nuanced left thinking around fighting to achieve hegemony, as differentiated from the crude notion of dictatorship of the proletariat or controlling centralism.

* * * *

After the bombing, when the old Penton Street press was moved from its temporary premises to Mackenzie Street near the Caledonian Road tube station, I was recalled from the IDAF to the fulltime service of the ANC to run the printing and finishing operations at the press. The Mackenzie Street media hub and printing centre was a cutting-edge operation. It had an editorial office, research room, typesetting room, printing press with two medium-range presses, a stitcher-folder-collator, guillotine, and process darkroom. We also had a layout and design section and a line despatch room. The entire two-floor building was secured with plate-steel shutters and doors, and there was a drive-in garage, also shuttered.

Gill Marcus was the overall chief and handled the oversight of the upper-floor research and typesetting, as well as the despatch, while I managed the origination, design, print production and finishing on the lower floor. Later, Hylton Alcock joined me on the ground floor as a graphic designer and Kwezi Kadalie joined Gill, Patti MacDonald and Lynnette Brown on the second floor. Before we mechanised, a team of elderly veteran women of the ANC women's section would come in once a week to make up a manual collating-folding-stapling and despatch production line. Sarah Carneson, Rica Hodgson, Mollie Marcus, Nancy Dick, Winnie Dadoo, Ray Harmel, Sarah Naicker and Dorothy Shanley were an amazing team. These are all hidden faces of our struggle who seldom are recognised in the public space.

The press produced everything from posters and journals to underground literature and international campaign literature, churning out millions of sheet-runs. It was the best ANC logistical centre, and ran from the dark early hours of the morning until late at night. So in some ways the bomb blast at Penton Street inadvertently benefitted us for media development in the liberation movement!

(Ironically, when the ANC was unbanned and ever since, it has never again produced this kind of media infrastructure, largely through mismanagement by new incumbents that took over the department of information and publicity function. If the ANC had brought the skills, political understanding, discipline and infrastructure back into South

Africa after their unbanning, rather than abandoning this in exile, it may well have avoided the kind of incapacity that would later manifest itself in the new conditions of being a legal organisation.)

Several MK combatants, on finishing their military training in the camps, were either sent to the press for a short course, or to the London College of Printing to do diploma or degree courses in printing, publishing, or film and video making. They would then come to the liberation movement media hub and press to do voluntary work or for practical experience and training. Some remained fulltime at the press after the conclusion of their courses. These were Mandla Maseko, Mafa Ngeleza, Prince Cassock, Kenosi Lerole, Celeste Naidoo, Miles Pelo, Maurice Maja, and Zodwa, who was the partner of Ndonda Khuze (Lazarus Hlekelo Mphahlele), the singer in the Amandla Cultural Ensemble.

Besides working together, we were like family and had lots of fun together too. We were all far away from our families in South Africa, and by the end of our time in exile had probably spent more time with each other than our own families. We spent almost every day together and socialised together.

My life became absolutely consumed by this work, although I was still sent on missions to Europe by SACTU as a speaker-representative, and by the youth section of the ANC as directed by my friend and close colleague George Johannes. George, a fellow Camissa African from Cape Town, who originally was going to become a Catholic priest but changed his mind when dedicating himself to the liberation struggle, would later become the South African ambassador to the Vatican.

I also served on the editorial board of *Sechaba*, the premier ANC journal, and as a journalist-contributor. I further served as a journalist and on the editorial board, as well as on the technical-production side, of ANC weekly news briefings; *Rixaka*, the cultural journal of the ANC (to which Miles, who was a talented young artist, and I contributed sketches and poetry, respectively); *Workers' Unity*, the SACTU publication; *Umsebenzi*, the SACP publication; and *Phakamani*, a religious affairs journal. And we produced information packs for use by the ANC missions in various countries and at the United Nations, as well as a great variety of underground pamphlets and booklets. These would be despatched to the frontline states and from there smuggled into South Africa. Furthermore, as various talks and think-tanks became the order of the day in the late 1980s, we produced all the literature, memoranda and press releases for those too.

At home in South Africa, our printed work was in every township, factory, church, university and school. Visibility, communication and presence were nine-tenths of the battle. Our little collective, working flat out, was one of the best fighting units that the ANC had at its disposal. Over thirteen years every piece of printed material, whether used in the underground or abroad, originated in one of the printing presses that I played a key part in developing, in South Africa, in Botswana, in Zambia and in the UK. Of this I am very proud.

Aside from my work in the ANC and SACTU, I was also active in my SACP cell, where one of the other members was Jabulani 'Mzala' Nxumalo. Mzala was one of my closest comrades and friends. He was a protégé of Chris Hani and a prolific researcher, writer and avant-garde thinker. He wrote the critical book *Gatsha Buthelezi: Chief with a Double Agenda* (Zed Books, 1988). He also frequently wrote for the *African Communist*, *Umsebenzi*, and the *World Marxist Review*, and contributed to a number of books.

Mzala would come and work with me on occasions at the printing press to share ideas, or ask me to read and give a critique on a piece of writing of his before publication. In his ever-cheerful voice, he would say, 'Chief, what job would you like me to do? And then we must talk. I want you to read this new paper I'm writing and don't spare the critique. I want your honest opinion.'

We shared a strong passion about what we called the 'national question' and on the ethno-nationalist tendency of some in the ANC. In our discussions, Mzala and I often speculated on what would happen if the apartheid regime unbanned the ANC and SACP; we could already see that it would happen soon. Much of the corruption of the ANC and its policies that would later come to the fore were part of our discussions, and we were fairly accurate in our assessments. The seeds of what was to come could be seen among some of our number then. We both said that the greatest weapon that our enemies had to use against us was if they were to unban the ANC.

Around this time, Uncle Harry Gwala had quietly been brought to London for his health and safety, and on a few occasions Mzala, who was looking after him, brought him to the press. He sat in our process darkroom in peace, reading and working. It was a privilege to have been able to briefly engage with Uncle H.

* * * *

During this period Maria and I talked about going back to Africa, to work at the ANC school and settlement at Morogoro. We differed on this proposed move and whether it was the best way in which we could serve the struggle. We were both also developing along different growth paths and effectively were becoming different people with different goals, activities and friends. We split up around the time that the MK cultural group Amandla Cultural Ensemble had come to do performances in the UK, and when Maria's sister Teresa Farelo was on a visit.

We were all taken up with the Amandla visit, and I was also caught up with SACTU assignments to Cyprus, Greece, and an ANC youth section representation to a United Nations global youth forum conference in Spain. It was a tumultuous period of upheaval for me when it was hard to think straight. I had to find alternative accommodation and ended up living in an awful boarding house with no heating (this was the middle of winter), and with one dirty bathroom that had a coin-operated gas burner for hot water. Our mutual friends felt awkward and felt the need to keep their distance.

In 1984 we got divorced. Maria and our three sons left the UK for Morogoro, to live at the Solomon Mahlangu Freedom College settlement for three years. The entire divorce and then the departure of the children with their mother was a painful episode in all our lives.

That same year we got the devastating news that my SACTU comrade, teacher and mentor in Botswana, Jeannette Schoon, and her six-year-old daughter, Katryn, Dylan's playmate, had been killed by a letter bomb at Lubango, in northern Angola. The letter-bomb had been sent by Craig Williamson, a security policeman who at one stage had infiltrated a range of organisations. Many had been wary of him and raised questions, while others were entirely taken in by him. He was behind attacks and assassinations of a number of comrades.

Jeanette and her husband Marius with their two children, Katryn and Fritz, had been warned to leave Botswana, as they had been identified as targets for assassination, and they'd moved to Angola because they thought it would be safer for them and the kids.

It was deeply distressing and traumatic. I recorded this in my journal simply as 'Katryn':

Six years old, Katryn, dead
killed by a parcel bomb in the dirty war
Sent by the fascist security police
of the Apartheid State, 28th day of July 1984.

You curly headed baby, how many comrades
was it that nursed you and Dylan?
How you used to laugh and cry
and sometimes drive Marius and Jenny mad
with your lovable antics, the roving carrycot-jawler
at each briefing and debriefing
oblivious of the war and danger around you
. . . on the backseat of the VW Beetle, sleeping away
while parents and comrades anguishing
about the enemy's next move.

You and Dylan and Moffat
ready to go on a long journey
find a paddle pool filled with water in the garden
and fully clothed get in, splash about in delight
your smile and gurgle, two little front teeth showing

and Jenny pulling her hair out, having just shut up home, ready to go out . . .
That's how I last remember you.

Your mother, she taught so many of us, also now no more
your bodies torn to pieces; her body that she energetically used
to confound the apartheid regime – how they hated her
– how our people loved her; your bodies now no more
but her spirit lives in us and thus her work continues.

Dearest Katryn, whenever I look at Dylan
I will always remember you, another young life
not allowed to develop, nipped in the bud
another child martyr of South Africa
One day we will ensure better futures for all our children
and your sacrifice will nurture them – farewell Meisie, Hamba Kahle
only six years with us, we will always love you little sister, Hamba Kahle Katryn

Assassinations were in part a propaganda exercise, and to sow fear and awe. The assaults on our morale came hard and fast as the tempo of the dirty war was stepped up. It was a different kind of war, but a war nonetheless.

It also became very clear that the security police were targeting a very particular calibre of cadre. Some high-ranking people, who often made very easy targets, seemed to be overlooked. The left within the liberation movement, legendary strategic thinkers and those carrying out strategic work, were the targets. This approach continued right up to the assassination of Chris Hani.

The killings kept coming. On 28 March 1988, in the morning as she was opening the door of her office in Paris, Dulcie September was assassinated. She was shot five times in the head. I'd worked with Dulcie in Lusaka, and the assassination weighed heavily on my mind and deeply affected me.

Dulcie was an outspoken woman who'd been investigating trafficking of weapons and nuclear materials between France and South Africa. It's believed that the arms industry in France, Belgium, Netherlands and Germany, along with the apartheid regime, considered her to be the effective face and voice of the sanctions campaign and wanted her out of the way. It has also been speculated that Dulcie had come into receipt of nuclear, arms industry and sanctions-busting secrets that would compromise those behind these activities. Dulcie's family revealed too that before her death, Dulcie had indicated in a letter that there were people within the ANC who were connected to the nefarious forces she was up against; she had written, 'The enemy is within.'

I penned a short piece of poetry at the time of Dulcie's murder, sensing what was to roll out in future years after we attained what we called freedom – 'Beware Comrade – the AmaMafiosi':

The godfathers of crime
stalk the corridors of power
confounding the theories
of political scientists
imparting new dimensions to entryism
wearing the colours of the day
be it red or blue, easily shed tomorrow
cloth of the church, or the solidarity of union
whether be they those who balance scales of justice
or fly the banners of culture, 'Liberation Heroes'
ideology overruled, smiling benignly,
playing the funeral march
for . . . 'Freedom'
Beware Comrade, beware the amaMafiosi.

10

LONDON:
THE LIBERATION PRINTER

In 1985 I paid a short visit to Moscow. This was pre-perestroika (the political movement for reform within the Communist Party) and glasnost (openness), and while it was great to see the sights and get a feel for the ordinary daily lives of people, the politics, party delinquency and behaviours of officialdom left much to be desired. They certainly didn't inspire me as a model for community-supported socialism and democracy. There was as much to learn about what mistakes we should not make, as there was to learn about positive features.

I also returned to Zambia for a SACTU conference. The political climate and tensions that dominated my time in Lusaka five years earlier had changed considerably, and it was good to see the city again under better circumstances. It was also good to reconnect with all the older-generation trade unionists – Ray Alexander, Aaron 'Ben Bella' Pembe, Ben Baardman, and so many others, including trade unionists from home. Hauntingly absent was our dear Jeanette Schoon, who had done so much work on the trade-union front and whose thinking was cutting edge.

The conference was a happy turning point for SACTU, as its purpose was nearing the end: the Congress of South African Trade Unions (Cosatu) was about to emerge, in December 1985. SACTU was part of the process of forming Cosatu, and some of those involved inside South Africa in those processes were at the SACTU conference, where the formation of Cosatu and what it would be called were part of the deliberations.

In that same year Denis Goldberg – 'accused number three' in the 1963-64 Rivonia Trial, alongside Nelson Mandela and Walter Sisulu, convicted of sabotage and sentenced to life imprisonment – was released from Pretoria Central Prison after serving 22 years. Denis Goldberg was taken by his jailers straight from prison to the airport and put on a plane to Israel, where he was reunited with his wife and children. He then came to the UK to work with the ANC. Once settled, he joined us at the Mackenzie Street media production hub, where he set up an ANC merchandising operation aimed at the solidarity arena, to build support for the ANC and the struggle of the people of South Africa.

In 1986 a call for designs for a new ANC logo was made to comrades across the ANC camps, residences, the Solomon Mahlangu Freedom College and branches, and the best of these was sent to us to process, leading to the adoption of a new logo. This was part of a new media enhancement strategy that was developed to coincide with the celebration of the 75th anniversary of the movement in 1987. Up until then we'd been using the ANC logo designed by Thami Mneyele.

None of the final few designs was usable on its own but each had elements of merit. Gill Marcus, Patti MacDonald, Sello Moeti (Michael Lebese) and I deliberated on the merging of elements of the best designs; we also agreed that the symbolic basics of Thami Mneyele's logo should remain in the new design. With this brief, the final design was produced by Patti, who was our main designer at that time, and soon I was printing the first publications using the new ANC logo.

With this innovation we built a recognisable ANC brand at home and across the world. Denis's first products in the merchandising division were mugs, caps and T-shirts with the new ANC logo emblazoned on them.

When the ANC was unbanned, one of the historic elements that was enshrined in the logo, the controversial four race silos represented by the four-spoked wheel of the Congress of the People, was changed to project the industrial multi-spoked wheel of a mineshaft head, representing both labour and unity in action, together with the spear, shield and ANC flag. (The colour red, for the bloodshed in resistance to colonialism and apartheid, and the colour of the working class, was in 1990 inexplicably removed from the 1987 logo brand.)

* * * *

That year I visited Tanzania to attend an ANC youth section conference and found my son Dylan in a very poor state of mental and physical health. The settlement at Morogoro had its own dynamics and rivalries, which couldn't have been easy for Maria and the children, and not only had Dylan become extremely depressed, but he'd also had some bad bouts of malaria. He returned to the UK to live with me, and from this time I took care of his upbringing while my other two sons stayed with their mom.

As a father who had never been fathered, I found the role of father very difficult, and it had been made more so by the divorce and by the liberation movement lifestyle. Dylan had learning difficulties, and at one stage I got a frantic call from his school teacher. During school lunch, he'd pointed and repeated, 'Ambush . . . Ambush'. I had to explain that in Tanzania when children asked for 'ambush' it meant that they were asking for seconds!

The children were going back and forth between Maria and me, and this presented its own problems. And as an exiled cadre working for the ANC, I wasn't earning a living but relying on assistance from the ANC welfare committee, plus a modest allowance for Dylan.

The 1976 and 1980s generation in exile found great difficulty in being able to make new lives or even just hold their lives together. We'd left South Africa under traumatic circumstances, often after years of activist ups and downs, and social problems abounded among us. That's why AnnMarie Wolpe and others took the initiative to establish a welfare committee to support those of us who were battling to survive in the UK, and the efforts of the ANC welfare committee made a huge difference in our lives. Still, life was no picnic.

* * * *

I served on the ANC religious affairs committee, with people like Catholic priest Father Selwyn (Sally Gross) and Methodist reverend Cedric

Mason and others, all ANC activists. I also handled some of the Catholic affairs and Muslim affairs work of the liberation movement, and was asked to be in correspondence with activists in these arenas. Some of our Muslim supporter-activists from Cape Town were studying in Pakistan, and I was consulted when they wrote to the ANC for direction.

As part of my work in the ANC youth section, I liaised with young white military draft resisters in winning them over to the ANC where appropriate. There was an organisation of draft resisters called the Committee on South African War Resisters, which also brought out a publication called *Resister*. My old friend and comrade Heather Garner was working with the Committee on South African War Resisters, together with Bill Andersen and Gavin Cawthra, two very sharp war resisters.

I also engaged in an initiative started and led by poet Mongane Wally Serote – a cultural organisation called A Re Kopaneng ('Come Together'). It was great fun, and involved singing, musical and poetry sessions. Eugene Skeef the percussionist-performer-poet was also involved, as was that great and wonderful spirited musician Bheki Mseleku, Lorna and Graham de Smit, and several others, like Mandla Maseko and Maurice Maja from the press.

There was a lot on my plate, and I would often have to shed activities to focus on my core work. After a while I had to rationalise what I was doing because it became too much.

During the period of my divorce, I met Peter Zochling, a builder-cum-renovator who came to do some work at the IDAF, and who ran a boarding house. I rented a room from him. Pete was one of the few English friends I made in the entire time I was in the UK. He had a two-person canoe which the two of us used to tour the London canals. This was one of the few non-political pastimes that I enjoyed.

It was while living with Pete that I met Celeste Naidoo. An activist who'd become a target of the security police, she'd left South Africa, going into exile in Germany before coming to London. Celeste was from Cape Town and had a vibrant personality. She'd managed to get a bursary to attend a publishing diploma course at the London College of Printing, and came to work at the liberation media hub and press at Mackenzie Street.

We grew close and were married on 9 February 1988. This allowed Celeste to remain in the UK. After her time at college, she was able to get a good job with Penguin publishers.

In mid-1989 Maria returned to the UK, with our younger boys, Manuel and Vuyo. She had received a bursary to do university studies. The boys had some trouble adjusting, and shortly after their return I was fielding yet another concerned phonecall from a teacher. She said that they had got under her table in the class, and were holding onto the table legs; they looked very scared and were pointing at the other children, shouting, 'Boers, boers!' Though little palefaces themselves, they had never seen so many white children together before, and I had to explain to the teacher that they needed time to get used to the new environment because in Tanzania all the other children were black.

Though Celeste had no children of her own, she rose to the challenge of mothering and did her best to ensure that Dylan had a good home, and that Manuel and Vuyo had a good second home. It would have been much more difficult without her at my side. I can only thank Celeste for everything she gave and for taking such a burden on her shoulders. I know it wasn't easy.

Others also helped, including Colin Belton and Maria Nobrega, the couple Maria and I were very close to in our first years in London, but who had split up by then; my old friend Heather Garner; and dear old Wolfie Kodesh, even though he was in poor health.

I tried my best to be a father under difficult circumstances, but I knew that it wasn't good enough. I had never been rooted in my whole life, and my children were now also not rooted. The suffering of the children of political activists is seldom acknowledged. They have no choice, just like their parents. The parents themselves are in a perpetual dependency state within the struggle machinery.

We were suitcase people, simply trying to survive against the odds. The struggle, or our war, wasn't just about danger and loss of life but was also a series of psychological battles.

LONDON

* * * *

My identity during these UK years of my exile was totally wrapped up with being the liberation movement printer. In 1987 I wrote a piece of prose in my journal, and these few extracts of 'Companero Printing Press' illustrate how I felt:

The still of the morning shatters as you awaken
to begin another day of production.
You wind your way into the pattern required for creation
and I mould into the process; you and I are one.
Without each other no product can materialise.
When you move in rhythm, I am at peace,
when you break down, I feel the strain.
The pattern of work it's always the same
Load, make ready, ink up, register – all systems go!
Through this eye I view your sentinel form
as an expression of dignity; my own dignity
Bound in part with this my vocation.

Only a printing machine they may say.
But I say that you're my AK47 and together
we fulfil the call that every Patriot be a Combatant.
You're my partner in labour, you're my cultural tool.
You're my instructor in discipline; I spend ten hours and more
working with you every day,
and spend even more time with you in my mental processes.

For days after production, I take pleasure
in admiring our completed work; you're an integral part of my life.
And when I hear the many stories of the usefulness
that the literature we produce fulfils at home
in forwarding our national and social liberation,
or hear of comrades who have been imprisoned

> *or worse still . . . killed, for possessing our product.*
> *then I stop for a second before awakening you*
> *and take a long look and say a prayer*
> *I think of millions of illegal sheets*
> *from this underground liberation press*
> *In thousands of hands struggling for freedom.*

In the late 1980s a woman by the name of Jessica was sent to work with us at the press, where I was asked to train her for a few weeks. She was one of those cadres sent for a brief period during which we needed to be sensitive about her identity, which needed to be protected: she wasn't to be exposed to many people, nor be expected to answer questions. In other words, the 'need to know' principle applied, and I didn't ask questions.

While training under my guidance in printing, during those periods during which not many people were around – mainly Gill and I – Jessica was chatty, and I began to pick up huge inconsistencies and contradictions in what she was saying. She was asking too many questions about things that shouldn't have concerned her. She was also giving away much about herself that made no sense. She said that she was from Cape Town but her knowledge of the city's political dynamics was exceptionally poor for someone who was supposed to be an activist.

I reported my concerns up the chain, but the top people in the SACP vouched for her bona fides and I was told there was nothing to be concerned about.

Some months later I discovered that I was right to have been worried. The real story behind Jessica's removal to London was that her husband had been treacherous, leading to deaths of comrades, and she'd been sent to the UK for her protection because it was felt that suspicion had unfairly fallen on her – in other words, she was being protected. Then, months after having been training at our press, she was caught red-handed in an act of betrayal.

Later, the one-time ANC chief representative in London, Solly Smith, and also the ANC executive member who was editor of *Sechaba*,

Francis Meli, were outed as working against the movement. The struggle wasn't easy terrain, and you never knew who you could really trust.

These were the tensions that we lived with while carrying out our work: there was constant fear and awareness that what we were doing was dangerous, and that though there was an illusion of safety in being in London, the war was always with us, as much as it had been when we were in the frontline states.

I began to suffer from an acute pain and headache syndrome, and it was arranged for me to see the same specialist doctor who'd treated our president, OR Tambo. I was working in an enclosed space, with chemicals and inks and the loud noise of machines, from the dark of the early morning to the dark of late night, and Dr Hindley believed that I should be doing something outdoors, in the fresh air. To this end, he allowed me to take over his urban vegetable-growing allotment. I was also dealing with a low level but constant traumatic stress syndrome. I was in my 30s and had experienced constant moving around, without any rootedness, since early childhood, enduring one traumatic experience after the other. Managing it was most difficult.

Unknown to me at the time, the condition I had was more serious and would dog me for the rest of my life, getting more difficult as time passed by. In 2016 I finally got a diagnosis of axial spondyloarthritis, a painful, chronic arthritis that affects mainly the joints of the spine, and also the joints connecting each side of the base of the spine with the pelvis. It can also affect other joints in the body, as well as tendons and ligaments. With this, I also have costochondritis, which is an inflammation of the cartilage that connects a rib to the breastbone, with inflammation of the intercostal nerves running from the spine between the ribs into my chest, underneath my burn scars. All in all, it's a lifetime of severe pain management and involves flare-ups that get triggered by stress.

While I was wrestling with pain and some symptoms of post-traumatic stress disorder, other comrades were battling with similar conditions, as well as alcoholism, depression, suicidal thoughts, and serious illness, including HIV/Aids.

One of my close comrades working with me at the department of information and publicity media hub, Sello Moeti (Michael Lebese), was a focused, disciplined, work-oriented and clean-living guy; you could set your watch by his timekeeping. He'd been living alone down Kings Cross way, and after two days of absence from work, we realised that something was wrong. He was so ill that he couldn't even crawl to the front door to open it. He had to be hospitalised, as it turned out that he had a serious illness that could not be successfully treated. After a difficult period, he passed away. Only months before, Sello had been able to contact his family in South Africa, who had long given him up for dead. Now that joy was shattered as they had to come to bury him.

Hardly a week went by without some tragic news, but work went on like clockwork. When I think back on those years, of around twenty cadres with whom I was closely associated in my work, fourteen died before we saw liberation.

* * * *

After 1985, the changes were fast and dramatic. As the years passed and our resistance work paid dividends, it became clear to the apartheid regime that change was inevitable, but the way they handled this awareness was clumsy, their responses coming nowhere near to meeting the crisis they were facing. Traditional securocrats, military men holding influential positions in the government, simply upped the intensity of their efforts using outmoded brutal counterinsurgency methods and poorly conceived processes of winning hearts and minds.

As conservatives within the apartheid regime increased repression, corporate business forces and foreign governments' security agencies clearly got the message, and realised that a much more sophisticated counterinsurgency on their part was needed, and that an endgame had to be developed, as well as the nurturing of relationships with future black negotiators of a settlement.

But the apartheid regime, the securocrats, the corporate world, white South Africans generally and many western governments had demonised the liberation movements, which were seen as USSR and communist aligned, and this left no partners with whom they could negotiate. So the first step was to create a new layer of society which would be able to be engaged, followed by a climate conducive to negotiations.

In going forward, the visionaries within the National Party, the corporate sector and their international partners realised that they needed to promote a new kind of social architecture on the ground in South Africa, while also building a relationship of trust with liberation movements in attempts to wean the ANC away from what they saw as dependencies on Soviet, Chinese, Vietnamese and Cuban relationships. The danger for them was that the liberalisation and friendship-building strategy in a country where people had a high political consciousness could blow up in their faces, but it was a risk that they couldn't afford to avoid. They had to be aware that by opening up and liberalising, there would be less control over outcomes, and the political space afforded could result in the very liberation forces they were trying to neutralise, seizing control of the way forward.

This new 1980s environment would be used by both sides as a struggle terrain. Time would show that the liberation movement used it much more wisely than did the apartheid regime.

The means used by the new counterinsurgency forces in the 1980s were layered. The charity and non-governmental organisation (NGO) sectors grew rapidly and quickly to over a hundred thousand organisations, through huge injections of cash and training from the corporate sector, international trusts and foundations, and foreign governments. The promotion of community-based and NGO initiatives created a relationship-building interface for the new counterinsurgency approach, and this became the ground for developing a new layer of leadership and civil-society organisations, as different from radical political liberationist organisations.

At the same time, the corporates, trusts, foundations and foreign government agencies learnt that this arena would carry the risk of also including more radical elements, and that these would have contact with the liberation movements. This at the time was seen as a positive rather than a negative thing, where the objective was to also engage with moderate elements in the liberation movement and marginalise the radical left. It was all about a negotiated settlement of the South African problem by ensuring a favourable balance of forces where white South African and foreign corporate interests were protected.

The new approach would assist in opening up dialogues necessary for the endgame, which was to see a non-racial liberal democratic government installed, and a neutralised SACP and Cosatu, and a demobilised MK. Effectively, it was a grooming process in the political arena to ensure that the inevitable change on the horizon would see black governance that kept white and corporate power in control in a more subtle manner, and avoid South Africa lining up with powers hostile to Europe and the USA.

Parallel to this, after the change to a more sophisticated counterinsurgency strategy by the 'verligte' (enlightened) elements of the apartheid regime, the ANC found more receptivity to having mission offices in many western countries around the world. In London in the late 1980s, for example, the ANC chief representative Mendi Msimang was provided with two bodyguards and a vehicle for security by the British government. For some of us, this most visible move was a clear sign that major change was under way. It was Thatcher's government that was doing this, regardless of the UK prime minister having been a vocal supporter of the apartheid regime.

Whereas before the 1980s, all ANC/MK students were sent to Eastern Europe and the USSR for studies, in the 1980s bursaries became widely available for liberation movement students and for students from South Africa in general to study in western countries. The emergent trade union movement in South Africa was nurtured away from the communist World Federation of Trade Unions to attend courses with the British Trades Union Congress and the non-communist International Confederation of Free Trade Unions headquartered in Brussels.

The ANC was feted with special status from the United Nations and International Labour Organization, and invitations were extended to the ANC in many world forums and institutions, almost as if it were already a government in waiting. The ANC utilised this and built a formidable diplomatic infrastructure which waged a successful campaign to isolate the apartheid regime.

This was the background when a range of mass-based organisations in South Africa, encouraged through its contact with the trade union movement and the liberation movement, came together to form the United Democratic Front in August 1983. This new organisation, and the broader front involving what became known as the Mass Democratic Movement (MDM), became an arena for contestation of ideas and the development of a new layer of leadership.

It also became a means or conduit for relationship building between a range of institutions – business, religious, media and academia – to develop enough of a trust relationship to be able to conduct exploratory talks with liberation movements. These new NGOs were often sponsored and brokered by corporates, trusts and foundations abroad. And thus 'talks about talks' emerged in the late 1980s.

The final part of this trajectory was ever more direct talks between the apartheid regime and its periphery on the one side, and a layer of liberation-movement leaders in exile and in prison on the other. This facilitated a loosening-up of the environment of imprisonment, and then the gradual release of older, iconic political prisoners, and finally the unbanning of all banned organisations.

These emergent steps were preceded by a jostling of corporates, academic institutions, political think-tanks and hastily composed leadership groups to make a pilgrimage to Lusaka, London, Senegal and elsewhere to meet with ANC leaders. White South Africans who'd previously either supported the regime or who had remained mute were also now making pilgrimages to meet the ANC in exile for talks. White youth leaders, church leaders, businesspeople, academics and politicians vied with each other to be seen as the most enlightened.

Only a few years earlier the word 'terrorists' had rolled easily off the tongues of many of these people when referring to the ANC. The 'Free Nelson Mandela' campaign had seen a backlash called the 'Hang Nelson Mandela' campaign. Now, suddenly, that kind of reaction was giving way to overtures.

Alongside the soft and nurturing modern counterinsurgency approach was a continuation of harsh repression of the old securocrat approach, particularly of those considered more radical in the ranks of the liberation movements, through stepped-up assassinations, as well as against those in the ranks of the United Democratic Front, the MDM and Cosatu, who were thought to be radical undesirables. It was a classic carrot-and-stick approach to neutralising insurgency.

Finally, the avant-garde within the National Party, together with the corporate sector and foreign governments, were ready in 1990 to take the step of creating a climate conducive for the kind of negotiations that they believed would give them a favourable outcome, and to remove the old guard on both sides from centre stage.

A perfect storm of opportunity for the modern counterinsurgency was also created by a paradigm shift in Eastern Europe and the USSR, in a rapid loss of power of communist parties. This almost instantly created a new kind of struggle terrain that we were not as well equipped to handle.

The mass of the population, including much of the ANC that had fought under illegal conditions, would be sidelined during a three-year marathon negotiation session of the elite. Like a tap, the power of the people would be turned on and off as needed.

The ANC under the circumstances captured much ground and the National Party lost much, but this didn't alter the direction of the new counterinsurgency strategists, who played a long game, in undermining the liberationist struggle.

11

HOMECOMING:
PREPARING FOR FREEDOM

On 2 February 1990 the ANC, the SACP and the PAC were unbanned, and on 11 February Nelson Mandela was released from prison.

We were all ecstatic. At last, our exile would be ended and we would be stateless no longer. Perhaps even we would be able to lead a normal life. We wept and we laughed. It was an emotional rollercoaster time.

Almost immediately key people like Gill Marcus left our media hub and press at Mackenzie Street in London with a small group of others to assemble in Lusaka. There, a small team of ANC leaders was being put together to return to South Africa as the leadership team, to begin to engage in the first talks with the National Party government – FW de Klerk and his cabinet negotiating team.

The ANC team from exile, along with some older political-prisoner leaders and a crop of new leaders from the United Democratic Front and the MDM, entered talks with the apartheid regime, and also organised the reopening of an ANC branch system and offices across the country. They established a totally new party infrastructure and appointed people from the broad democratic movement inside the country to key posts. They also made overtures to the bantustan leadership and people within the black administration of the apartheid state to come on board the new freedom train. The doors were literally thrown open to all and sundry, while its longstanding loyal tried-and-tested foundation base were kept at bay.

This marked the beginning of the ANC's trajectory towards a meltdown. It became an organisation that was neither fish nor fowl, effectively a new ANC.

The more liberal democrat, as well as social democrats in the white opposition were drawn into what within months had become a very different ANC to the one we'd known till then.

My last job at the department of information and publicity media hub and press at Mackenzie Street was printing thousands of yellow handbooks with the modified ANC logo on the cover, emblazoned with the words 'Joining the ANC'. The centrepiece photo was of Nelson Mandela and OR Tambo waving, and this was surrounded by pictures of the early-twentieth-century ANC delegation to London and a joint gathering of the ANC and the African Political Organisation, followed by pictures of other key moments in the long history of the ANC. The handbook covered every aspect of the 'then and now' of the ANC, and explained how people could join the party, as well as publishing its own constitutional framework as a legal political body in South Africa. At the back of the booklet was the address of the new ANC headquarters at 54 Sauer Street in Johannesburg.

It was both joyous and sad to be printing and publishing the first ANC publication, with the party operating as a legal entity inside South Africa.

This coincided with the publishing of adverts in South African newspapers offering jobs in the ANC to the general public – the very jobs that we'd been doing over many years in a sterling manner as cadres. The problem was that we were still stuck outside South Africa and couldn't apply. Many of us felt abandoned by the new leadership core, and it didn't escape us that this was exactly what the apartheid regime wanted. They had worked hard to drive wedges between what they regarded as radical liberationists in the ANC, MK and SACP fighting a liberation struggle, and those they regarded as reformist civil-rights activists with ideas closer to nationalism and liberal democracy.

A highlight of those last months in exile was when Nelson Mandela came to London and met with all branch members for the first time. It was a beautiful, momentous occasion that I will never forget.

A couple of months earlier he'd gone to Sweden to meet up with OR Tambo and a select few of the older cadres with whom he'd had relationships in the old days, among them Wolfie Kodesh and Rica Hodgson.

When they got back to the UK, Rica was ecstatic; she grabbed me and said, 'Kiss the lips that kissed the man!' Wolfie gave me a photograph of himself with Madiba on one side and OR Tambo on the other side. It was so beautiful to see these men, friends and comrades, together again after almost 30 years apart.

When Madiba met with us it was like our father gathering his flock together. There was something spiritual about that first meeting under his gaze and listening to his voice. He'd spent 27 years in prison, but he took to the platform and held the crowd before him spellbound.

* * * *

In August 1990 I applied to the chief representative of the ANC mission in the UK, Mendi Msimang, for permission to return to South Africa.

Uncle Mendi sent me a letter to notify us that we'd be able to return but that the ANC wouldn't be able to provide any assistance with flights, nor financial support once we were in South Africa. I'd need to report to a government clearing officer in September 1990, soon after our arrival in the country, and I would be issued with a South African ID document and passport to replace my United Nations travel document. Uncle Mendi also wrote that we should report to the ANC office in Cape Town, with a letter of introduction supplied, to receive instructions on our political reintegration into ANC structures.

Celeste and I sold as many of our belongings as possible to raise some money, and sent a few of our things home to my brother-in-law Kevin Patel's address. We left London and my thirteen years in exile behind, to once more face the harsh realities of a South Africa that had not really changed. The reintegration process, I would find, was as difficult as when I'd first gone into exile so many years previously.

It was an emotional time, filled with feelings of joy and trepidation. I had butterflies in my stomach all the way on that flight back to South Africa – we had been called dangerous terrorists and now we were going back to those who'd labelled us as such, and who had been assassinating our friends and comrades.

We approached the immigration officers at the airport in Johannesburg with foreboding. On seeing our United Nations travel documents, the immigration officer had to call his superior, who had a list of all who'd been given clearance to return. I showed him the letter of clearance that we'd got from Uncle Mendi, and after some further questioning and instruction to report to an official in Cape Town, Celeste, Dylan and I were cleared into South Africa, officials glaring at us from all sides.

Once through to the main hall, I had a feeling of relief which turned to joy when my dearest friend Jimmy Dryja had come to meet us. He was so happy. He'd made a 'welcome home' placard and was jumping around, trying to look like a large welcome crowd. His happiness was contagious as we hugged.

We had a day to kill before our flight to Cape Town in the evening, so Jimmy took us to his flat to meet his wife Gertie and daughter Chanel. He also took us to his business, the Mini-Cine in Hillbrow, where we met up with his brother Stefan, who'd been just a little boy when we left South Africa. James and my friendship had lasted the test of distance and time, and that meant the world to me.

On the flight to Cape Town, it was strange to be sitting in a plane filled mainly with white South Africans, who were drinking and noisily talking to each other in Afrikaans or strongly accented South African English. A man got on the plane holding some roses and immediately the boisterous guys started teasing him and calling him Rosie. 'Rosie, your wife is going to know you have been up to mischief. Only a guilty man would bring her roses!'

It's a strange thing to remember but it emphasised the surreal anonymity of my return: for us, there would be no roses.

As the plane approached the Mother City, it was still light enough to see that wonderful sight of home beneath me. My mother, my half-sister May and her children, Celeste's parents, and my brother-in-law Kevin Patel and sister-in-law Marcella Naidoo were there to meet us. The emotions are too difficult to explain; they were beyond what words can convey. Physical body contact after years of separation – it was the happiest I'd felt in a lifetime.

On the drive from the airport into the city, I found myself staring at everything around me and retreating into myself. The infrastructure had changed but all the familiar features that had been in my Cape Town dreams over thirteen years were still there.

* * * *

Kevin and Marcella had renovated a building with a second entrance in their yard, and made it into a comfortable first home for us. They were so thoughtful, gracious and accommodating. Without them and the care they showed, life would have been extremely difficult. Their welcoming home, and our new home, was in Surrey Estate on the Cape Flats.

Once settled in, I went to see my mother and May, and her now grown and working kids (who all had jobs at the nearby Groote Schuur government hospital), all living together in their home in Lower Main Road, Salt River. Their socioeconomic conditions hadn't changed, and walking into the house, just a short distance of 100 metres from the old house on the corner of Cole and Nansen streets, was like walking back in time. It was a difficult experience of reunion, as I'd become a very different person over the intervening years, while for them it was as though time had stood still. We occupied very different worlds. But it was lovely to see them and to get hugs all round.

Kevin and Marcella had joined the new ANC and were continuing in their activism as former United Democratic Front activists. Down the same road as them, in Surrey Estate, was Paul Joemat and Rhoda Joemat (later a member of parliament), who were members of the ANC, as were others in Surrey Estate, like Ebrahim Rasool (later a premier of the Western Cape and ambassador to the USA) and Rashid Seria (one-time editor of the newspapers *South* and *Grassroots*, which faced bannings on multiple occasions). I was introduced to all these activists who were involved in establishing the new ANC structures in Cape Town. These were all impressive people who engendered hope that there were those who could outbalance the retrogressive elements coming to the fore in the new ANC.

As soon as I was able to, I paid a call on the ANC office, which was near the railway station in Athlone. When I entered the room, I was immediately struck by the lack of decorum – there were young, ill-disciplined people arguing with each other. I tried to get someone's attention and was asked to wait in a curt and uninterested fashion by someone who came across as a loudmouthed lout. The only thing remotely recognisable as representing the ANC were the T-shirts the people were wearing.

I was dumbstruck. Were these the people I was to report to after thirteen years of sacrifice and service? I found myself thinking, Oh, my God, what have we done to deserve this?

As I stood, frozen and shocked, from out of another room appeared Uncle Reg September. He took one look at my face and said, 'Come, let's take a walk.'

I quickly showed him Mendi Msimang's letter, and he shook his head and said, 'There's nobody in this office for you to report to or who can help you in any way, but let's not talk here. It's not safe.'

Out in the street, Uncle Reg finally looked me right in the eyes and said, 'Welcome home, Pat.' Then he shrugged and added, 'It's not quite what you thought, hey? We opened the doors of the ANC and all sorts of characters flocked in. I don't trust some of those characters – there are askaris everywhere. And that office isn't safe – it's probably bugged.'

As we walked along the pavement at a relatively fast pace, I noticed that Reg was greeting a lot of people, everywhere – on the opposite pavement, in doorways, even in cars that passed. 'Uncle Reg, you seem to have gotten to know a lot of folks around here,' I commented.

He said, 'No, I don't know any of them, but I'm sending out a signal to anyone watching my movement that I'm not alone. It's a defensive measure. Those of us who returned are under constant surveillance wherever we go. Even in the office there are security police agents among us.' Uncle Reg gave me a stern look and said, 'Keep your head down for a while, and Ray, Jack and I will see where to fit you in. Take all the security measures that you've been taught and trust nobody.'

Uncle Reg asked if I had a job lined up and I said no – I'd been expecting a position at the University of the Western Cape but it had fallen through – but that Celeste had been offered a job in the publishing industry in Johannesburg. He enquired after the children, and I told him that only Dylan had come home with me, and that he had a lot of learning difficulties, partly as a result of the kind of life we'd led and his many moves, not to mention that he'd never done mathematics or Afrikaans language in his schooling before. Reg promised to make some enquiries. He asked how I was getting around, and I mentioned that I was reliant on the minibus taxis and the train.

'Ooh!' he exclaimed. 'It's dangerous to be moving about on your own. I don't mean from skollies, but the enemy will be tagging you continuously. People are also getting bumped off.'

By this time, we'd gone around the block and zigzagged through the side streets.

He said, 'Here's my number. We're both going into the corner shop ahead. You come out again and turn right, and I'll come out after you and turn left and go back to the office. Don't take a taxi here. Make your way to the station and take a train to the next stop and then get a taxi. Keep your spirits up and goodbye for now.'

It was all surreal.

* * * *

Celeste and I moved out of Surrey Estate to Rose Street in the Bokaap in town, as it was more central and easier to get around from there. No sooner had we done so than Celeste went up to Joburg to the job she'd been offered.

At this time, I joined with Reg September and others in critically looking at our communities of people classified as 'Coloured' and what interventions we could take to build a stronger sense of belonging as stakeholders and beneficiaries of our struggle for liberation. We particularly wanted people in our 'Coloured' communities to reclaim and be proud of their African heritage, and also to engage in self-empowerment. We committed to building African consciousness among people still classified as 'Coloured' and to address a more positive approach around pride of place within the diverse South African family of peoples by reclaiming our African identity.

We began a process of critique about the word 'Coloured' in order to start looking at a non-racial, non-ethnic, non-tribalist and non-colourist way to talk about ourselves and our history and heritage. This would ultimately draw inspiration from the old Camissa river system in Cape Town and freshwater river systems all over Africa.

We agreed that to simply attack people for using the term 'Coloured' was shortsighted if we didn't educate them as to why there was a difficulty with being proud of this term, and also without providing an alternative paradigm of thinking. But it couldn't simply be about changing terms. We were concerned by approaches that artificially recreated European stereotype versions of tribes existing in the seventeenth century as a twentieth-century solution to complex identity issues. It was African consciousness and reclaiming our African identity that had to be the focus, and also finding a way of expressing our indigenous roots and the African-Asian roots of our enslaved ancestors.

Our overall aim was to find a positive manner to express our unique ancestral-cultural identity as a subset of people who had the commonality of facing a basket of crimes against humanity, from slavery and genocide to de-Africanisation and apartheid – and who rose above these adversities. Over the following decades, the concept of Camissa Africans evolved.

But we also recognised that within communities labelled 'Coloured' there were groups of people who had never lost their indigenous identities, regardless of all the attempts by the colonial and apartheid administrations. These were the San peoples, the Nama, Korana, Damara, Griqua, Orlam Afrikaner, and some Cape Khoe communities. They, too, had every right to revive such communities, without resorting to seventeenth-century European stereotyped tribalism, or notions of Verwoerdian firstism or primacy notions. There was no one-size-fits-all approach when it came to self-determination.

We also recognised that there was a conservative tradition among some people classified 'Coloured', who were close in thinking to white

Afrikaners, and that they may be happy to call themselves 'Coloured' or 'Brown' people. Regardless of how others may feel, they, too, have that right to self-identify.

But we were clear that the state and political parties should desist from classifying, de-Africanising and labelling one sector of African society as the colonial and apartheid governments had done.

The word 'Camissa' comes from the Kora (Cape Khoe) ǁkhamis sa, meaning 'sweet water for us all'. It refers to the river that flows from Table Mountain down to the sea, a freshwater system with over 40 tributaries and springs that today runs beneath the city of Cape Town. This work was woven into all that I did over the next three decades, by means of research and writing, public participation sessions, focus groups, producing TV series, publishing, and finally creating the new Camissa Museum.

A lot was on my mind and there was much to do for community and family. The repatriation committee structures were largely unfunded and were also ill-equipped to deal with the problems many of us were experiencing. For example, they got our children into schools that we couldn't afford. In my case, Dylan was placed at the expensive Marist Brothers school in Rondebosch, but after a month it was clear that I wouldn't be able to pay the school fees, and I had to take him out. We didn't have any money and I was still needing to find a job.

I managed to get Dylan into Trafalgar High School in District Six, Uncle Reg's alma mater. Dylan would remain there for six years because he also needed to do the standard-nine year over. I couldn't have made a better choice, and the school did marvels for him, thanks to the dedicated teachers and the school's strong political outlook and tradition of struggle. Trafalgar High has my utmost respect.

Still, trying to deal with his school placement myself within my modest and fast-dwindling means made me feel like I had when I'd first left school and was trying to find a job. It was the exile experience in reverse, and weaning ourselves off dependency on the movement was a painful experience for many.

After all I'd done and thirteen years of experience in the ANC and as a representative of the ANC in international forums, I'd gone back to zero, like I didn't exist. I was again pushing huge boulders uphill. Our media hub and printing press back in the UK were rendered redundant within months, and we felt abandoned. Effectively, the ANC as an organisation was taking leave of those who'd been working for it over a long time, and depersonalising and alienating itself from its loyal membership. In time many even felt betrayed.

The thousands of activists in exile, soldiers of MK and political prisoners were kept at bay in exile, and in camps and in prisons, as spectators, for up to three years. It was something over which we had no control. We certainly were estranged from the strategy of creating an instant new ANC with no vetting or candidature membership, with no accountability of leadership to the thousands in exile and prison who were now cut adrift by the small elite who returned to South Africa and were totally preoccupied with negotiation and establishing a new, legal ANC. And by the time most exiles had returned, the ANC structure and leading personalities were a fait accompli that we had to accept.

In fact, right up to the unbanning of the ANC and the SACP, we were still being told by those spearheading negotiations that they were not in negotiations with the apartheid regime. New branches in South Africa that kicked off with much fanfare were quickly controlled by cliques, which then purposefully kept control over the size of the membership and how its business was conducted. This was to ensure that small elites became entrenched elites for life, and would be mobile right up the chain and secure parliamentary and council seats. The awful so-called democratic centralism system, which Joe Slovo had critiqued as being the bedrock of non-accountability of leadership and institutionalisation of a corruption of democracy, interplayed negatively with the seizing of branches by self-serving opportunists and nefarious elements.

We'd been told that a new underground front, Operation Vula, had been opened inside South Africa and that some of the top leadership had entered South Africa to pursue this strategy to intensify the struggle. ANC leaders also promised that there would never be round-table negotiations with many role-players, and said that they would insist on a two-sided negotiation table with all liberationist forces on one side to present a united front, and the apartheid regime and its quislings on the other side. That just did not happen.

In this way, the modernised counterinsurgency strategy of our enemies was successfully used to deradicalise the liberation movement and steer it not even in a social-democratic direction, but rather along a liberal-democratic trajectory. The ANC and the SACP continued to use the currency of left rhetoric and slogans, but it was a case of talk left and walk right. The messages and posturing were used to ensure the poor electorate continued its support while a new estate of professional politicians was cultivated, and through the aberration of the discredited democratic centralism, a small band of leaders could literally do what they liked, without any accountability. This was exploited to the full by the real power in South Africa – the large corporates and their foreign-state protectors. It was a South Africanised formula of neo-colonialism.

When looking at the list of the new interim leadership in 1990 it was shocking to see the low calibre of some of the internal representatives. Proximity to power rather than leadership qualities catapulted some into the leadership, and the ANC would pay dearly for this mistake in future years. Even some of the external ANC names were questionable.

So our initial joy quickly turned to concern and later to dismay. At our greatest moment, the liberation movement was being outwitted by opportunism. There were plenty of people clamouring for careers and a place in the professional political sun – on the gravy-train – who were quite willing to turn a blind eye to what was happening. It was a feeding frenzy, and an alienating experience for those who'd suffered and sacrificed so much for a differently envisioned future in South Africa, for the poor communities from which we'd arisen. For liberationists, it was demobilisation by default, and the turning of the ANC into a liberal democrat nationalist party.

* * * *

For those who didn't know the history of the ANC, it may have seemed like a dramatic shift to conservatism was taking place post 1994. But the ANC never claimed to be a socialist party, and those of us in the ranks of the ANC who were socialists understood this very well, even though we were dismayed about how much of a conservative lurch it took after 1994.

However, the ANC and its fuzzy ideology were full of contradictions, because while saying it wasn't a socialist organisation, it was a member of the Socialist International of social democratic parties worldwide. Until the 1990s, the ANC still had a soft social democratic character, and formally the ANC was an associate member of the (SD) Socialist International. In 1999, the ANC actually became a full member for South Africa of the (SD) Socialist International, and it's a member to date, even though proclaiming that it is not a socialist organisation but rather a broad church. In 2013 a split took place in the Socialist International, with many parties leaving the Socialist International to form the Progressive Alliance, although some parties chose to be members of both. The ANC, however, chose to remain in the Socialist International and not to join the Progressive Alliance.

Even the ANC's adoption of a 'national liberation' character over a purely 'narrow nationalist' character was rooted outside of its ranks. The ANC was created in 1923 out of the old nativist-nationalist movement, the South African Native National Congress, with an emerging black middle-class base, allied to traditional leaders, that was relatively conservative even for its time. In 1935 a broad left platform, largely communist led by people who had multiple membership in the African People's Organisation, trade union movement, Communist Party of South Africa and the ANC, formed the National Liberation League. Also in the League were representatives of the Workers' Party of South Africa, the base of the Unity Movement that was formed in later years. Those involved as the drivers of the National Liberation League were also building the anti-fascist United Front.

It was the National Liberation League that brought the ideas around 'national liberation' and building a 'united front' as political tools distinct from narrow nationalism into the ANC, and these ideas were challenged by significant conservative forces within the ANC from that time. It was the 'Three Doctors' Pact' – the joint declaration of cooperation signed by Dr AB Xuma, president of the ANC, Dr GM Naicker, president of the Natal Indian Congress, and Dr YM Dadoo, president of the Transvaal Indian Congress, in the recognition that all 'non-Europeans' should unite in the struggle against the National Party government and its segregationist policies – together with the emergence of the ANC Youth League and the National Liberation League, that dramatically changed the ANC into a liberation movement. But this progressive approach didn't happen without internal resistance from conservatives within the ANC. It's often forgotten that the ethno-nationalist bantustan quisling leaders were conservatives who broke with the ANC, and many had familial ties and friendships that crossed the divide, particularly with the next two factional upheavals in the ANC.

The first upheaval was the split of the Pan Africanist Congress (PAC) from the ANC, which has had much airing. Later, the Gang of Eight was a dissident Africanist faction within the ANC that since 1964 had been objecting to the influence given at the last of three conferences at Morogoro (up to 1969) to those that they called non-African minorities and the SACP. The leaders of this faction, which called itself the ANC-African Nationalist (ANC-AN), and were producing their own documents as ANC-AN, were eventually expelled from the party in 1975. This ended a lengthy upheaval that had dominated discourse and effectively sabotaged the ANC approach of creating a formidable international solidarity movement in the 1960s. It had all the hallmarks of a counterinsurgency programme by the apartheid regime's bureau of state security.

Though the eight were expelled, the Africanist faction remained a significant force within the ANC. To hold the movement together, a compromise was reached whereby it was agreed that none of the three minority groups 'Coloured', Indian and white, could be in national executive leadership positions. This compromise position held sway until the Kabwe conference of 1985 when the ANC opened up membership and leadership positions to all South Africans regardless of their 'race classification'. As soon as the ANC was unbanned, those quislings and factionalists and their bureaucrat beneficiaries of apartheid came flooding back into the ANC, where they bolstered the old ethno-nationalist tendency sometimes referred to as 'Africanist' based on the notion that only those of sub-Saharan ethnicity are Africans.

Nonetheless, in the early 1990s we had little choice but to go along with the way ANC leaders were taking us forward and hope that we could influence the direction of this new political creature carrying the ANC brand. Mzala and I had had a long discussion in London during which we agreed that the unbanning of the ANC by the regime would be used as a manipulative tool by an enemy who knew our weaknesses better than we would admit. It certainly came true.

My dear friend Mzala passed away in London in 1991 before he could be part of the return to South Africa. With him passed the five different aliases under which he wrote so much of the cutting-edge political discourse of the left within the ANC. He was 'the other Chris Hani' who is not mentioned as much.

The enemy within our ranks would be bolstered, and liberationism would be held to ransom. The chilling last message of Dulcie September to her family said it all – 'the enemy is within'.

12

SETTLING:
SHIFTS AND TRANSITIONS

I had a personal archive of over 1 950 items that I'd printed over the years, which I'd sent on to South Africa ahead of me, hoping that it would get through. I realised that it needed to be kept in a proper archive, so I lodged it at the University of Cape Town's African Studies Library for a modest price of just R1 500. That was what thirteen difficult years of work was worth.

Jackie Selebi, ANC Youth Section leader and representative on the council of the World Federation of Democratic Youth from 1983 to 1987 while he was in exile, was responsible for the repatriation of ANC exiles back to South Africa, and a 'returnees' fund' was controlled by him in Johannesburg – but he seemed to treat the fund as his own bank, and few were getting assistance. We were desperate for money to survive, while some former comrades were living it up, becoming instantly rich overnight. After much pleading, Celeste had managed to get a modest once-off payment from the returnees' fund for herself, Dylan and me. It helped to take the edge off the survival pressures before I managed to get a job.

The way 'returnee aid' was being handled was one of those early warning signs of the ascendance of criminality within the ANC at the highest of levels. We'd seen these signs before within the ANC in exile, and there was a clear co-relationship between political power in positions of authority and criminality. Left unbridled, it would pose a great threat to the aims and objectives of the liberation movement in future years, as we have all come to experience.

I was also highly aware that the past had taken a huge toll on my mental wellbeing, and at least at this level, the returnees' assistance committee were helpful in getting psychological assistance for some of us. The counselling was well meaning but the counsellors didn't really have the skills or understanding to deal with the multiple traumas many of us had suffered. Still, it was useful simply as a catharsis of unburdening in a safe space.

In 1991 I applied for a job as a community media coordinator at Grassroots Educare Adult Education and Training Trust in Athlone. Anita Marshall, who worked as librarian at Grassroots, phoned me and said, 'Welcome home, comrade. It will be so good to have you with us. I will put in a good word for you.' It was the first time in the few weeks since I'd returned that a stranger had reached out to help me, and it made all the difference. I got the job, and started working with four other new people who started on the same day.

Grassroots was an organisation that grew out of the trade union movement and the needs of workers' children for safe care and education while they were at work. (Some of the trade unions continue to play an important role in Grassroots to this day.) So getting to work at Grassroots was a real coming back to my roots in Cape Town.

Ginny Richards was the director and Eric Atmore the deputy director. Eric, a Woodstock boy, would go on to do his doctorate and found the Centre for Early Childhood Development, one of the most successful NGOs in South Africa. Grassroots was a great place to work in that I was surrounded by like-thinkers and comrades – people such as the late Dr Daniel Plaatjies (who would become a major advisor to the president and cabinet on economic affairs and social advancement for the poor), Philip Balie, Anita Marshall, Sharon Reynalds, Raymond Schuller, Rose Sonto, Ursula Oliphant Evans, Harold Coetzee and Esme Matshikisa.

Our work was among the poorest of the poor in the sprawling shantytown shacklands of Cape Town's informal settlements, and in the subeconomic townships of the Cape Flats and similar areas across the rural areas of the province. We were also connected to similar networks throughout South Africa. We trained de-facto teachers of preschool children, and community leaders, who had taken spontaneous action in creating their own social advancement path by creating preschools for their children. It was very much the Steve Biko philosophy of self-help and creating sufficiency models of educare, where Grassroots played a facilitative role led by expressed community needs.

Our mode of work brought educare together with providing literacy, numeracy and adult education, for informal teachers, parents and community members who created the preschools themselves. It was an empowerment model rather than a dependency model that we facilitated. We also supported the modest infrastructure of these poor schools – often little more than shacks – and provided appropriate learning and teaching materials and resources.

With my feet planted at Grassroots and doing meaningful work using some of my media production skills, I now felt that my sword of struggle was at last being turned into a ploughshare. I was with working-class people on a daily basis with whom I shared a deep connection. The work was practical, and the results were tangible. My colleagues were wonderful people who became my circle of friends too. I felt like I was back home in a real world.

Reg and Ray had asked me to go work in the National Education, Health and Allied Workers' Union (Nehawu) as an organiser, but I told them that I had already moulded into work at Grassroots, and I was now also single-parenting Dylan and wouldn't be able to leave him on his own for long periods. I said that I would give Nehawu and the Food and Allied Workers' Union as much support as I could locally, but not as a fulltime official. At Grassroots I was the Nehawu shop steward.

Besides the work I was doing at Grassroots, I was active in an ANC branch and in an SACP branch, but it really was a far cry from the old disciplined, well-coordinated, intellectually stimulating branches that had had ideological cohesion, direction and practical outputs. These branches were packed with people who had very little political understanding and were directionless, and most were just looking to climb up the new ANC ladder as quickly as possible. Discussions and decisions at branch level had no impact on people at the top, who were a law unto themselves; the branches weren't being moulded and nurtured at a higher level. They were more like social clubs.

Celeste and I got divorced around this time. From the beginning it had been clear that ours wasn't a marriage that would last long – there was a significant age difference and we were quite different personalities. The marriage was one of convenience, companionship and comradeship, and it supported us both through those difficult last years of exile.

I gave up the rented house in Bokaap and took out a bank mortgage bond on a cheap semi-detached house in Devon Street in Woodstock that needed a lot of work done on it. I got stuck into turning it into a home.

During those early days at Grassroots, I met Thembi 'Eva' Makona, who ran a family cultural music group while working fulltime for the International Red Cross. Thembi had grown up as a servant on a farm, sleeping on a blanket at night under the kitchen table, until one day she stole a horse in the early hours and rode away as fast and far as she could. It's an image that remains imprinted in my mind.

While Grassroots made me feel at home at last at work, politically and at a friendship level, Thembi made me feel at home at a deeper personal level. Her children were all engaged in the cultural group she ran, and the two of us took them around to their gigs across Cape Town. She was a fun and caring person. We enjoyed some wonderful times together, but I wasn't ready for another committed personal relationship. I could see that Thembi dearly wanted that, and Wolfie, who loved and respected Thembi, also told me that she was growing attached to me and that I should make up my mind and not lead her on because that wouldn't be fair.

I began to slowly spend less time with her and focus more on work. When Thembi died of tuberculosis within a year of our slow parting, I was deeply saddened. Tragedy continued to hit her children and grandchild, who all lost their lives a few years later in a deranged shooting at their home by a Mozambican boyfriend of one of Thembi's daughters. All this had been foreseen by Thembi's mother many years before, as she was a seer. Thembi herself had had the ability to sense what was on the horizon.

Thembi had been willing to snatch whatever happiness that living for the moment could offer, and I frequently think of her and how much light she brought into my life in those early months of my return. She made all the difference at an otherwise tempestuous time.

* * * *

The South Africa we returned to wasn't a very safe place at all, both within the ANC and from without. We engaged frequently in mass protest, and the security police and collaborators were operating among us everywhere. Paranoia was rife, but at one level it was a healthy thing that kept us alert to the great dangers that lurked just beneath the veneer of the unbannings and negotiations taking place. The apartheid regime remained very much alive and well for more than three years before a new South African political dispensation was in place.

There was also a 'third force' operating, linked to global interests and international organised crime. Where there's conflict, there's money to be made; and likewise with political chaos. The old names for the third force – which was at work during the American Civil War, the Boer War and both the World Wars, the Chinese nationalist war, the Korean war, the Vietnam war and the South African Defence Force war in Angola and across Southern Africa – are 'black-marketeers' and 'carpet-baggers'. In South Africa, the third force brings together rogue politicians and civil servants, political factionalists, old apartheid securocrats and old bantustan quislings, as well as prosperity churches and elements among the new entrepreneurial class. Via the old sanctions-busting networks of global organised crime, which were repurposed in the post-1990 era, along with their old intelligence and securocrat accomplices, new relationships were cultivated with old and new role-players in the political-economic arena.

The third force is more like an octopus network than an organisation per se – a perfect storm of opportunism and nefarious destabilisation activities. It continued to operate post 1994 and still does in South Africa today. It interfaces with global crime portfolios and the oligarchs behind these across the world. It involves money laundering, sabotage, mercenaries, prostitution and drug rackets, grey-goods rackets, arms smuggling, energy fuels smuggling, human trafficking, people smuggling, artificial shortages and so on.

Third forces also offer services to governments where a government can't be seen to be doing certain things. South African politics has unfortunately fallen foul of this type of undermining and it has threatened our economy, parliament, judiciary and executive government, as well as poisoned much in the civil society arena. It's a dimension that ideological politics has never come to grips with, and it taints left and right politics equally, but it particularly thrives under fascist-militarist type governments.

By the end of 1993, after three years of intense round-table multiparty negotiations, horse-trading and compromises, an interim constitutional framework was put in place for two years, so that elections could be held to establish a non-racial legislature for the first time, and also a second house, a senate, which was indirectly elected by members of each of the nine provincial legislatures, with each province having ten senators. Together, these would serve as a constitutional assembly for drafting a new permanent constitution and a bill of rights. There was also a commitment to establish a multiparty government of national unity after the first elections, which would take place on 27 April 1994.

The ANC leadership over three years had spent much more time with the negotiation parties – those we regarded as our enemies – than it had with the members and structures of its own party. They were getting used to a different kind of lifestyle and a different kind of professional political career. The ANC as an organisation was neglected at a time when it desperately needed an organisational development intervention and modernisation. The now new mass membership were left in the dark and couldn't always understand what was happening in their name. Still, the ANC as a brand and its leaders under Madiba had much street credibility and that, plus a whole lot of hope, is what kept people's loyalty.

Whenever the leadership had difficulties at the negotiating table, the membership would be called on to protest in the streets. There were strong feelings that the negotiators were giving far too much to the National Party and other right-wing parties, but the loyalty levels were still very high among us, regardless of how we felt about how the leadership treated those below them. We'd all been through too much to give up on political struggle, to simply walk away and switch off because we were unhappy and feeling that there was a trust deficit between ourselves and the detached leadership hierarchy.

We were asked to be patient and to understand that while we'd successfully created conditions of 'ungovernability', we hadn't won a war where the ANC could just impose its will on the process. The leadership under Nelson Mandela said that civil war had to be avoided, and that that required some give and take.

Madiba kept us focused on achieving the goal of wresting control away from the white minority, and presented that loyalty to the ANC brand was about this core factor, which could bring about opportunity to advance the interests of the poor and eradicate the racist system that had dominated our lives. That was good enough for me as a first step for us all to unite behind. We also hoped that once we crossed the threshold into a new democracy, then there would be a real focus on social and economic advancement for the poor.

Madiba's 'civil war' comments weren't without foundation, and during the entire period of the negotiations the high levels of deaths and injuries were comparable to a low-level war. There were several serious armed conflicts during this period, including one in the 'independent homeland' of Bophuthatswana, when chief Lucas Mangope tried to get out of the negotiations, saying he wished for his homeland to remain independent. Sixty people were killed and 300 injured, including three members of the private army of the Afrikaner Weerstandsbeweging, an Afrikaner nationalist neo-Nazi white supremacist paramilitary organisation that had allied itself with Mangope and his government.

There was the march of 80 000 protestors to Bisho (today's Bhisho) in the 'independent homeland' of Ciskei in the Eastern Cape, which led to soldiers firing indiscriminately on protestors, killing 28 and injuring 200.

There was the shooting incident at Shell House, the then headquarters of the ANC, when about 20 000 Inkatha Freedom Party supporters marched in protest against the elections. When the ANC opened fire, nineteen were left dead.

There was the Afrikaner Weerstandsbeweging's assault on the World Trade Centre in Johannesburg, where the negotiations were taking place. They used an armoured vehicle to crash through the glass windows of the building.

In Natal (today's KwaZulu-Natal), meanwhile, armed incidents resulting in killings were the order of the day in a conflict between ANC and the Inkatha Freedom Party, fuelled by a third force – a network of security and ex-security force operatives, frequently acting in conjunction with right-wing elements or sectors of the Inkatha Freedom Party, as well as criminal profiteering elements.

There was much to worry about, especially for those of us in long service with the liberation movement. We all lived with an awareness of having a target on our backs, yet we tried to live as relatively normally as was possible under these conditions.

And while our leadership tended to keep their distance from us, the people didn't do the same. The mass of people time and time again came out to support the ANC and its leaders. We went out on the streets and put our lives on the line. On one of these occasions, I found myself arrested and imprisoned once again, and appearing in the dock – I'd thought that those days were behind me. The charges were later dropped but spending time in the Caledon Square underground police cells reminded me of my own experiences that sometimes seemed so long ago.

Around this time, Maria let me know that she would be returning to South Africa with Manuel and Vuyo, and I felt I needed to get myself settled. I was in a relationship with a colleague at Grassroots Educare Trust, Ursula Oliphant Evans, and we hastily decided to get married and move in together. I sold the house in Woodstock for a small profit, and Ursula and I took out a mortgage bond on a house near Kenilworth Centre, in the same road as Jimmy Matthews, son of the poet James Matthews who had been mentored by Wolfie in his youthful days.

Ursula helped me to get perspective on the present and not to be overly locked into the past. She impressed on me that if I was going to be able to contribute to how the future panned out in South Africa, I needed to improve my formal education. 'With just a junior certificate and technical diplomas, many doors will shut you out and leave you feeling bitter,' she told me. Following her advice, four years later I would embark on a master's degree.

My sons Vuyo and Manuel returned to South Africa in 1993. My three children and I had much baggage from years of disruption, and it was more than Ursula and her daughter, Woody, could handle. They had their own problems and baggage to contend with too. We painfully took leave of each other although we continued to work together for a while at Grassroots. Some months later, Ursula got a post in the civil service in Pretoria, and left Cape Town.

It was distressing for both of us. I felt condemned to not being able to have a workable relationship, as though I was jinxed.

* * * *

In 1993, I took a conscious decision to resign from the SACP. I had lost confidence in its commitment to provide a public rallying point for democratic socialists to have a direct voice in a future legislature with a formal new type of electoral alliance. The quality of discourse and debate within the party had dropped radically. Had the SACP followed a different approach in forming a broader left democratic-socialist party with African characteristics, as some of us had proposed, there would have been an institutionalised left critique in parliament rather than simply a right conservative approach to critique.

Up until the unbannings, the SACP had been having dynamic discussions rooted in the processes of glasnost and perestroika that had emerged in the Soviet Union and Eastern Europe, which had then spread across the world. We were doing much introspection and reviewing what had gone wrong. In 1989 Joe Slovo had produced a booklet, which I'd printed, titled *Has Socialism Failed?* I read the booklet while printing it, and when he came to fetch it (with a bottle of excellent whisky to thank me for the quick turnaround time), I said that I believed that the title was wrong. It should have been *Has the Communist Party Failed?* and the answer was unambiguously 'yes'.

The booklet outlined the departures from socialism by the communist parties with the replacing of democracy with democratic centralism, which was dictatorship by a ruling elite and more akin to fascism. Slovo outlined the corporatist nature of nationalisation, and critiqued the party and its self-appointed vanguards as being part of the problem, together with militarism. The origins of the communist brand of socialism were rooted in the commune and soviet (town councils), which were all about smaller non-corporate forms of government and economic production, taking what corporatism and nationalism had created back to the people. But socialist countries had instead installed rule by a vanguard elite that subjected people to tyranny backed by militarism and the creation of huge nationalised corporate monopolies run by bureaucracies that still exploited and alienated the working class.

After our short discussion, Joe said that I was making some good points and hoped that the booklet would spur such debates in party cells. Instead, however, when the SACP emerged as an unbanned organisation in South Africa, all the critiqued elements about the Soviet Union and Eastern Europe were ignored; the ushering in of a new democratic-socialist approach didn't happen. Everyone got caught up in the hyperbole of the unbannings of the SACP and the ANC, and the negotiations fever that went with it. Everything else in discourse just went to pot.

The SACP, blindly following an outmoded path, was on a road to nowhere. As a socialist, for me there was no point in carrying on being a member of a non-party, so I resigned. I could only hope that civil-society organisations of community action networks would arise to fill the gap left by the SACP in conscientising and mobilising 'people power' for a stakeholder-driven political framework. Only such a new drive dedicated to rolling back poverty and holding the emergent middle-class detached political estate accountable would give us hope that our liberation gains had not been hijacked.

I put my heart into working in community-based organisations and into work for the ANC to win the elections based on a level-headed view of the limitations of any future ANC government. It was an important first step to create the kind of space that a non-racial democracy would offer.

In the run-up to the first democratic elections, I was seconded from Grassroots Educare Trust to serve on the Independent Electoral Commission as a director for voter education in the Western Cape. This is where I first met Clive Newman, though we were sure that we had met in Woodstock as kids. Our genealogy research also showed that we had cousin connections a few generations ago. I engaged with Clive Newman, Randy Erentzen and Ray Brink, when Unathi Njokweni, myself and others were running a parallel voter education programme to theirs. We each had outreach teams.

It was an amazing experience, with so many permutations. One day we would be educating soldiers in a military camp, another ordinary people on the streets of Manenberg, and yet other labourers on farms. Most people we addressed were happy and enthusiastic to vote.

Once, we gave a talk to workers at a fish-packaging factory. The boss insisted that the education session happen half an hour before the end of the working day, in the changing rooms – so we had before us about 30 women in various stages of getting out of their overalls and into their going-home clothes.

They were peeved that the boss hadn't given them time off earlier in the day to listen to the talk, saying that they didn't give a damn about voter education because getting transport back home on time was more important. 'Praat ma djulle IEC ouens. Wie hettie tette gesien, hoh? As ek nie worrie nie, dan moet djulle oek nie worrie. Os wiet hoe werk die move. My vote is my secret. Ken djy? Die antie wiet mos hoe ek gat stem.' ('Go on and talk, you IEC guys. Who hasn't seen women's breasts before, go on, tell me? If I don't care about it, then you shouldn't worry either. We already know all about this voting business. My vote is my secret. Do you know that? This aunty knows just how I'm going to vote.')

We had to take on the employers about their attitudes and practices, as they needed to give people a proper opportunity to learn how the ballots worked so that their employees didn't unintentionally spoil their ballot papers.

The election day result was a testament to our job well done in the arena of voter education. It was a highly satisfying task.

The election results, though disappointing at a provincial level for the ANC in the Western Cape, where they'd scored only 33 percent, saw us jubilant – the ANC had taken 62 percent of the vote nationally.

There are fundamental flaws in the voting infrastructure in black areas of Cape Town that quite frankly amount to jerrymandering, and short-change black voters. The demographics do not lie. The largest population demographic regularly comes short, while a tiny white minority is overrepresented. Something has clearly been amiss since 1994 and requires an independent civil society investigation, in my opinion.

But the night of the results saw us drive through the streets, waving the black, green and gold flag of the party and the new South African flag out of car and truck windows. It was an unforgettable experience, nothing short of an amazing moment in time – and the world celebrated with us. Regardless of all the problems still with us, this is something that we should never take for granted.

* * * *

Dylan completed his schooling at Trafalgar High School in 1996 and he had the privilege to address a reunion at the school of the graduate class of 1956, the year I was born. Vuyo and Manuel were living with Maria and still at school, already taking an interest in eastern spirituality and martial arts which they later followed as a life path.

Professionally, I was at a crossroads. Fighting for something is often more difficult than fighting against something. It hit me that I wasn't equipped to engage in the fight for a truly new South Africa, and that I needed to both identify what I would focus on and equip myself with the education and skills to do so.

In our new model of legislature based on proportional representation, professional politicians were accountable to nobody but their party. Even though constitutionally they were public representatives, practically they were party representatives, with the broad public having no say in their appointment by parties. There was a real danger that the 'people power' we had fought for would turn out to be 'party power' that would get captured and criminalised, and work against the people.

There was, however, an open process for people interested in working at parliament to present themselves to a panel that sat for a few weeks to consider new appointments. You had to submit a CV and express an interest in an area of work at parliament. I did so in 1994, expressing interest in public-participation management, and was called to appear before the interview panel, which was made up of senior parliamentary officials.

A few days later I was offered the post of sergeant at arms, which was an honourable post but security and ceremonially oriented. I wasn't interested in simply being a kind of mascot for parliament, albeit with considerable status, so I turned down the position.

Over the next eighteen months I carried on working at Grassroots Educare Trust and got involved in the work of promoting the Congress for Early Childhood Development along with Daniel Plaatjies and Eric Atmore. I continued working in community-based preschools development. And I became part of the founding of the NGO Coalition, whose aim was to promote civil society by uniting and strengthening the non-profit sector, and served as a representative on its national committee.

This was all in preparation to continue along a path of ensuring that public participation would be prioritised and embedded in the new constitution. It also meant that I engaged in public lobbying around moulding the content of our new constitution.

Around this time, I was in a relationship with Zainie Misbach, and Dylan and I were living in Bokaap with her and her children. Zainie was an amazing person and great fun to be with. We'd entered into a Muslim-rites marriage, but ultimately Dylan and I found the cultural norms and regulations too restrictive. Dylan and I moved into a flat, and I began to prepare and equip myself in earnest for changes in my life.

With the adoption of the new constitution in 1996, a constitutional obligation was created of the legislatures and local councils to ensure that no legislation was passed without due public participation. Furthermore, public representatives in the legislatures had to hold the government accountable. If we could build a strong element of entrenched public participation built on these constitutional provisions, that could act as check and balance. There was a unique opportunity for our new parliament to be a very different creature than other parliaments in Africa and the world.

I wanted to be part of this process of ensuring that parliament worked for the people.

13

CONTRIBUTIONS:
WORKING FOR THE PEOPLE

Early in 1996 posts were advertised for the team that would lead the public education department at parliament, and I applied for and got the post of head of public relations. This was one of the key posts required to implement the public education and participation programmes that were to be embedded in the new constitution.

The post was a challenging one. It involved managing all elements of public relations, as well as the staff of twelve who made up the public reception office, tour guides and the public tours programme, a parliament merchandising shop, and the team responsible for all events and functions, including the annual state of the nation address of the president, and all international heads of state visits.

At the same time, I embarked on a three-year part-time distance-learning master's degree. A mix of business and management sciences, heritage tourism and history, it focused on Cape and Indian Ocean slavery, together with Cape indigenous peoples, travel and migration studies, and tourism impacts on countries. I was getting minimum sleep and pushing maximum output, going to bed in the small hours, only to rise again at dawn's crack.

I still found time to be social, however. One evening, after an outing at Randy Erentzen's Riffs Jazz Club in Wetton Road with Clive Newman and his wife Denise, my friend Melanie Jacobs and I met Stephen and Gail Smith and Cheryl Osborn. Cheryl was also originally from District Six, and daughter of one of the artisans at my first job in the jewellery manufacturers, M Obler & Son, all those years ago. The relationships born on that evening 25 years ago would be enduring, and our close band of buddies was called 'The Usual Suspects' by Clive. Cheryl and I would get married later that year.

My old passion for fishing returned. Stephen, Clive and I would frequently go out on the trawlers from Kalk Bay, on trips that were as much a cultural experience as they were about fishing. Stephen, Rowland Jethro – another dear late comrade who always addressed me as Tavarish – and I were also keen rock anglers. In those moments nothing mattered but the bite of the fish at the end of the line.

* * * *

At work, my main interface was with the speaker of parliament, Dr Frene Ginwala, and the chairperson of the national council of provinces, which would replace the senate in 1997. The first presiding officer of the national council of provinces was Govan Mbeki, and thereafter Naledi Pandor.

I interfaced on a minute-by-minute basis with the speaker's special advisor, Lawson Naidoo, who I knew from London when he'd worked at the ANC mission office in Penton Street. I also worked closely with the head of security at parliament, Russell Christopher, and on the visits of heads of state I liaised with the protocol team of the office of President Nelson Mandela, headed at that time by John Reinders.

From the perspective of my interest in building an institutionalised public-participation culture and processes, I also interfaced with the director of the parliament public education department, Alf Karriem, and others working with Alf, like Neeran Naidoo, Merle Brown, Phil Mahlangu, Razia Adams Kafaar, Beben Cadman, Melanie Jacobs, Barry Streek and many others. Each of these people had a special place in my work and life.

The job at parliament was all-consuming, and I had huge responsibilities to live up to. But it was an empowering growth period for my life too. I often pinched myself and asked whether I was dreaming. I had come such a long way from my roots, and I'd also overcome the difficult manner in which I transitioned back home from exile.

In five years of applying myself to the challenges presented in the new democratic parliament I pioneered much, including new protocols for parliament and its ceremonials that ensured the greater involvement of the public, particularly community-based constituencies. In the public education programme, we talked about the old culture of what we called 'fortress parliament' and broke down the barriers between parliament and the people. Working closely with Russell Christopher, I organised for police to be taken away from the gates, and public access made easier by a less in-your-face approach to security. Together with colleagues in the public education programme, we came up with two important slogans: 'The doors of parliament are open to all' and 'Parliament – making democracy work for you'.

People were encouraged not only to visit parliament on tours, but to observe how members of parliament engaged, through attending sittings in the public gallery. Even more importantly, an obligation was entrenched as far as portfolio committee sessions were concerned. Portfolio committees are at the core of parliamentary work in terms of developing and preparing legislation to be passed by the national assembly and the national council of provinces. The chairs of those committees had to produce adverts and other means of communications inviting the public to not only come to observe committee meetings, but also to participate and put forward views and proposals or challenge positions in draft laws. Public petitions were encouraged too.

The other job of parliament is to hold the executive government to account, by listening to public complaints and concerns, and call the president and ministers to be questioned and to give account. Here, too, the public has a constitutional right to fully participate, and it is the job of the portfolio committees to ensure that the public has that opportunity. It's the core of our constitutional democracy.

During the heyday of the new public education department, this feature of the constitution was diligently followed. Later, in the Zuma era, there was a breakdown of the vibrancy and effectiveness of this feature as members and leading figures of parliament lost touch with the essence of what constitutional public participation involved. After Dr Frene Ginwala, there just was not a passionate person at parliament to drive the public-participation obligations, nor to effectively hold the executive to account.

Without a return to this essence of our constitutional democracy, we effectively do not have the democratic system that was envisaged by the constitutional assembly. If this was working efficiently and effectively, parliamentary issues wouldn't be constantly in the courts to find resolution. It's a proper public-participation process via portfolio committees that ensure that members of parliament are public representatives and not there simply to follow party dictates. It would seem that most members of parliament across all parties don't really understand this part of constitutional democracy in South Africa.

The public education programme became a watchdog body to ensure the committees maintained their obligations, as well as consistently facilitating high levels of public participation. We made sure that South Africans could exercise their collective and individual right to promote their interests in decision-making and oversight processes. We also facilitated and enhanced the process by which parliament consulted with the people before decisions were made. (Unfortunately, under the Zuma administration, all of the excellent public participation work and infrastructure to meet parliament's constitutional obligations to 'people power' unravelled, and parliament once again became a fortress under 'party dictatorship'. Hopes that the Ramaphosa administration would get back to basics and right-track 'people power' quickly fizzled out too.)

We also developed a programme to take parliament to the people, where parliamentarians would go to communities around the country to hear their views and inputs. Parliamentarians were encouraged to go to schools in their communities, through our 'flags to school' programme, where a new South African flag was flown over parliament every day, then packaged and given to a member of parliament, who had to go and give a talk about parliament and its work. The parliamentarian would then present the flag to the school and encourage them to hold daily flag-raising ceremonies and discuss our constitution and bill of rights to raise youth consciousness about public engagement with parliament. I remember one member of parliament asking if I could write his speech for the school;

my response was that if you can't address schoolchildren without a speech written by another, how can you be representing the public in parliament?

I must have done a few hundred ceremonials, events and functions in my time at parliament, and much troubleshooting around public-relations issues. Modern-day public relations has become all about denial and putting a spin on things that are clearly wrong. Excellence in public relations, I still maintain, is about acknowledging where things went wrong and telling the public how they will be fixed.

It was a challenge balancing supporting public participation in the legislature and ensuring that high-profile guests, local and international, had the best possible experience of parliament. I coordinated visits from Cuban president Fidel Castro and Palestinian leader Yasser Arafat at one end of the spectrum, and US president Bill Clinton and British prime minister Tony Blair at the other end.

On the day Fidel Castro was to address parliament, the public works department was sprucing up the pillars at one of the entrances with white-wash. While talking in earnest with the Cuban ambassador, I stepped backwards into a freshly whitewashed pillar, which deposited a wide white streak down the back of my suit. I had to call Cheryl and have her rush down another suit before the ceremony began.

(Fidel Castro and I had a chance to converse through the interpreter, and he gifted me a box of Cuban cigars. At the birth of my first grandson, I gave one to my son Dylan to enjoy on his special moment on a balcony outside of the hospital.)

The speaker had a rule of 'no arms in the house, even ceremonial swords'. When Bill Clinton was visiting, I had the delicate task of approaching the chief of his security detail, a highly trained tall African American man by the name of Snipes, and inform him that he and his fellow security detail weren't to carry arms in the house. I said my piece, and Mr Snipes looked down at little me with a broad smile, and with the bulge of his weapon clearly visible under his suit-jacket. 'Certainly, Mr Mellet, I can give you the assurance that we are not carrying arms,' he said. I thanked him and communicated to the speaker that the assurance had been given. There certainly was not more that I could have done.

During a subsequent luncheon with the speaker, I had to get one of my female support staff to escort Hillary Clinton to the toilets. President Clinton then said that he might as well go, too, so I escorted him. Coming out of the toilet, he reached out to shake my hand and began some small talk. Chuckling, I said to him, 'I hope the dampness was from washing your hands.' He smiled and took it humorously.

Later, we were in the gardens of parliament, and Clinton and Madiba had a joint press conference to wrap up the visit. They were seated at a table with microphones, looking out at the pond in the garden. When asked about his relationship with figures like Castro and Arafat, Madiba looked directly at Clinton and, with a smile, said, 'My response to anyone who tries to tell me who I should have as a friend, even the president of the United States, is to tell them to go jump in that pond.'

After Clinton's visit I was invited by a US state department (the equivalent of our department of international relations and cooperation) to visit the country as a guest. I accepted, on condition I could plan my own multi-state tour to look at the underbelly of democracy in the United States – namely African American, Native American and Hispanic American social realities. Accompanied by an African American former diplomat, I visited Washington DC, including the poor ghetto area of Anacostia, then Virginia, New Jersey, New York City, Maryland, Birmingham in Alabama, and the Sioux reservations in South Dakota, San Jose and San Francisco in California. I visited police stations and jails, Native American homes and spiritual sites. I visited Capitol Hill, Congress and the White House, as well as soup kitchens for the poor in proximity. I was awarded the freedom of the cities of Birmingham in Alabama, and Rapid City in South Dakota; I refused the latter because of the discrimination against Native Americans I'd witnessed there.

I also visited many sites of interest, museums covering slavery history and sites of memory, as well as the Civil Rights Museum and Baptist Church that had been bombed, killing three little girls, during the civil rights campaigns of the 1960s. And I was able to join an elder to burn sage and pay my respects at the Wounded Knee massacre site.

CONTRIBUTIONS

* * * *

Working with Madiba and his protocol team over those years was a privilege. My first time engaging with him in my new role was seeing him flanked by his security as he was moving up a passage in my direction. I thought to make way for him by stepping back into a doorway, but he stopped and said to me, 'You don't have to hide away and give way for me.' He had a big smile on his face.

I mentioned that I was one of OR's lads who'd been mentored by his old friend Wolfie Kodesh. He brightened and said 'Very good. Very good. You will have had the best teacher in the world. Give my best to Wolfie.' I would go on to have many more engagements with Madiba, who always availed himself for public participation events.

One day the entire Colombian senate, including the president of the senate, and their wives, unexpectedly turned up at parliament. They had been brought by the internal relations ministry, hoping to get a chance to engage Madiba. Of course, we accommodated them in the speaker's gallery from which they could see the president seated below. It was a week during which the debate on the president's state of the nation address was taking place, and the sittings would go on until 8 pm, which was exhausting for Madiba.

The Colombians' protocol officer and our international relations ministry official were begging for a chance for them to meet the president and have a photo opportunity. This was at a time when every VIP in the world was coming to South Africa with one thing in mind – a photo opportunity with Nelson Mandela. I sent a note to the speaker, who was presiding over the house, to convey the request, and got a response: Madiba could see them for five minutes in the corridor of the house as he left the chamber at 8 pm.

It was then 3 pm, and they wanted to go back to their hotel to put on fresh clothes. They returned at 6 pm, and for two hours the senators and their wives stood in two rows in the corridor, waiting for Madiba to come out of the chamber. All the senators were quite old, but the wives looked youthful and were dressed like stars out of the TV show *Dynasty*.

Finally, the moment arrived, and Madiba stepped out. I introduced him to the president of the senate, then he brushed past the line of old men and went straight to the row of women, taking one of the wives' hands in his in a warm two-handed handshake. 'Pleased to meet you. You must only be sixteen, my dear,' he said.

The photographs were taken, including the old men but featuring Madiba with a bevy of ladies around him – clearly delighted though also visibly tired.

There would be many more of these close encounters over the time I worked with Madiba on high-profile visits, and he was always willing to fit in a 'meet and greet' with groups of the public who were visiting at parliament.

In those days I had the reputation of being a Mr Fix-it, someone with access to anyone right up the chain to the president and the speaker. I was always rushing up and down the corridors of parliament, orchestrating one event or another. Those times were a bit of a magical, fantasy world, pregnant with possibilities.

There were a few occasions when I became the news too. One evening, as I had a drink with a few of the journalists in their pub at parliament (no longer a feature), I was asked to share a bit of my own life and thoughts with them. At that time, I wore a little self-made lapel pin of a remembrance rose, a socialist symbol as a tribute to fallen MK comrades. It was a useful prop that often started a conversation, allowing me to engage in political education and the longer history of the struggle in the form of storytelling. And here I was telling stories to a group of journalists hanging on my every passionate word. They were stories of a world they hadn't known and of which they were keen to get a glimpse.

I also spoke of the feelings I had of the sense of place of parliament, about the building, its corridors, its woodwork, its artworks, its network of underground tunnels, the bunker and the Camissa pool in the subterranean level. I spoke about the theatre that parliament became and the theatrics we all witnessed there daily, from comedy to tragedy and high drama.

That weekend the newspapers carried a half-page story of the interview with me, with a photograph, under the headline 'The phantom of parliament's opera'.

* * * *

I got my M.Sc in 1999, and this formal qualification was useful in opening doors to work opportunities and a way to serve our people at a level that could make a difference. The academic training had also given me good research skills and opened new avenues for historical and genealogical research, and had greatly improved my writing and speaking skills.

My dissertation – for which I was awarded a distinction – was entitled 'Heritage of the Cape Enslaved and Indigenous Peoples as a tourism niche to advance entry of Black Entrepreneurs in the Cape Tourism Industry.' This became a new starting point for my excursion into research, writing and publishing of news media articles and books, and engaging on these subjects on social media and in film making and broadcasting. It was a qualitative leap forward.

In 2001, the year I left parliament, I was called back to create and manage the implementation of a historical tableau on six stages representing the period of 1600 to the present, along a walking route of parliament. I did this in cooperation with the Artscape theatre, and with the parliamentary staff dressed in period costumes and trained to give short three-minute enactments. As the premiers of the provinces, judges from across the country, deputy president and president walked past each stage, the short enactment took place, then froze. It was a great show, unlike anything done at parliament before.

In all of the public relations work and these complex ceremonial events, I was supported by a great team, including Somayah Fortune, Beben Cadman, Colleen Louw, Veronica Rhoda, Obed Plum and Kenneth Mbange. I had previously worked with Somayah at Grassroots Educare Trust, and she was a mainstay of our team at parliament.

After moving on from parliament, I was asked to serve on a parliamentary committee to introduce a cultural history exhibition in the old assembly chamber. It was recognition and affirmation honouring my five years of contributions towards shaping the parliament of the people.

* * * *

In 2001 I took up a position as a director in the University of Cape Town's (UCT's) fundraising and development office. It was a Eurovarsity that needed to be transformed to embrace the 'universal' that a great university must be. It also still needed to find Africa's bright light. Instead, in its crest, Africa was still represented as a dark background, with the lamp of European civilisation bringing light to its darkness. Dr Frene Ginwala warned me that UCT would definitely frustrate me as there was no will and commitment by its well-entrenched old guard to entertain real transformation.

I was focused on turning around their alumni department to be able to address the concerns held by black alumni who felt alienated by the domineering white colonial culture. We were trying to guide the university, which I found really did not want any guidance, even though they were struggling with transforming a rather alienating and colonial campus for both black students and black alumni. I worked with Professor Andrew Sillen and Shelagh Gastrow, and first Dr Mamphela Ramphele, who was vice-chancellor, and then her successor, Prof Njabulo Ndebele.

But we made hardly a dent in transforming campus culture from white South African coloniality. During my two years there, I produced a wall exhibition and booklet, with a foreword by Prof Ndebele, about the difficult struggle of black alumni at UCT over the years. The university's *Monday Paper* published correspondence that noted archly, 'This is what results from taking into management someone who is not one of our own. This is a made-up history distorting the facts.'

My colleague and friend in the UCT development office, Shelagh Gastrow, and I then travelled abroad and did a global study of UCT alumni across colour lines on attitudes towards their alma mater. We interviewed 200 successful alumni, in South Africa, Ireland, the UK, Australia, the USA, New Zealand and Canada. Black alumni spoke of their humiliation under apartheid and the earlier colonial regime, saying that they couldn't fully identify with a university for which they had to get state permission to attend as second-class students, unable to engage in extracurricular activities and even excluded from some academic experiences. Many white alumni, meanwhile, complained that with all the black students and academics at UCT it was no longer the same, and they too felt that they couldn't identify with the university any longer. But there were many, both white and black, who welcomed change and wanted to see more transformation, and said that they would contribute towards making it possible.

All the old guard in the UCT administration could see was criticism, however, and the entire print run of this excellent and expensive study was embargoed and pulped. The candid views from both white and black alumni critical of UCT from differing standpoints was too much for the university to handle in an open and transparent manner.

A spinoff of Shelagh and my otherwise wasted trip was that we learnt a lot about how universities abroad raise money to improve their services beyond what the state can fund and beyond what fees, already too high, can deliver. The most successful institutions overseas had what they called institutional advancement offices, which had strategies to raise capital from donor-investors, trusts, foundations, corporates and alumni.

Professor Sillen pioneered this new approach but we found that UCT had little appetite for these new ideas, even though their implementation was bringing in much-needed funds. Shelagh and Andrew Sillen were valuable fundraisers for the university but they were not appreciated and faced much animosity for their forthright approach to many of the academics who had big egos and lived in very narrow worlds.

UCT had become a dead-end street for new ideas around transforming away from its colonial and racist paradigm. As much as this was abhorrent to many black students, academics and broader society, it was a colonial comfort zone for the old guard who felt alienated by a changing South Africa. The university also refused to shift from its narrow approach to raising capital, or acknowledge the necessity for such efforts to be transformative in an environment where fees couldn't continue to rise and where the state had a ceiling on what it could contribute.

We found that other universities were much more receptive to change, so Shelagh and I resigned from our posts and went off without any money to see if we could establish an institute for institutional advancement that taught the ABCs of raising partnerships and funds in the manner that we'd seen successfully done abroad.

We founded Inyathelo – The South African Institute for Advancement, which we got off the ground with a lead grant. We established a small office and training campus in an upmarket new Cape Town precinct in the Cape Quarter, and we set off on a phenomenal growth path that soon saw us teaching our methodology to universities, museums, hospitals and other institutions across South Africa and across the continent. Our brand gained attention and became recognised in the arena of institutions of excellence.

Our message was that you don't chase money; rather, you build relationships and partnerships. It was all about matching people and organisations that had the same goals, rather than trying to coax people into parting with funds for projects they weren't interested in.

Deciding I wanted to pay forward the life lessons and opportunities given to me by my own mentors, I employed Samantha Castle, the niece of notable jazz vocalist Mervyn Castle, as a receptionist. Sammy, who was from Elsies River, was living with her grandmother and siblings. From her teen years she'd often had to play the role of mother to her brother and sister. Life had dealt her some difficult cards. She was mentally ready to find a lucky break wherever it appeared, and to take it and run.

I saw something of myself in Sammy, and she became a great source of pride in my life. She was passionate and internally driven, and prepared to embrace risk and innovation – a diamond in the rough. We sent her on short courses, and I coached her in her written assignments, and she bounced ideas off me, and she blossomed. We also gave her opportunities beyond being a receptionist, and soon she was running her own youth development programme, Youth in Philanthropy South Africa.

To meet all her commitments, she worked hard and studied hard. She created and engaged in small-business activities like making accessories and chair covers for the events industry and selling shoes via youth networks that she created. She called me 'Father' and I called her my daughter or dogtertjie – my spirit daughter.

* * * *

On one of my trips with Shelagh to Ghana, we visited the notorious slaver castles, El Mina and Cape Coast Castle, and I felt that I was on a spiritual pilgrimage. I saw the dungeons where thousands of human beings had been incarcerated before being ushered through the gate of no return and loaded onto boats and rowed out to sea, to where ships lay at anchor, waiting to receive them into cargo holds. From there, the enslaved were taken to countries far afield in the Americas and the Caribbean – and they were brought to the Cape.

As I stared through the gate of no return, I could see Sister Mary Martin talking to eight-year-old me about St Martin de Porres and slavery. I had walked the resistance road, putting one foot in front of the other, and had come to the genesis of the story.

It was a deeply spiritual experience to be in that place. Marks along the walls half a metre from the floor evidenced how excrement would pile up. Water was thrown over the bodies from vents above. One of these vents was next to the entrances to the chapel where religious services were held near to the cries of humans in distress. The stench of what they had to live in wafted up to drift across the noses of those who prayed above the hell below. It's something that I won't forget.

During that time, I began working in earnest to engage in the transformation of historical narratives and the museum sector from a decolonial perspective. I began writing alternative histories from a decolonial perspective. I engaged with Prof Jatti Bredekamp, then the executive director of Iziko Museums, which is the flagship organisation for a basket of museums, art galleries and cultural heritage sites in the Western Cape. I was commissioned while at Inyathelo to develop a business case and plan for transforming the old colonially oriented Cultural History Museum into the Slave Lodge Museum.

When the new Slave Lodge Museum was completed and launched, I was thrilled (though just a little bit intimidated) when Prof Bredekamp invited me, a relative unknown and not from the established academic community, to deliver the keynote address at the launch. It was indeed a great honour.

On one of the walls in the museum, a quotation was inscribed with something I had once passionately said, under the heading 'Cultural Echoes': 'All around us every day we experience the echoes of cultures from Asia and Africa – the fruits of the labour of the enslaved people. This great contribution of so many men and women, our ancestors, has for too long been blotted out by over-amplified colonial narratives.' With the establishment of the Slave Lodge Museum, I had made an indelible mark for transformative museology and for restorative memory which I believe is a prerequisite for restorative justice and decoloniality.

This experience inspired me to make even more efforts to research, write and teach about the Indian Ocean slave trade and slavery at the Cape. I researched my own family tree, and visited archives, libraries and graveyards in the quest to find out about the enslaved in my genealogy.

I created a travelling exhibition called 'The Ties that Bind Us'. It started off on display at the Slave Lodge Museum as a pop-up exhibition, then was taken on a tour across the province.

I also established a year-long 'Black Entrepreneurs in Tourism' course which was funded by the Swiss government. This pushed me to write preparatory notes for what was a focus on heritage tourism rooted in Cape indigenous peoples and Cape slavery. The outcome I expected was that each participant on the programme would produce a brochure for their company, a marketing video, and an article for a magazine. It was a great success.

* * * *

Shelagh Gastrow and I travelled to other African countries to deliver our services, and universities from other parts of Africa travelled to our courses in South Africa. The Inyathelo brand attracted further funding, and we established a prominent board of trustees. Shelagh was the executive director and I was the managing director; both of us were ex-officio board members too. Cyril Ramaphosa and Dr Mamphela Ramphele became our patrons, and the late Prof Richard van der Ross was chair of our board.

I visited New York and the Ground Zero site in the first week after the planes flew into the towers on 11 September 2001. It was a sobering experience. We were able to walk right up to the cordoned-off site, and along the way there was dust everywhere and people had posted notices on walls asking if anyone had seen their missing relatives. We popped into fire stations where little shrines with candles and loved ones' pictures and holy cards had been placed; clothing hooks still had clothes on them from firemen who hadn't returned. I thought of my previous visit to the USA, when I'd gone up to the rooftop of one of the twin towers. I remembered the staff working there, and realised that they had perished.

New York was a different place. Photo-ID was demanded at every building we entered, and foreigners were overcompensating by wearing US flags to show patriotism. Foreign men with beards, like me, were treated with suspicion, and because one of my names was Tariq, I would be profiled and pulled aside and asked questions about my beliefs.

In our collaboration in Inyathelo, Shelagh and I travelled together on journeys that took us to the USA, Australia, Canada, New Zealand, the UK, Ireland, Nigeria, Ghana and Mozambique. On these many trips we experienced many cultures, peoples and learning paradigms, and this helped us to mould the institute's programmes. I collaborated on the writing of a few publications on fundraising and development, and learnt many new skills. In that period of five years, I read and researched more widely than ever before and started writing in earnest. For years I'd written prose and poetry in my journal but now I felt able to write on the issues that I felt could affect national discourse.

* * * *

There came a time when Shelagh and my common vision had run its course and we began to move along different trajectories and employ different critiques and outlooks.

While Inyathelo focused on building philanthropy, I wanted to move away from a 'charitable benefactor to beneficiary' approach. My ideas were focused on what makes a society have true social cohesion, moving along a trajectory of social advancement through self-help and building a sufficiency economic philosophy to create a stakeholder society that takes charge of its own destiny. This was less about top-down philanthropy and more about self-help and popular social giving, and social mobilisation of effort, rooted in social solidarity.

Popular social giving is what poor to lower-middle-class communities contribute to the needs of societies around them. They do this through volunteerism, financial contributions, church work, community or civic organisational work, doing collections, running fundraising fetes, and so on, through a help-each-other ethos. The sum total of this has been measured and quantified, and has been shown to be the largest social giving culture in South Africa. In fact, studies have shown that popular social giving in communities actually had a stronger footprint in South Africa than high-level corporates, foundations and trusts, and was a bedrock of social capital and social cohesion in South Africa.

I saw the concept of a 'development state' touted by the government and the ANC, which involves a paradigm of 'a developer and the developed' as a neo-colonial approach. This is where development was premised on notions of playing catch-up with the so-called developed or first world – namely, the imperial superpowers. We then borrow huge amounts of money at high interest rates and we invite the imperial powers to match what we have borrowed and to come in and graciously invest in helping us. It's a recipe for debt bondage. Borrowing isn't always bad if it supports real growth and empowerment, but it's not beneficial if it's used to subsidise the rich, political patrons, consultants and foreign company ventures.

I believed in a 'social advancement' paradigm as the alternative to the 'development paradigm', based on empowerment of the population, not elites, planned multiplier-effect self-help projects and a sufficiency-for-all economic policy. This is what we should focus on. And we should not be cloning our country on Europe, America, Australia and Canada, but rather look at comparisons with similar countries to our own around the world. The model of social advancement keeps a focus on for the many, not the few.

Political leadership in South Africa has no original ideas around 'social advancement with African characteristics'. The 'development' approach objectifies people and their circumstances, and has no mobilisation strategy for self-advancement. It fully relies on foreign corporate investment and the notion of a trickle-down effect which over time will 'naturally' benefit the poor. The economic philosophy of sufficiency is what I believe is needed. This is rooted in an African consciousness, which was advocated by Steve Biko. It is also the successfully implemented economic philosophy in some eastern countries, like Thailand, where unemployment is just over one percent. We should be looking at some of the amazing and simple approaches there for full participation in the economy, rather than at western imperial models.

Sufficiency for all is an economic philosophy that consciously aims to avoid a scenario of a huge wealth divide between rich and poor, instead promoting a more flattened-out spread of wealth and benefit. It actively orientates the state, business and society to ensure that across the country the poles of abject poverty and super wealth are not nurtured, but instead 'sufficiency for all' becomes the focus at all levels of government and the economy. A culture of modest but decent and secure living standards for all characterises the nation. Inherent within this approach is that all are stakeholders and all are mobilised to self-help in a collective drive nationally. This envisages that nobody is left out in the application of effort; there's no situation of passive spectators and active doers, nor developers and developed – but all pulling together. It can be characterised as a social advancement paradigm involving all of society in working towards a common goal, where the accent is on working.

Inyathelo was focused on building philanthropy and institutional advancement, which at one level was okay, but I wanted to promote a different type of social giving, and get back to the frontline of social advancement, serving at the coalface of poverty. I felt that I needed to get closer to the social problems that people were facing in coping with everyday life. If I could step back into the community-service world and then step forward again into the arena of government service, I believed that through this I would be equipped all round for making some meaningful contributions to our post-apartheid society and the challenges faced. So in 2007 I left Inyathelo.

Twenty years later this successful institute is still doing great work and owns its own campus in Cape Town five times bigger than our first rented premises. Substantial investment has flowed into many institutions and projects throughout South Africa and the African continent through the work done – a lasting developmental footprint arose out of the Inyathelo project.

After I left Inyathelo I continued to mentor Samantha, who landed a job at the University of the Western Cape. At the same time, she began and completed her BA, then passed her honours, then entered a master's degree programme with a focus on drone technology; she later changed the subject of her master's to a business discipline, started over again and did exceptionally. She is now busy with a doctorate. She did all of this part-time, at night, while she was working.

She was also rising in her work, and got opportunities to give addresses at international forums and came into her own. She would relate how she used to sit in the open-air quad at school in Elsies River during assembly, where the principal addressed the children. The planes coming in to land at a nearby airport would fly noisily overhead and disrupt the principal's speech. She would look up and say to herself, 'One day I am also going to fly to distant lands on one of those.'

And Sammy has also paid it forward, by mentoring the next generation. I had instilled in her that never mind how successful you become on the ladder of life, you must never forget the class of people that you come from – the working class – and you must give back.

14

CHALLENGE: TACKLING CORRUPTION AND CRIMINALITY

Unfortunately, my next move didn't give me the opportunity to live out the potential of my convictions. I took up a position in the South African arm of a UK-based international NGO serving the needs of the poorest of the poor in South Africa and India.

The work of the organisation in South Africa was focused on the HIV/Aids pandemic and specifically on getting antiretroviral treatment and support to pregnant mothers, children and child-headed households. In South Africa they employed doctors, nurses and pharmacists across the country to implement the programme where government either couldn't meet the need or met it poorly. This focused on deep-rural areas and subeconomic peri-urban and urban ghettos. The organisation paid for more doctors, nurses and pharmacists to be recruited and employed, and deployed at state hospitals and clinics. They also funded community worker programmes that provided primary healthcare community assistants and advocates of the antiretroviral treatment. It was a huge logistical operation and managing medical personnel, especially doctors, was difficult. I managed a budget in excess of R300 million, and it was a huge responsibility.

That group of high-level philanthropists were nice enough people but were nonetheless elites. The directors-trustees were super-wealthy businesspeople in the financial sector based in London, and some were South Africans. They were a totally different breed of people to anything I had yet come across in life, and it was a complete culture shock for me. These guys lived in a world of hedge-fund wealth acquisition, and they applied that methodology to the world of NGO poverty challenges. Their manner of thinking just didn't fit with our social reality in South Africa. For instance, it was nothing for them to fly us all to a meeting in a Swiss Alps chalet or in London – they were the kind of people who have their own private jets. Money was no problem, and these influential movers and shakers with their global reach sincerely believed that they could make the right impact. When they held fundraisers, the super-wealthy came out to play and funds raised were in double-digit multiples of millions of pounds.

The form of the organisation in South Africa wasn't the typical NGO with the built-in checks and balances around good governance. It was more of a private company operating with a centralised approach. The donors were both directors and participants in the programme, and used business methodologies on a highly complex social challenge in South Africa. In that sense, it was a social experiment, where the business concept of an investment with measured returns had to be implemented and carefully monitored for a narrowly defined outcome and impact: investment expended had to be monitored for producing as much 'bang for the buck' as possible. It was a culture shock for the medics drawn into this work.

The South African NGO sector had itself changed from the culture of the 1980s and early 1990s. As a result of the contraction in funding post-1994, there were far fewer NGOs, and these were competing for funds. A distinct separation had occurred, in which community-based organisations operated on a shoestring budget while NGOs commanded salaries and perks that matched those of members of parliament and government executives. (It's pertinent to note that many members of parliament had originally been nurtured within this NGO arena, where there had been little accountability for funds, and for output and impact. This culture was migrated into government post-1994.)

I was very disappointed to find the same unaccountable and opportunistic NGO culture where I worked. The donors, though aware that something was wrong, clearly had no idea as to how much of a problem existed, and continued to be most generous. The high cost of the organisational base infrastructure was out of sync even with the ethos and methodology of the UK organisation. Monthly personal expenses charged to the organisation were often as much as the astounding salaries, and all of it was under the tax radar. It was an impropriety time-bomb waiting to explode.

The generous patrons had woken up to the fact that something was going wrong and decided that they needed some management competence to be hired to work alongside the medical professionals to turn things around – and that's how my post of managing director was created. They hoped that bringing in a managing director would solve a problem that couldn't be managed from the UK. But the action had come too late. A few rotten apples could be removed but the entire programme was built around personalities, making such an option unviable.

It was a catch-22, where removing the problem would collapse a programme on which thousands of people were reliant. After only a year, I had no option but to spell this out to my employers and leave. My recommendation was to put the whole operation under temporary curatorship, and for the UK organisation to sever its relationship with the local NGO.

The donors called it a day soon after I left. It was a pity because the London funding consortium had invested a huge amount of money, and their lives and passions, into an amazing programme at the coalface of poverty.

The local NGO, which had secured a second funding vehicle that had been running parallel to that of the donors for some time, seamlessly metamorphosed into a new entity almost overnight, with support from the United States Agency for International Development.

I became painfully aware that there was something deeply wrong in South Africa. Whether politics, government departments, religious institutions, the sports sector, business, organised labour or NGOs, a toxic corruption culture was deeply entrenched. Worse still, the vehicles used for corruption and exploitation for personal gain always seemed to have the veneer of serving the poorest of the poor.

This was a far bigger issue than just being a problem in political parties or the state. South Africans had lost their mojo. The ethos of sacrifice, passion and hard work in the struggle years had disappeared and been replaced by something monstrous.

* * * *

Over the next eighteen months, I was unemployed and I focused on research, writing and publishing. Social media was just taking off, and this gave me the opportunity to test public reaction to my decolonial approach to history and heritage, as well as the area of identity exploration.

In 2008, I envisioned writing a book on the many lenses through which we can examine identities that don't proceed from colour, race, ethnicity and nationalism. I set myself a goal to produce one historical paper that looked at identity in the winelands of Franschhoek. The product was 'The Black Fruits of the Vine'. That gave me the confidence to research, write and publish *Lenses on Cape Identities – Exploring Roots in South Africa* (Dibanisa, 2010).

It was through publishing this first book and the feedback I got, as well as the feedback I was getting from hundreds of people following my blog and Facebook posts online, that I was encouraged to take on further writing projects.

Media personality Dali Tambo contacted me to do a series of biographies, 30 in all, for the 'Long Road to Freedom' project for which he was commissioning the production of the first of an envisaged 400 sculptures for the Oliver and Adelaide Tambo Foundation, which would tell a different kind of history of South Africa. They were the stories of exceptional personalities from all communities and all walks of life over the preceding 400 years. Being given this commission, which included advising the sculptors, further honed my abilities and gave me greater confidence.

I was also in later years approached by producer Nhlanhla Mthethwa and award-winning film director Mandla Dube to join them in producing a three-part TV series on history and heritage – *Mapungubwe: Echoes from the Valley*. After that success, Mthethwa teamed up with award-winning director Keitumetse Qhali for another three-part TV series, *The Ties that Bind Us*, based on my work.

In 2009 I was awarded provincial honours in recognition of my contribution to the promotion of intangible heritage in the Western Cape.

* * * *

In early 2010, the last chapter in my formal working life began when I joined the immigration services inspectorate division of the department of home affairs.

Initially I came into the department to deal with the overall management of ports, visas and enforcement in the Western Cape, but this quickly changed as the department restructured. Executive management, out of touch with reality, moved away from having specialist personnel at a senior level; and then all the immigration specialist senior managers became generalist managers of district offices, without any regard for the nature of how immigration services interfaced with the South African Police Service and other security sector structures. I would find that the department was prone to madcap and hasty decision-making that defied logic.

I was drawn to the sector by my lifelong study of transglobal slavery and migration from the fourteenth century to the late nineteenth century, as well as my study of modern-day human-trafficking and people-smuggling rackets. My M.Sc had involved examining human migration, migratory trends and systems of migratory management, and I wanted to use my studies in my work and not simply become a pen-pusher.

Becoming a general manager of an office, rather than a specialist in a branch of law enforcement relating to combatting human trafficking, wasn't what I'd signed up for, however, and I was prepared to leave immediately after having been recruited. I protested, and was allowed to continue as Officer Commanding Cape Town International Airport, Cape Town Harbour, Saldanha Bay Harbour and Mossel Bay Harbour.

South Africa is thoroughly in the grip of organised crime that goes all the way up into the business sector, politicians and government, and also involves rogue legal practitioners and immigration practitioners. The racketeers operate inside and outside of home affairs. Allied to this is a host of side rackets, including false stamping, printing false asylum-seeker permits, and organising fake permanent residence visas, ID documents and passports, as well as illicitly acquiring genuine documents. The incompetence, organisational chaos, inappropriate systems and poor technologies that constantly break down (sometimes because they've been sabotaged) within an inappropriately structured, staffed and technologically equipped home affairs guarantees that criminality will thrive. The fish of corruption and nefarious activity survives because they swim in a sea of chaos. The challenge was to drain that sea of chaos.

My first brief was to tackle a malfunctioning and corrupt visa and permitting operation in the Cape Town home affairs office. This involved a collection of nefarious forces both internal and external to home affairs, and not only local and Southern African organised crime, but also global organised crime syndicates from several countries. Mafias were literally running the visa office with impunity, and with the cooperation of thoroughly corrupt civil servants in a chain right up to Pretoria headquarters.

A lucrative trade in migrant laundering, people smuggling and human trafficking was afoot. Other rackets were drug-mule smuggling along the Cape Town, Dubai and Sao Paulo routes, brides for sale, prostitution, grey goods smuggling (fake-brand goods that are imported into a country through unofficial distribution channels), blackmailing and money laundering. False documents, from certificates and visas to IDs and passports, were all available on the black market. Rackets abounded to such an extent that civil servants were leaving their jobs to become immigration agents, because there was a fortune to be made.

I immediately inherited cases involving a few nightclubs in Cape Town that had been illegally supplied with hundreds of worker authorisation certificates by home affairs officials. These special certificates made it easier for corporate bodies to bring large numbers of remittance technical workers into South Africa for projects of up to five years' duration. In the right hands, a corporate permit, which essentially is a company-vetting mechanism that allows for the issuing of worker authorisation certificates for a mass of skilled persons, leads to a simplified issuing of visas, but in the wrong hands it can be used as a currency for human trafficking.

Nightclubs that should never have been issued with these certificates for the 'scarce skill' of exotic dancing were issued with hundreds of them. Clubs were engaging in the chain of trafficking women, and then passing these women between clubs. We tracked almost 600 women who had come into South Africa over a five-year period. Some of them had been reported missing, and the international criminal police organisation Interpol had also tracked some to nightclubs and brothels in Cape Town.

My job was to teach officers how to investigate cases, collect detailed evidence, draft charge sheets and follow through with court action. Generally, I found that over 80 percent of immigration services inspectorate cases in Cape Town were not followed through by the national prosecuting authority prosecutors, who were compelled to declare case dockets nolle prosequi (not prosecutable), or they were found by the court to be poorly recorded or poorly written up. The literacy levels of immigration inspectorate officers was extremely poor.

Home affairs, which was also notorious for having poorly compiled cases, had repeatedly been beaten by racketeers in court, but over three years, with the assistance of a dedicated enforcement team and an excellent legal senior counsel, I was able to successfully retrieve all the certificates being used by the various nightclubs. The judge ordered a full investigation of human trafficking in this arena.

I also inherited arrest and deportation cases of undocumented migrants – people without legitimate visas, or having false papers, largely from Southern Africa. Because South Africa has no unique visa system for Southern African Development Community (SADC) countries, anyone wishing to work in South Africa from an SADC country must meet the same almost impossible criteria that people from Europe and the Americas must meet. This flies in the face of the fact that the South African economy was built first on slavery, then indentured labour, then migrant labour and labour-brokering from SADC countries for the last almost four centuries.

Also active was an SADC-wide revolving-door people-smuggling operation focused on economic migrants being laundered through the asylum-seeker refugee system, which crippled and overwhelmed the poorly managed genuine refugee processing system. Large numbers of people across SADC countries are brought into South Africa without visas by racketeers who charge people for their assistance, and then continue to blackmail and exploit them once they're in South Africa. Alongside this has been an industry producing fraudulent documents of various types, all for sale in a highly profitable racket.

Periodically, as the incoming trade of migrants slows down, the same racketeers whip up local antagonism and aggression towards these economic migrants and refugees, and call for their expulsion. So every few years we see a spike in attacks on SADC migrants, particularly taking on an Afrophobic character. Once these migrants are deported (which is a complex and expensive process), the same criminal syndicates that pressurised for the migrants to be deported, restart the racket to bring them back in, in a repetitive supply-and-demand cycle.

This revolving-door racket exploits South Africa's poor policy and practice regarding the management of people and conveyances movement within the SADC community. (Conveyances are all cars, trucks, trains, aircraft and ships passing through a declared official port of entry.) As a long-term scholar on Cape slavery, I found that all the countries in Africa and Asia from which people were enslaved in the seventeenth, eighteenth and nineteenth centuries are the very same countries where people smuggling and human trafficking are occurring today, with South Africa as a destination. Human trafficking out of South Africa is also rife, making us both a sending and a receiving country.

I would go out on joint police and immigration services operations to get first-hand experience of what occurred on raids. In one operation in Saldanha Bay, in one room of a flat above a popular shopping store, we found a pitiful situation. The room was subdivided into six by cords across its length and breadth draped with cloth and towels to create privacy for each group of occupants. Some were single, while others were couples, and some had children. Twenty-five people were in that one room, each paying a daily rate as rent to a syndicate. The space was full of smoke and fumes, as people were using primus stoves, which was also a fire hazard. It looked just like a hold in a slave ship or a dungeon in the old slaver forts. There were three of these rooms. These people were being provided as labour at a price, and were being exploited by their controllers.

In my time I found all sorts of variants of this phenomenon of twenty-first-century slavery – five kilometres from where anyone stands in an urban or peri-urban space, there's an enslaved person being kept against their will and exploited. We found people sleeping under counters in spaza shops in townships where the business belonged to a syndicate of white South Africans and global criminal network crimelords. Labour rooted in debt-bondage to syndicates in home countries – Pakistan, Bangladesh, Thailand, China, Somalia, Nigeria, Tanzania, Eastern Europe, Russia and elsewhere – was rife. The exploitation involved cheap or free labour, prostitution, brides for sale, body-part harvesting, drug trafficking via human mules, and service positions in organised crime.

At the end of 2011, the minister of home affairs, Nkosazana Dlamini-Zuma, asked me to take her around Cape Town harbour to explain the environment and the failings of the department, and to follow up with a written briefing. I knew the harbour well; in my teens I'd worked on deep-sea fishing trawlers and visited the ships on which my cousins Herbie and Edgar were seamen. It was an amazing feeling for me to now be taking a minister on an orientation and investigation tour of the harbour and pointing out the problem areas.

That done, at the request of the minister, I was recruited by the director general of home affairs onto an inter-agency clearing forum (IACF) to examine the security flaws in all South Africa's harbours, with the ultimate aim of recommending a new inter-agency strategic approach to security management in maritime ports. The forum included the highest-ranking police, defence force, revenue service, home affairs and state security office bearers and generals dealing with border and port issues and management.

Together with a seconded state security agency (SSA) official with navy experience, I was briefed to develop and oversee to completion a pilot infrastructure at Cape Town harbour that would become the model for maritime port security management of a border management authority. The brief further included examining all maritime ports with the view to establishing cruise-liner terminals, and establishing a pilot cruise-liner terminal in Duncan Docks in Cape Town harbour.

Before my intervention, four immigration services officers had been responsible for clearances of conveyances and crews coming into the international port of entry in Cape Town harbour. They'd sat in a terrible office outside of the harbour, sharing shifts between them over 24 hours, during which it was virtually impossible to diligently do their jobs of being inside the harbour, mobile over 22 square kilometres, and boarding ships to clear the vessels and to clear the crews. (I estimate that it would require at least 30 people to deal with the large harbour.) They were also responsible for checks on the Saldanha Bay and Mossel Bay official ports of entry, and to regularly check on all fishing and yachting harbours too.

Visiting seamen, instead of having themselves and their ship cleared while on board their conveyance or in a premises inside the port, as per international best practice, were illegally entering South Africa to voluntarily report to an office outside the secured harbour. The conveyances weren't being cleared in the prescribed manner. Stowaways were walking into the country and camping under bridges or highway flyovers.

I made two trips to Cuba to inspect the maritime security arena there, and learn from their internal affairs department and naval guard; this led to my getting the nickname of 'Mr Maritime' among department colleagues. We also hosted the Cuban sailors in South Africa, and we worked together to do an assessment of all maritime ports to see how we measured up to international standards.

We flew helicopters over part of South Africa's wild coastline right up to Mozambique to see how nefarious activity between small fast-moving vessels and offshore shipping occurred and to look at what was required to stop this.

My changes brought in 25 officers, sufficient vehicles to cover the

22 square kilometres of harbour, and mobile communications packs for movement-control coverage on vessels. We also identified a two-storey building in Cape Town harbour and renovated it, and established the first Inter-Agency Command Centre to house all the services and expanded personnel within the IACF under one roof with modernised equipment. Opposite the centre we identified and renovated premises to establish a new professional cruise-liner terminal to the same standard as Cape Town International Airport, complete with shopping, eateries, a viewing deck and adequate parking linking seamlessly with the new developments at the V&A Waterfront.

Similarly, where Cape Town International Airport had previously had passenger-clearing operations in a narrow passage for international flight departures, I motivated for and accomplished the building of a new spacious and security-oriented departure section. I also almost tripled the officers at the airport.

All this wasn't easy to achieve. It was an extremely difficult terrain within which to work and a relatively lonely path to tread, and with much malice to negotiate. The secondment work hadn't replaced my other duties, and I was also dealing with the combatting of human trafficking, working on special investigations, running an incident room on criminal activity, and managing high-profile and complex court cases. I was also managing the ports control operations at Cape Town International Airport, thankfully with some good shift managers, and a very able deputy, Geneva Hendricks, who was a remarkably proficient inspectorate officer at assistant-director level. Despite doing the work of five officers, and excellently, she was always overlooked for promotion. Her knowledge of the legislation, the role-players in airports and harbours, and the systems within law enforcement were invaluable to me during my time in the service.

* * * *

For my first three years in the immigration services inspectorate, I was popular and my successes in the legal arena and in the maritime environment, including my successes in curtailing corruption, were lauded by all. But everything changed after another occasion of corruption crossed my path, and the finger pointed to someone or some people at an executive level.

One day, at my office at Cape Town International Airport, I received two invoices for R800 000 apiece for transport services rendered to staff at the airport, from a company unknown to me. Both invoices were already stamped 'paid'. I was being asked as the officer in command to sign off these payments.

I immediately said that I wasn't prepared to do so, for three reasons. First, I hadn't procured the services of this company; second, I hadn't been the person who'd paid the company according to documented proof of services rendered; and third, there weren't many staff on my rosters who were without their own vehicles and deployed between 6 pm and 6 am requiring transport that would be so expensive – only around eight officers.

I carried out a forensic investigation, beginning with finding out as much as I could about the company that had been given the staff-transport tender, and I immediately found out that at the time it was a shelf company (a pre-registered company with no assets or liabilities and which has never conducted business), with no public details available on a blank website landing page.

I tracked down the contract won by tender process and found that it was clearly an approved sweetheart tender. There was a one-way price of R270 applied simply for having a sedan car and driver available for each trip, with the capacity for three officials to be transported. Then there was a R75 fee for each official actually transported, and a R15-per-kilometre fee. This was an inflated and unjustifiable exploitation of state resources. No taxi service charged anything near this exorbitant price. Whoever in the department agreed to this tender had to have done so in cahoots with the company.

Tracker reports showed trips of these drivers to destinations as far as Knysna, Worcester, Malmesbury and Saldanha Bay, whereas the few officials using this service lived within a maximum of twelve kilometres from the airport. Effectively, what was also evident was that more cars and drivers were being charged to our account than we could possibly need; more personnel were getting into those cars than were on shift; and more kilometres were being charged to our account than was possible.

Finally, I discovered that the company that had been awarded the contract was subcontracting the transport services. I asked for an invoice from the subcontracted company. It was for R70 000, which means that the two company invoices I'd received and refused to authorise had been inflated by R1.4 million. At OR Tambo International Airport in Johannesburg, where they had 400 staff, the company was being paid over R7 million per month, and at King Shaka International Airport in Durban, where they had a third of the staff that Cape Town had, their invoices were around R1 million. And the same company was working across several government departments and ministries.

All this infuriated me: for the preceding six years, there'd been 'no money' for the replacement of the tatty uniforms of my officers, yet here was piles of free money being given away.

Armed with this information, I went to see the executives of home affairs. In spite of the fact that I had already completed an investigation and had proof of wrongdoing, the director-general and chief financial officer handed the matter to the chief director of procurement to investigate, and she insisted that she had to bring the chief executive officer of the company concerned to see me.

We met in a boardroom at the airport. The chief executive officer was an unpleasant man with a toothpick stuck in one side of his mouth who immediately started berating me for not following the orders of my superiors in Pretoria. They had been wondering who this character in Cape Town was who refused to cooperate, he said.

The chief director had clearly brought this guy to intimidate me.

'Now that your curiosity has been satisfied, I want to apprise you of a few things,' I responded. 'I don't operate based on superiors in Pretoria ordering me to do this and that. I apply what the law says I must do. I've done a full investigation on your invoices.' I then threw out some bait: 'I won't even look at or dream of signing an invoice that hasn't been cut by at least 50 percent of the figure presented in your original invoices.'

The man fell for it and within a week sent new invoices cut by 50 percent. No genuine business would have responded in that manner.

I told the department that I wasn't going to sign any invoice coming from this company. The upshot was that I was removed from Cape Town International Airport.

I was told to focus on my maritime project across South Africa and particularly on the pilot project in Cape Town harbour. In this interagency forum work, I worked well with my colleague, a former South African Navy officer from the SSA, the government department with overall responsibility for civilian intelligence operations. Our aim was to develop a plan and roll out in each of the eight maritime international ports of entry – Cape Town, Durban, Richards Bay, East London, Port of Gqeberha, Port of Ngqura, Mossel Bay and Saldanha Bay – an interagency command centre and a cruise-liner terminal to boost harbour security and facilitate a more efficient and effective dockland business and tourism.

Three years later, at the tail-end of the pilot project in Cape Town, I finally became exhausted with dealing with the corruption. I drafted a twenty-page report for the new minister, Naledi Pandor, who asked me to come and see her. She persuaded me to go to work in her office as a special advisor on secondment, as she had her reservations about whether all that was conveyed to her from the department was reliable. Her phrase was 'my word is my bond', and she didn't want that to be compromised.

I attended the launch of the Cape Town harbour project in my new capacity, which was a highlight of my career. As special advisor, I was at the side of the minister at the march-past parade of the inspectorate as it was formally launched.

I was proud of what we'd achieved: we'd established a physical footprint of modernisation and integrity in the harbour, with an inter-agency command centre linked to a newly built cruise-liner terminal complete with a shopping and eatery precinct fully occupied by small black-entrepreneur businesses.

CHALLENGE

* * *

In 2013, the department began replacing the old green bar-coded South African ID book with a new smart identity card – and it was while working with Minister Pandor on this that I uncovered yet more chaos, incompetency, possible corruption and dishonesty at a high level. Department executives had lied and misled the minister along the way towards the launch, and I found that for this super-expensive project, there was no comprehensive project plan, nor a project manager, and that top officials were spontaneously managing it without following any formal plan.

Ultimately, there was a showdown between the minister, with me at her side, and a range of senior officials from home affairs and the government printer. A project plan was demanded and finally received, a project manager was appointed, and a monitoring desk was established under me in the minister's office. If looks could kill, I would have been dead, but the ID card was successfully rolled out as a result of the minister's intervention. I have great respect for the manner in which she paid attention to detail, diligence and good governance. If only all our minsters operated in this manner.

Not long afterwards, I had an epiphany of sorts when, in 2014, I attended an ANC executive meeting to represent the minister. As there were a few new faces at the committee round table, we were asked to introduce ourselves. I explained my professional role, and added that I attended the Wynberg branch of the ANC.

One fellow laughingly piped up, 'Don't worry about mentioning your branch, comrade. Here, branches are irrelevant. We don't take things like that as a prerequisite for being at our executive meetings.'

I said nothing but I thought, Now the ANC that I knew is truly dead. This organisation, whatever it is now, is not worthy of my being a member if branch membership is meaningless. The ANC made much about being a democratic organisation, with branch membership its most important foundation because that was really where decisions were made and filtered up. But it simply was not true in practice.

It was a serious moment for me that was comparable to other seminal moments when I made choices along the resistance road that underpinned my own personal liberation.

I had become acutely aware of the criminality chain in South Africa and that it led up to the doors of the ANC national executive. Our state apparatus and government had gone rogue. I felt compromised by having my name associated with things that I had always opposed and took the decision of saying 'not in my name'.

When Minister Pandor was being replaced after the elections in 2014, all the staff in the ministry were asked where we wished to be deployed. My first choice was to head the inter-agency command centre at Cape Town harbour so that I could further implement the border-management authority plans for the maritime environment. It was the logical position for me.

Curiously, Minister Pandor wasn't told this; rather, she was informed that I had resigned. Disbelieving, she asked to see my file and resignation letter and, of course, they couldn't produce this. Minister Pandor warned me that I had ruffled a lot of feathers and that the executives were going to be nasty.

She was right. The director-general of home affairs simply ignored my existence. I approached deputy minister Fatima Chohan, who had stayed in the same role after the elections, and with whom I enjoyed an excellent relationship, and she took my problem higher up the chain. She managed to persuade the executive not to go with their first choice, which was to deploy me to the worst operational office of home affairs at Marabastad – where non-corrupt officials went to die, often literally – and the decision was made that I would relocate to Johannesburg to clean up the corruption at OR Tambo International Airport.

Two years previously I'd been part of a process to deal with corruption at OR Tambo, whereby we'd removed the entire staff complement and replaced them with military-trained officers, with the intention of dramatically reducing corruption. Instead, and quickly, the corruption, indiscipline and rogue behaviour set in among the soldiers. The problem was that the head of the fish that was home affairs was rotten.

However, I would at the same time as my redeployment to Johannesburg, be demoted from a chief director position back to a director position. It was all about teaching me a lesson and putting me in my place.

I was going through some serious re-evaluation in my personal life at the time, too. My eighteen-year marriage to Cheryl had begun as a source of joy and companionship, but had turned into a very difficult partnership fraught with problems and difficulties in communication, without a shared vision. This became much more difficult when in the course of my work I came under threat. I had to reluctantly accept that my wife and I were incompatible. I cherished the good times and had hoped that we could be friends, but I couldn't go on with the marriage. I proceeded with divorce, which was concluded some months later. It was a sad time of loss for me.

* * * *

After relocating to Johannesburg, I rented a flat in Germiston and commuted to work daily. It was a lonely and alienating environment, so I threw myself into work issues.

I had to mend several broken relationships between the immigration services ports inspectorate and the airline community, the Airports Company South Africa, with the two trade unions, the National Education, Health and Allied Workers' Union and the Public Servants' Association. Also, the morale of the almost 400 immigration services inspectorate officers, all previously South African Defence Force soldiers, was low and discipline had eroded.

First, by just a few smart interventions, I managed to turn around the climate of distrust and build excellent relationships between the role players at the airport. Then I began compiling an investigation report into the corruption and lack of due diligence there.

I dealt with deep-rooted corruption syndicates involving many state and private role players, including the Guptas, as I carried out my investigations. Ajay, Atul and Rajesh Gupta had arrived in South Africa from India in the 1990s and quickly established themselves as influential businessmen. They'd met Jacob Zuma in 2002 and cultivated a relationship with him. When Zuma became president seven years later, they allegedly used their access to him to wrangle all manner of government contracts and redirect billions of rands of public funds to their companies.

Together with a colleague from the SSA, we identified the nefarious chain at the airport as including people within the airlines staff, the Airports Company South Africa, home affairs, the customs arm of the South African Revenue Service, the South African Police Service, a company specialising in providing services to government called Bosasa, and even the cleaning staff.

I produced a 100-page detailed report on what my investigation had found, and sent this to Minister Malusi Gigaba's office and to the director-general. It identified 46 immigration services officers at the airport who were thoroughly corrupt and who could be prosecuted. It also identified 100 officers who seriously lacked due diligence and how this undermined the work. And it identified a culture of indiscipline where officers on night duty were using blow-up mattresses to sleep on duty.

Furthermore, there had been gross violations of human rights. There were cases of people arrested for infringements and unlawfully detained for over a week at police stations in Germiston and Kempton Park. In one case, a gay couple had been humiliatingly interrogated about their sexual lives by an officer at passport control. In another, an old Brahma Kumari religious leader in a wheelchair had been incarcerated because she was processed five minutes after midnight where her visa entry date terminated before midnight. And there was a rude and unlawful challenge to mother and daughter third-generation Chinese South Africans, returning from a holiday, who were stopped and asked, 'How can people like you be South Africans?'

These types of violations were not the exception but rather the norm, and I could associate many of these human-rights violations with the culture of the apartheid era.

The way staff were treated by superiors was also awful. I came across bullying, misogyny, psychological abuse, sexual harassment, death threats and rape by seniors on juniors. Stress levels and early death related to stress were high in the department. In all my working life I had never seen such a disgusting approach to staff relations.

In home affairs, antagonism towards and purging of Camissa African staff was rife; at OR Tambo International Airport, out of close to 400 personnel, only two were classified 'Coloured'. Within government departments across the board, I witnessed marginalisation and crass victimisation and purging of 'Coloureds'. This was causing a retrogressive backlash from those classified as 'Coloured', with further negative behaviours emerging and causing a vicious cycle of hate. The politics of non-racialism and anti-racism and anti-colourism had vanished.

At OR Tambo International Airport my eyes were opened even wider to how politicians and government officials flouted the law and enabled criminal activity at the highest levels. There was the case of a Saudi Prince who apparently had visited South Africa a few times for shopping sprees, and was just allowed to do as he pleased. The next time he arrived in his private jet with an entourage, including armed bodyguards, I ensured that, together with colleagues from other agencies, we surrounded the aircraft, had the bodyguards surrender their arms, and processed them all the same way as others entering South Africa.

There was a case, too, of one of the Guptas' senior employees who had three passports but no visa enabling him to live and work in South Africa. Clearly, officialdom had been assisting him with illegal entry into the country for a long time: all three passports were full of entry and exit stamps, and he had a letter from home affairs in Pretoria exempting him from the normal procedures. It was unlawful. I told the officer dealing with the case that he should be refused entry and put on the next flight out.

I later got a call from someone who didn't identify himself, but who had an Indian accent, saying that they wanted me to go out with them to a restaurant in the evening for dinner and to have a discussion. The tone was persuasive and insistent. My response was that I had an office at the airport, and an appointment could be made with my secretary for any meeting, as I had an open door to any legitimate complaint.

There was also a brewing scenario around the development of the Fireblade Aviation project, where a private jet facility was being developed at OR Tambo International Airport using private money. I got wind that the Guptas were interested in getting a share of this facility as a 'black empowerment partner' without having invested anything in the project.

Previously, the ministry and department had said that it had no objection to developing private jet facilities in Cape Town and Johannesburg, but for these to be included as recognised international ports of entry, they were given a long list of boxes to tick, establishing physical and procedural requirements for recognition. The various agencies – health, customs, immigration, the police and the SSA – were to monitor the progress, and each finally give clearance that all conditions had been met.

I was the senior officer doing the final sign-off for the Fireblade private jet terminal of all the checks by the various agencies. Thereafter it was out of our hands, and a matter for a submission to be made to Minister Gigaba for final approval. After I had left the service, I followed the court cases pursued by the investors in the facility, and the misrepresentations of the facts by the ministry. I could see yet another reason why it became important for the nefarious forces to see the back of me at the airport – I could contradict their version.

I also detected that racketeering and human trafficking were on the increase. We found that young Malawian girls were being spirited away to the Middle East, and managed to save a thirteen-year-old dressed in hijab being escorted by an old Saudi man. When a female officer took her into a private room to identify her face against the passport, it turned out that she spoke no African language but spoke very good English. She said that she was a Christian girl and that her 'mother' had gotten her a passport and that the nice man was taking her to see her sister, who'd left the week before. This 'mother' was not her real mother, of course, and had groomed the child; she'd also clearly had a means for getting genuine South African IDs and passports.

Finally, it became apparent that the new ID card and passport, which the state had implemented at huge expense as an unforgeable means of identification, was increasingly finding its way into the hands of criminality. In other words, genuine documents were getting into the hands of criminals by unlawful means, and this pointed to high-level corruption within the department.

My carefully compiled report was ignored.

Not only that, but I had changed the shift system to break up the concentration of criminal activity on one shift, and these people were lobbying top officials, including the director-general, to revert to the old shift system. Without consulting me, the director-general brought in a junior official from Cape Town as an 'expert' to make recommendations to undo what I had instituted. So, for every step forward in combatting crime at the airport, headquarter officials were forcing us to take two steps back.

While about a third of my officers were corrupt or lacking in due diligence, two thirds were officers of excellence, but they were being put between a rock and a hard place, between my instructions and the counter-instructions they got from headquarters. They kept saying, 'Who do we listen to, sir?' Some officers were receiving death threats and feared for their lives.

15

AT REST:
LEARNINGS FROM A LIFETIME IN THE STRUGGLE

On 16 October 2014, I received a letter from human resources, which had been signed by the director-general on 7 October 2014, charging me on three counts of misrepresenting my financial situation in my annual statement of financial interests in 2011 and 2013 – charges that were reputationally damaging and completely false. The letter alleged that I had not declared three entities as financial interests – two non-profit entities for which I was an unremunerated trustee, and a past employment position as a managing director from which I had resigned, and all before I started working for home affairs.

Without having served me first with an audi alteram partem ('let the other side be heard too') letter to give me opportunity to respond as to why I should not be charged, the letter further stated that I had to appear before a pre-hearing – which had already taken place the day before I received the letter, on 15 October.

The unlawful manner in which this matter proceeded showed me that there was now no doubt that people high up were trying to get rid of me.

My annual statement of financial interests for each of the relevant years was fully up to date and actually much more detailed than required. There also was a copy of my detailed CV with human resources, declaring and recording what my relationship was to the three entities noted as undeclared 'financial interests'. I'd meticulously noted my affairs, as I knew how important this was. These were non-charges.

I submitted affidavits and proof that these were not financial interests but long-defunct entities not relevant to 2011 or 2013, and that human resources did have proof of declaration in my CV, which was on file. I appealed to the director-general, who refused to give me a hearing. I made it clear to the director-general that there was mischief afoot in the human resources department, and that the department had not allowed me to put my side of the case before charging me and moving to unlawful disciplinary proceedings.

I refuted all the charges in a legal challenge supported by legal counsel and with affidavits, despite which I was found guilty in a bizarre ruling. It stated, 'In terms of the sanctions available to me I have ruled out a Final Written Warning as too lenient a sanction considering the nature of the misconduct and your own conduct throughout the disciplinary process. I deem that you are in fact incompatible with the organisation as you refuse to submit yourself to its processes as required by an employee. I therefore deem dismissal to be appropriate.' This was followed by five pages of dishonest, convoluted and contradictory statements before concluding, 'Considering the length of service with the department, your age and other mitigating factors, I am of the view that one month suspension without pay and a final written warning will be corrective and sufficient.'

My legal counsel, today a judge, said that we could challenge the finding in court, but that the department would drag it out for a few years, and though they would be found guilty, it would cost me financially and be very stressful. He advised me to walk away for my own peace of mind. So, in 2015, after just a year at OR Tambo Airport, and a few months before my 60th birthday, I resigned in disgust.

The political arena that I had dedicated my whole life to as the vehicle for the liberation of our people from poverty and exploitation had become an unrecognisable monster.

* * * *

During my year in Johannesburg, I slowly began to make a circle of friends, largely in the Southeast Asian community, who introduced me to the Chinese Buddhist temple in Bronkhorstspruit and another Thai temple in Midrand. It became a time of contemplation, reflection and getting my head together about what was happening in the South Africa that I loved and had served for so long.

Through a South African friend, a relative of one of the boys who'd been in the children's asylum with me, Peter Addinall, I learnt of a Thai woman in Cape Town who was seriously ill with an unknown ailment. She required time off work, a diagnosis and urgent medical treatment. Peter asked me to assist him to achieve these things for her.

Peter, Asirawan 'Leenah' Deeying and I communicated via Skype and phone, and I saw that she was indeed in a bad way: her face was covered with a butterfly rash, much of her hair was falling out, and her eyes were puffy and closing. She also had joint pain and looked like she was at death's door.

I explained to Leenah that she needed to go to Groote Schuur Hospital to see a well-known doctor who specialised in blood-related ailments and cancers. Peter agreed to take her to see the specialist. I then spoke to the doctor via Skype while she was in his surgery to get a diagnosis and to be advised of costs and treatments.

In December of that year, 2014, I travelled to Cape Town for a week and used the time to see Leenah. Her condition had been diagnosed as a combination of thrombocytopenia (a bleeding disorder involving a low blood platelet count) and lupus (an inflammatory disease in which the body's immune system attacks its own tissues and organs), and would take at least a year to get under control. Even then, it was a lifelong condition that required close medical supervision, with blood tests every six months.

She didn't have medical aid, and had to accept that it would be too expensive to treat in South Africa. I advised Leenah that she should go back to Thailand, where she would be covered by their excellent and affordable medical system, but she was reluctant to do so, and wanted to remain working in South Africa until her visa ran out in two years' time.

After my short holiday in Cape Town, I went back to Johannesburg, and Leenah and I kept in touch via Skype. In 2015, I travelled with her to Thailand to meet her family – and we got married there. Seven years later, I can say it was the best decision I've made: we've had a happy and productive time together.

In the meantime, I took out a mortgage bond on a house near the sea in Cape Town. It was a great leap of faith: I'd developed a business plan for a small Thai health spa, guesthouse and heritage reflection centre in a place that would double as a home. By the end of our first financial year, Leenah and I were doing well in the business, and her health had improved – her hair had grown back and all the scarring and disfigurement on her face was gone.

* * * *

The judicial commission of inquiry into allegations of state capture (chaired by then deputy chief justice Raymond Zondo, and frequently shortened to 'the Zondo commission'), held between 2018 and 2022, may have uncovered some of the malfeasance that underpinned state capture, but it barely scratched the surface.

The ANC and the president and cabinet just didn't share the shock and horror that the broad public felt at the revelations. They dealt with the entire thing defensively and arrogantly, with much denial, and without really taking the blame. Most importantly, there were no consequences for the corrupt, who still hold positions in the ANC as an organisation, and many of the questionable characters are still deployed in the legislatures and in cabinet. The reports indicate that the ANC itself and its top officials have a case to answer in terms of presiding over a culture of malfeasance in which the organisation looks as if it was beneficiary.

For many veterans and the general public, the perception gleaned from the entire Zondo Commission hearings and reports is that the leadership of the ANC over at least the last fifteen years presided over the organisation's own moral ruin, trust deficit and loss of esteem in the country, engineered from within. What apartheid had tried to do and failed, those among us entrusted with leadership accomplished.

Together with advocate Rod Solomons and several other former activists who were, like me, deeply troubled by and concerned about the continuing corruption and political and economic meltdown in South Africa, we founded an organisation called South Africa 1st – For

Constitution, People and Country (not to be confused with the xenophobic Put South Africa First organisation). Through this non-partisan medium we made our critical voices heard on all the major issues that were arising, and joined with similar organisational formations in the non-party civil-society arena across the country.

Indeed, many of us have tried to start building civil-society initiatives and campaign for renewal and meaningful change, but largely those in government and the ANC are scornful of anything that takes place outside of their inner circle. They're also most adept at demonising critics.

I have supported the new growing movement of community-based organisations, community action networks and calls for an all-in national convention for renewal, transformation, constitutional integrity and deepening democracy, as has been forwarded by many other organisations across South Africa, such as Defend Our Democracy Campaign. For we older people who are veteran activists, we can now only focus on what is possible for us to do. In my case, my focus is on changing mindsets and empowering people with knowledge and the thinking skills to motivate them to become change agents.

During this time, I involved myself in several research, writing and film-making heritage projects, and began to work on a few book projects simultaneously. I was also appointed to serve on the South African Heritage Resources Agency Council, and by 2020 my book *The Lie of 1652 – A decolonised history of land* was published, and held its own as a bestseller for much of the following year.

The content of my research and writing involving a decolonial critique in the history, heritage, restorative memory and restorative justice arena, seeks to change mindsets so that people can understand the deeper reasons for our problems and find ways to use restorative memory to build restorative justice. In so doing, I also promote innovation and social entrepreneurship. I continue to walk down the resistance road that I set out on as a child.

Reg September and I had been keen for two decades to establish a place of history, heritage, learning and memory at the Castle of Good Hope. There was no ANC support for the idea. When Reg passed away in 2013, I made it my mission to find a way to realise this dream.

During the writing of *The Lie of 1652* I began to construct and develop a concept of a Camissa Museum project that could be developed at the Castle, and connected with Angus Leendertz, Colin Jones, Calvyn Gilfellan and ambassador Robina Marks to take this forward. By April 2021, having raised the funding ourselves, we were able to launch a mini exhibition for the museum at the Castle, and to also launch an online version of the museum. The physical museum will be complete by October 2022 and now has a dynamic new board of directors.

The Camissa Museum concept is rooted in a tool known as the 'seven tributaries matrix' that I developed to explain the roots of people classified as 'Coloured'. In this, we're in rejection of the term 'Coloured' and refer rather to 'Camissa Africans', which is a non-colourist, non-racist and non-tribalist term. Within these seven identified tributaries we unpack the more than 195 streams of origin of Camissa Africans, and the ties that bind us to our fellow diverse African communities.

For this concept, I also drew on the work of the late Dr Neville Alexander, and his use of water and river systems to explain the fluidity of identities. He spoke of the coming together of various tributaries of peoples using the Kai !Gariep River as an analogy for human identity development. In his paper, 'The politics of identity in post-apartheid South Africa', published in *Challenges of Globalisation: South African Debates* (Maskew Miller Longman, 2001), he said:

> The Gariep River is one of the major geographical features of this country. It traverses the whole of South Africa, and its tributaries have their catchment areas in all parts of the country. It is also a dynamic metaphor, which gets us away from the sense of unchanging, eternal, and God-given identities . . . It accommodates the fact that at certain times of our history, any one tributary might flow more strongly than the others, that new streamlets and springs come into being and add their drops to this or that tributary, even as others dry up and disappear; above all, it represents the decisive notion that the mainstream is constituted by the confluence of all the tributaries,

i.e., that no single current dominates, that all the tributaries in their ever-changing forms continue to exist as such, even as they continue to constitute and reconstitute the mainstream.

I also am involved in building international relations between communities in South Africa and all along the old slave routes of the Vereenigde Oostindische Compagnie, the Dutch United East India Company, through telling the stories that highlight the ties that bind us and combatting xenophobia and Afrophobia.

The Camissa Museum is also used to expose youth to the many unsung role models in our communities who have risen above adversity in their lifetimes to go on to make great contributions. This is the best way that I can continue to serve the communities from which I come as a Camissa African, while paying tribute to the great mentors and leading South Africans I've met in my life.

* * * *

I have learnt some important things on my journey.

Perhaps the first is to recognise that as human beings we find our own human worth in giving service to our fellow human beings. If that social contribution is missing, there's nothing that sets us apart from any other life form.

For those who are from my background of poverty and deprivation, as you improve your circumstances and make social advances, if you forget where you come from and do not give back, you will have lost your soul. Everything will have been meaningless. It's important to pay it forward for the next generation. Your measure of achieving social advancement is all about measuring this alongside the social reality of others and ensuring that they have the opportunity to advance as well.

A show tune from the 1949 Rodgers and Hammerstein musical *South Pacific*, 'Happy Talk', includes the lines, 'You've got to have a dream! If you don't have a dream, how are you to ever have a dream come true?' It speaks for itself, and it has worked for me. Dare to dream and dare to envision. Then follow your dreams and make them happen. But never trample on others as you do so. Spread the message of daring to dream.

Draw on that which is greater than yourself – the spiritual dimension of life. Over my life I've created my own simple spiritual framework as I came under the influences of many faith traditions – Catholicism, Islam, Buddhism and Afro-Asian shamanist animism, where a commonality appears around way of life, saints and ancestors. Those who quote from Marx that religion is the opium of the people, using an incomplete translation, do not look at the dimensions of what Marx said in his full observation: 'Religion is the sigh of the oppressed creature, the heart of a heartless world, and the soul of soulless conditions.' In liberation theology, this aspect of faith and spirituality centres on envisioning or dreaming of a better life – of rising above adversity – and focuses on walking the vision by working to realise it. It's moving from the 'sigh' and 'heartlessness' and realising the claim to 'soul' in the 'soulless world' that defines the spirituality of syncretic faith. It has worked for me.

Indeed, it is my belief that those who hold syncretic beliefs are far more in number than those who adhere to formal mainstream religions. I'm of syncretic faith which has five simple principles, each of which speaks for itself, and contain lessons that are rooted in my journey through life. Everyone must find their own path and I'm not a person who embraces proselytising.

The five principles of my syncretic faith are:
- Be at one with the positive unifying force.
- Be balanced and of service to humanity.
- Be attuned to the ancestral continuum.
- Be quiet to regularly reflect, meditate and learn.
- Be sure personal advancement always benefits others.

I acknowledge that I'm born of a people, Camissa Africans, who have over 195 roots of origin, and who have faced many adversities – crimes against humanity such as colonisation, slavery, wars of ethnic cleansing, genocide, de-Africanisation and apartheid. My ancestors rose above that adversity. I'm proud to be an African of Camissa ancestry and I love to burn Kharo Khun (mphepho – wild sage) and commune with my ancestral continuum. I nurture their memory and to allow their stories that travel on the winds from afar to enter my receptive ears.

As I've traversed the world supping with many cultures, I've grown older and, I hope, wiser. I've learnt what it is to be an internationalist, and that this is incompatible with colourism, racism, tribalism and nationalism. Find ways to travel. Travelling is the best teacher in life. To always be in a narrowly confined world results in having a narrow view of others. The one thing that is more certain than any other is that each of us has a date with Santa Muerte, Holy Mother Death, the patron of non-discrimination. She discriminates against nobody and will take all to the ancestral world.

My resistance road has involved a life in which politics was prominent. Five formal political influences were dominant – socialism, anti-colonial national liberation, pan-Africanism, anti-fascism and anti-racism. Over time and with experience, I've learnt to critique the mainstream of each of these and their rigidity. I've also learnt that you can be fanatical, turn political beliefs into a secular religion, and go so far 'left' along these formal political trajectories that your approach becomes 'right'.

I've also found that as I discovered more about our continent and about the people of Africa, I became more aware that our pan-African outlook isn't always African, and has its own gremlins, made in America. We just don't spend enough time in scholarly exploration of Africa's repository of knowledge and inspiration, free of the filters of coloniality. European political and economic philosophies dominate the traditional left political paradigm, which has projected its own forms of white supremacy in the world of ideas.

In my own thinking, in these latter years, I've been influenced to a degree by the observations and ideas of two men of politics who, although from different political realms, were close friends and confidantes and who engaged each other frequently – the unorthodox late Deng Xiaoping of China and the equally unorthodox Lee Kuan Yew, late former prime minister of Singapore. I've also looked at the thinking of Deng's successor, Xi Jinping, who built on Deng's new thinking.

Both Deng (or Xi Jinping) and Lee Kuan Yew use the deep culture of their societies as social capital for dealing with modern-day challenges. Deng and Xi developed modern China's approach of socialism with Chinese characteristics. Lee Kuan Yew developed what he called the 'middle way' with Singaporean characteristics. Both dared to move along a path that said that whether it was European capitalist or European socialist thinking, it was not appropriate as a one-size-fits-all to be imported by other countries and peoples across the world. Each country had to dig deep into their local culture and conditions to chart a way forward and inspire their people to work to achieve better lives for all. The European way, right or left, and the imperial propagation of that way, along with a neocolonial mindset about what constitutes civilisation and 'world order', would never result in motivating people nor advancing their societies to a better life.

Singapore's neighbour, Thailand, found the same path albeit along a different trajectory, and it came from an unusual quarter – a benevolent royal. Thailand's King Bhumibol Rama IX took a similar approach to Lee Kuan Yew when after the Second World War he inherited a devastated country with widespread poverty, and was challenged to find a social-advancement path that was appropriate for Thailand. He came up with a simple vision – 'I want my people to be happy, safe and secure in every way' – and realised that radical agrarian reform linked to education reform was required.

He also saw the need for levelling in Thai society, where abject poverty on the one hand and vulgar rich lifestyles on the other were a threat to building social cohesion, and he therefore propagated the idea of 'sufficiency for all'. He drew on local Thai culture and faith to create his own theoretical and praxis framework, of social advancement with Thai characteristics – the Sufficiency Economic Philosophy.

I'm not a disciple of Lee, Deng, Xi or King Bhumibol, who has now mechanically adopted all the thinking of these influences. Rather, what has impressed me about all these figures has been their ability to reject paradigms of orthodoxy and come up with innovative new thinking in political applications that break rigid old east-west and north-south dividing lines. What has been interesting for me is the convergence of thinking among these giants of Asian political thought along the lines of social advancement with non-European characteristics for their own countries.

Now, this was also not foreign to me because I had already heard this type of thinking in my youth, here in Africa. Julius Nyerere had presented his version of social advancement with African characteristics back in 1962 in the form of Ujamaa African Socialism ('ujamaa' means 'family' in Kiswahili) and the village culture was at its root. Kwame Nkrumah also presented social advancement with African characteristics born from the African humanist tradition. Patrice Lumumba, whose focus was anti-imperialism and anti-colonialism, exposed what he called a 'middle way' of social advancement with pan-African characteristics, calling on Africans to stop being enamoured with European solutions, be they left or right.

Steve Biko was the strongest African philosophical voice in my youth, whose focus was the liberation of our minds from European domination and self-doubt. He fundamentally questioned the European way, European civilisation and European domination in left thinking and solution finding. Self-realisation and self-sufficiency as black people and Africans were the core of a consciousness that we had to cultivate if we wanted to build a path for actualising social advancement in South Africa. Only by believing in ourselves and appreciating the worth of our continent, its peoples and cultures, will we be able to liberate ourselves – achieving socialism with African characteristics, a social and economic construct fashioned by ourselves.

Changing material conditions was reliant on changing mindsets, which colonialism and European imperialism had sowed with self-doubt. Even our visualisation of our futures was tied to European left cultural and intellectual models of social and economic development politics. Biko challenged us to find our own way in South Africa and on our continent as a whole. He wasn't a narrow nationalist, as he could see this same consciousness developing across Africa, Asia and Latin America among all black communities in our diverse shades and cultures. His 'our own way' was essentially an anti-colonial and anti-imperial internationalist paradigm. Core to his thinking was that we can't move forward without consciousness, without a philosophical framework, and in this way he, like all of the aforementioned, realised that we would be floundering (and we are) if we had no guiding philosophical framework for social advancement.

Modern-day politicians in South Africa are bankrupt of appropriate and innovative new thought, largely because the ANC has ceased creating and promoting a culture of intellectual discourse. In fact, under Zuma's influence, it embraced anti-intellectualism and made enemies of intellectuals. Since around 2005, slowly but steadily a crass form of anti-intellectualism has taken root and smothered healthy intellectual discourse in the political realm. As a result, the same bankrupt ideas just keep being regurgitated.

* * * *

I believe that we also need a totally different approach from the 'party power' dominance in the political realm, and a real move along the trajectory that OR Tambo advocated – building infrastructure of political engagement that is communitarian in character and roots, to realise 'people power' – demos kratos – the root of democracy. OR was passionate about this being the cornerstone of a new South Africa that he envisaged.

This requires community-based organisations and community action networks. It also requires an assembly of people's organisations made up of civil-society organisations rooted in community action networks, as a second house alongside the elected legislature, the national assembly. This should replace the white elephants the national council of provinces and provincial parliaments, which are founded on the old apartheid bantustans.

Such a second house would have non-remunerated representatives who would play a watchdog and lobbyist role in terms of drafting and passing legislation, but also a strong role of demanding accountability of public representatives in parliament, and of cabinet and government. This is a concept that my old comrade and friend, the late Mzala, and I discussed, as being able to make a huge difference in the political life of our people – A National People Council (of civil society organisations).

Our representatives unfortunately are not accountable public representatives, because they're formally engaged in the practice of the narrow party interests under the present system. This alienates people from a class of new nobility – a political estate.

Every ten years an all-in national convention for renewal should be institutionalised, to ensure regular broader accountability to the people.

My critique of 'party power' and the aberration of democratic centralism, which naturally creates unaccountable corrupt political elites, has led me to believe that across the world, and not just in South Africa, the same framework of a multiparty democratic legislature should be used to create a multiparty governing cabinet. Put another way, a governing cabinet should always be a proportional multiparty cooperative institution, just as in the legislature. In other words, instead of being led either by majoritarianism or by temporary coalition governments, stability is reached by institutionalising governments of national unity and having robust engagement in cabinet.

All parties should have a constitution that doesn't allow the democratic-centralist model, but instead has strong checks and balances to always keep leadership accountable to its membership base, with provision for impeachment. Transformation for the poor, and political renewal, with the principle of strengthening maximum public participation in creating and adopting legislation and in holding government accountable, is vital.

Today's political culture has totally watered down the constitutional obligation for vibrant public participation in legislature and government business. We had this originally under speaker Dr Frene Ginwala in the first years of the life of parliament when we removed 'fortress parliament' and worked hard to ensure that the doors of parliament were open for all.

From a lifetime as a political activist, I believe that if we want the liberation of our country and continent that we dream of, we need to deal with the colonisation of our minds by both the imperial European left and the right, and to come up with new political and economic approaches, and institutions with African characteristics.

South Africa must focus on addressing the following issues:
- hunger and poverty alleviation
- job/economic activity creation
- provision of homes and improved built environments
- land and agrarian reform
- quality education and skills development for all

Economic advancement projects are required so that money revolves within South Africa and Southern Africa, and we need to curtail the explosion of mall culture and multinational corporate franchises that has killed local small business, self-employment, entrepreneurship and innovation. For this, we need:
- SADC-wide joint infrastructure projects – road, rail, airports, harbours, tourism
- building manufacturing/beneficiation industry and buy-local cultures across SADC
- curtailing mall and franchise culture, and promoting a mass small-business culture such as covered and serviced stall-parks in close proximity to all existing malls and transport hubs, like in Asia, with procurement chain support and business practices development support.

South Africa not only has the lowest employment rate, it also has the lowest rate of informal sector, and it stands out globally for this in comparison to similar countries. Indeed, similar countries thrive on informal sectors, whereas our government and local government effectively criminalise self-help in the informal sector and tie it up with prohibitive red tape. Spatial apartheid and city by-laws, and aggressive policing, sanitise urban space and the regulatory environment, and are just as antagonistic to the informal sector as was the Group Areas Act.

Furthermore, government at its various levels drives the informal sector into the arms of syndicated crime. The neocolonial mentality in government simply blocks this kind of observation, and solutions to rapidly grow and facilitate the informal sector as it exists in Asia as a major employment sector. My experience is that such proposed solutions, with practical suggestions for implementation, fall on deaf ears. I once put across a practical and inexpensive plan, along the lines of this analysis, to President Ramaphosa, after his 'thuma mina' ('send me') call to summon the spirit of our country's struggle history to tackle the problems of today, that would create 500 000 employment opportunities over five years, and he didn't even have the courtesy to acknowledge receipt and give a reply.

South Africa needs a simple and motivational charter and socioeconomic political philosophy with the five focus issues at its core, giving attention to the three project priorities, along with establishing an anti-racist national platform for building liberation and national unity. Spatial apartheid in this context needs urgent addressing. Political leadership should be about galvanising people to ensure self-advancement and social advancement.

A social advancement state is what South Africans need, not a neo-colonial developmental state, dependent on a paradigm of 'developer' and 'developed'. All of this requires a mixed economy, private-public cooperative and state, and full engagement in the economy by all. Currently, our country is being fought over by a range of imperial forces, with global criminal network interference. When these elephants and their local collaborators fight, it's we the grass that gets trampled. Our foreign policy should be non-aligned and aimed at strengthening a global non-aligned movement.

This, in a nutshell, is my political framework for social advancement with African characteristics in South Africa.

* * * *

There are those who ask me if I'm disillusioned and regret my past dedication and service in the national liberation movement. Not at all.

I've been under no illusion that all those things for which I stood and fought, would just naturally emerge if we simply dislodged the apartheid regime. Dislodging apartheid was but just a first step. As we often say, 'A luta continua' – the struggle continues. The struggle against apartheid involved all sorts of people with all sorts of ideas and ambitions, and it's natural that these differences would come more clearly to the fore once apartheid was removed. For those of us who envisioned greater things – social advancement of the poor – that struggle will continue.

I have no regrets for taking the resistance road in fighting apartheid, and standing together with a broad church in fighting for freedom from that repressive racist system. I would do it again if I had my life over. I'm proud that I could serve with so many fine, outstanding human beings. That there were scoundrels among us – yes, I know that only too well. That we didn't all share the same politics is only too obvious if you look at the broad framework that held us together. But this doesn't negate the fact that we had to fight the apartheid regime with as broad a force as necessary. No narrowed-down political faction could have accomplished what we did.

We've seen similar outcomes with fraternal movements in Nicaragua and East Timor, and all over the world. Nirvana doesn't exist in real-world politics. Struggles have a permanence and will always be with us. It's when complacency sets in that we must worry. Dissatisfaction isn't a bad thing. We only get one life, with limited days. I've tried to use my days wisely in the service of my people.

In what remains of my life, I will continue down the resistance road that I set out on, in the hope that many more from impoverished lives may also find the personal liberation that I found in doing so. My energies now, in these days of the evening of my life, are focused on the decolonisation of the mind. I believe that nine-tenths of all our battles is overcoming mental slavery and allowing ourselves to envision a different world to that to which we've become accustomed.

I focus also on simply being a mensch, striving to be in tune with the positive in people and with the environment, and cherishing the inner liberation reaped through taking the resistance road.

16

IDENTITY:
THE HERITAGE WHISPERER

One night in 1997, I had a dream that I had a sister in a far-off land – Rosa. In the morning, I just couldn't shake it. Maybe I did have a sister called Rosa somewhere. In our family tradition we take dreams very seriously.

This opened the door to something I'd been putting off over many years: I needed to find my father, deal with changing my name – and perhaps find out if I really did have a sister. It had been almost 30 years since Pieter Francois Mellet had returned from the dead, and then for all of five minutes.

I asked one of my colleagues, Beben Cadman, to assist me, and we collected together as many telephone directories as we could find. We then made a list of all the Mellet phone numbers. Next, we embarked on the phonecalls.

We didn't find my father. But we did find his brother, and he and his wife agreed to meet me.

Giel and Lettie Mellet were an old couple. When I met them at their home, my heart pounding, they were sitting on the edge of a settee, tightly gripping each other's hands.

Immediately, Giel began to talk. He said that he knew that I was his brother's son; he'd last seen me when I was just a toddler. Then, very seriously, he said, 'I am very sorry for how my brother treated his children. He just left them and did not care for them.'

He'd used the plural – children. I'd learnt from my half-sister May that my father had been married to a woman called Ruby, and had had four children with her, while he was seeing my mother, but maybe there were more?

I asked Giel whether I had other brothers and sisters, and he said, 'There's a sister in Australia who's older than you, called Kathy Rose, and there's a brother up in Joburg who's younger than you. There are others but we do not know them.'

Then, the crux: my father was still alive, married, and living with his wife in Vereeniging. Lettie said that she was in contact with the wife.

I asked Lettie to see if she could get a phone number for the sister in Australia. If anyone was going to be able to guide me through this story, it would have to be my older sister. It was she who'd come to me in the dream. Her surname Rose, was close enough to Rosa.

Before I left them, Giel and Lettie gave me some photos of my father and a brass pestle and mortar that he had made. Again, they both apologised profusely for all I'd been through as a child without a father.

That same evening I received the phone number for Australia. Even as I dialled, I wasn't sure what I was going to say. Once Kathy was on the line, I simply blurted out, 'I'm phoning from Cape Town and my name is Patric, and I think I'm your brother.'

'What? Another one!' said Kathy in a broad Australian accent. Then there was disbelief. 'You're not having me on, are you? Are you sure? How do I know this isn't a prank?'

We spent a long time on the phone. Kathy explained that there were three other mothers, besides my own, that they knew of and perhaps more. And there were eight half siblings altogether, including me, and she knew all the others – Reg, her full brother, then half-siblings Francois (who had a learning disability for which he'd been institutionalised his whole life as though he was mentally handicapped; he died of brain cancer as an old man, still institutionalised), Andre, Peggy Lee and Jimmy (who both lived in Johannesburg), and Lynette Inauen (in Switzerland).

I have another sister, Laura, also living in Australia, but she's May's half-sister by my mother's ex-husband, which means that she's not a direct blood relative. Laura eloped and left South Africa to marry her husband Noel Maslamoney. We think of each other as siblings.

I had grown up as a single child but, counting my mother's other four children, I had twelve siblings!

My father's children and I seemed to have one thing in common: we'd all experienced being welfare kids and being in foster homes; in fact, at one stage four of us were in foster homes only a few streets apart but without knowing of each other's existence.

Kathy gave me the phone numbers of Lynette, Peggy and Jimmy, and I phoned them. With each conversation, more and more of the puzzle pieces tumbled out. By the end of the week, I had a pretty good picture of my family situation, and I'd realised that Peggy had more knowledge than all the others – she'd known a bit about me through another of my father's brothers, Ben Mellet. She'd met our father before, she said, and had no interest in meeting him again.

I arranged with Peggy to go up to Joburg to see her, and we planned a get-together in the Kruger National Park, where even Kathy from Australia and Lynette from Switzerland came for the first-ever meeting of us all. There were some uncanny similarities between us, given that we'd grown up in different cultures and under different influences, and had never known each other, and of course this gave rise to some lively 'nature or nurture' discussion.

Through my meetings with all my siblings on my father's side, I learnt many truths about him and of their experiences of abandonment.

One day, out of the blue, I got a call from the sire. There was a little chuckle on the other end of the line and then, 'Guess who this is? It's your dad!'

That was difficult for me to digest: 'dad' means something very different from being a sire, and I was speaking to a stranger. But I agreed to go to Vereeniging to meet him, if only to satisfy my curiosity.

On meeting me, my father kissed me and hugged me, and he and his wife made lunch for me. He then pulled out a photo album and showed me pictures of him and our youngest sibling, Andre, and his grandchildren. 'I love children,' he said, stroking a photograph.

'Really?' I said. 'So, how many children do you have?'

My father shifted in his chair, then said, 'Andre, Kathy, and now you.'

I was dumbfounded. 'You have many other children,' I said. 'I've met them all.'

'No, that's not right,' he said. 'Anyway, if your mother hadn't forced me to leave, and made you grow up without a father . . .'

I realised in that instant that nothing had changed: he was still the liar I'd been told about, unwilling to take responsibility, and there was no point in talking to him any further.

I wouldn't see my father again, and I made my peace with what my mother had always told me: my father had died a long time ago.

In 2002 when he passed away, his brother Giel phoned me after he'd been buried, to express his condolences. My dead father had died a second time.

* * * *

I decided it was high time that I spoke of these things to my siblings on my mom's side. My half-brother Henri had died by then, after a hard and miserable life on the streets. He'd had to have his legs amputated due to diabetes, and I was one of six family members who'd attended his funeral service.

My half-sister May, who'd been a constant presence in my life while I was growing up, recalled a time when my father had tried to force himself on my mother, and had cut her hand with a broken bottle in the process; and there was indeed a jagged scar on my mother's hand. May also told me that my father had tried to mess with her; she'd told my mother, who hadn't believed her, and had sent her away to a convent.

I tracked down my half-brother John, who was then in his 60s. After our mother and his father's divorce, he'd grown up with his father, Alan, who'd remarried a woman called Frances. They'd had a daughter, Laura, who lived in Australia with her husband and two children.

John and I had a sad and difficult first meeting. He said that he'd been old enough to understand the breakup between my mother and his father Alan, and that my father had played a part in it. Both our mother and his father had their faults, as far as he was concerned, rather than one or the other being to blame. He also said that there were things that hurt too much for him to talk about, and I didn't press him. But, he said, there was one thing that he wanted me to know: when I was a child, my mother had secured a letter of restraint from a lawyer forbidding him to see me or to communicate with me in any way. He explained that our mother never wanted me to know anything about her marriage or divorce, my father or the circumstances of my birth.

John said that in recent years he'd called my mother and they'd had an argument. I told him that I knew about it. I'd gone to visit my mother on that day and found her crying. She was 80 years old then. I asked what was wrong and she said that Johnny had been 'funny' with her on the phone.

'What do you mean when you say he was funny with you?' I asked.

'He asked me whether I ever thought about his father,' she said, 'and I told him that I never think about Alan.'

John had apparently wondered how our mother could have just moved on so easily from Alan, when she'd had four children with him.

'I told him not to get any stupid ideas because in those days a woman went to the doctor, and he would give her a teaspoon of special medicine, and that is how she got pregnant and gave birth to children,' she said.

John had apparently become angry and told her that she was talking rubbish, and slammed down the phone.

I looked at her, astounded, and said, 'How can you tell a man with children and grandchildren of his own, that he exists because a doctor gave you a spoon of medicine to get pregnant? No wonder he got angry. So, tell me, Mom, was that the same way you had me?'

A flicker of a smile broke out on her face before she said, 'Gwan voetjeck, I don't want to talk about this any more.'

Some time later, I decided to try and have a closure conversation with my mother. The occasion saw what I call my mother's two personas come to the fore, with both Annie, her pleasant persona, and Gladys, her pained and difficult persona, making an appearance. As a child and teen, I'd warmed to Annie and learnt to tolerate Gladys, but I loved them both in my own way.

I took her some photographs of my various Mellet half-siblings, dreading the conversation with her.

'I remember them all so well!' my mother exclaimed, smiling, looking closely at each photograph. 'Look how well they've all turned out!'

'Mom, why did you never tell me about them?' I asked.

She looked me in the eyes, full-on Gladys, and without a smile said, 'It was none of your business.'

I said, 'But they're my brothers and sisters'.

Staring coldly at me, she snapped, 'They are nothing to you.'

And that was that.

My mother was also a closed book on her siblings and my cousins. In my journey to get to know my hidden family, I would find that cross-colour and cross-race relationships were a family norm, beyond those that I knew. I only had full relationships with my Aunty Doll's family, and as a child I had limited contact with my Uncle Bob's children and my Aunty Mabel's children. But I knew nothing about my Uncle Bill or my Uncle Charles and their children.

Two years ago, I was pleasantly surprised when a woman contacted me on social media, and after comparing information, she turned out to be the granddaughter of my mother's brother, who I only knew as naughty Uncle Charlie. Meralyn Barry's husband Michael turned out to be a brother of a woman with whom I'd worked at parliament and on a film project, Shelly Barry. We subsequently connected, so I have another treasure in my life.

My journey of discovery of my family seemed to prove what's known as the law of the seven degrees of separation, meaning that any two people in the world are separated by at most seven connections.

* * * *

What remained to be done was to present my case to the department of home affairs, to clear up the matters left in limbo when I was sixteen.

I researched my father's details, then made an affidavit for me and my children to have my rightful surname and my real identity was restored to me – Patric William Tariq Mellet. And, just like that, that's who I became, in 1997.

My formal identity was restored, but my life experiences between the ages of 16 and 41, together with my childhood years, are what really made my identity, the person I am. Zinto became a passionate heritage whisperer over the years, a person who assists others to find their stories – and we all have a story to tell.

It was liberating but also strange shedding such a major part of my identity. I'd carried the name 'De Goede' for 41 years. Now in some ways De Goede was dead.

This was a pivotal moment in not just my life. It was also important in the life of my three sons, whose ID documents were also changed to reflect my family surname. Each had to answer lots of questions from friends and teachers about the name change, just as I had to explain the same thing across parliament and the various ministries and presidency with whom I interacted every day in those years.

Dylan, Manuel and Vuyo have gone through many of the experiences over the years as elaborated in this book. They've had difficult lives but despite the hardships each has blossomed and in his own way has risen above adversity. They really should take a bow for being survivors who, like me, had to cope with much on their own.

Dylan, a chef, has been married twice and has fathered three sons, my grandchildren – Caleb, Tyler and Celeo. Manuel, a physical-fitness trainer, also divorced, has been battling with overwhelming post-traumatic difficulties rooted in the past; he's father to Aryan and Ella, another two of my grandchildren, who live with their mom Maite Castillo in Andalucia, Spain. Vuyo is married to Nazli Jugbaran and they run a spiritual wellness centre in service to humanity.

It's not been easy for the children of activists who've had to survive the many moves of refugee life, dangers, deprivations and broken relationships. I salute their fortitude and survivor spirit, as they cope with sadness and often self-reliance in dealing with the difficulties they've been through. I love and appreciate each one of my boys for their spirit, and for what each finds they have to live with mentally.

* * * *

IDENTITY

In 1999, at the time of my graduation with an M.Sc, the certificate was in my rightful name. Proudly, I went to see my mother, to show her my accomplishment, along with my graduation photographs.

Mom looked at my degree certificate, then, in a response that pushed me all the way back into my past, back to when I was Cleaners' Boy, she said, 'What's that any good for, mastermind? You haven't even got a matric.'

She had no understanding of what a master's degree was; she wanted to see a matric certificate because that was a 'real education' as far as she was concerned. I took it as a little lesson in humility.

My mom died on 23 March 2001, and we buried her on her birthday, 26 March. Before her death, Alzheimer's had set in and she was just a slight, frail, confused woman. She'd been the saddest person I've ever known.

Wolfie Kodesh stood by me to give his support as she lay in her coffin at the church door. During the service, I read the poem 'Mother to Son' written by social activist Langston Hughes (1901-1967).

Well, son, I'll tell you:
Life for me ain't been no crystal stair.
It's had tacks in it,
And splinters,
And boards torn up,
And places with no carpet on the floor –
Bare.
But all the time
I'se been a-climbin' on,
And reachin' landin's,
And turnin' corners,
And sometimes goin' in the dark
Where there ain't been no light.
So boy, don't you turn back.
Don't you set down on the steps,
'Cause you finds it's kinder hard . . .

The following year, at the age of 84, Wolfie died. We'd spent some of the most important moments in history together, and shared 22 years of friendship. He'd been decorated with three service medals, bronze, silver and gold, for over 50 years of service to the liberation movement.

ACKNOWLEDGEMENTS

I would like to thank and compliment my dear wife, Asirawan 'Leenah' Deeying, and her parents and extended family in Thailand, as well as our daughter, Watsana Thanomputsa, and our son, Cheyttha Thanomputsa, his wife Yao and our granddaughter Nongnaam. They have all brought great value to my life and much joy. Their country, Thailand, has become my home from home, particularly the farm at Sinakhon in Sukhothai.

A big thank you to my sons Dylan Mtshali Mellet, Manuel Bram Mellet and Vuyo Beyers João Mellet for everything that you sacrificed and for everything that you are. Keep striving to give of yourself to others. May you and your children be blessed.

To my spirit daughter Samantha Castle, thank you for always being there and everything you've managed to achieve – keep paying it forward.

I also wish to thank my commissioning editor, Mbali Sikakana, for her amazing support and skilled interventions to improve the presentation of my story. Also, many thanks to editor Tracey Hawthorne for all your assistance, and particularly with your structural suggestions to ensure the best reader experience.

To Nestor Paz and Fr Camilo Torres, who, in sacrificing their lives in the frontline of the struggles of the poor in their countries, and leaving us their written advice so many years ago in my teens, I thank them for setting me off on the resistance road.

And to you, my dearest comrades, Sello Moeti, Miles Pelo, Mzala Jabulani Nxumalo, William Khanyile, Jenny and Katryn Schoon, and Dulcie September, who were never able to return home, it was a privilege to have worked with you along the resistance road, and you are never far from my thoughts.

Love you all xxx

INDEX

Abdurahman, Abdullah 21, 46
Addinall, Peter 240
Africa Education Trust 141, 147
African Communist 153
African National Congress (ANC) 23, 46, 63, 81, 85, 87, 93–95, 100–102, 104–105, 107, 110–114, 116–120, 122, 124–126, 128–137, 139–141, 143, 145–148, 150–154, 157, 159–161, 164, 167–173, 175–176, 179–186, 190–192, 194, 196, 200, 214, 231–232, 241–242, 249
African People's Organisation 182
African Political Organisation 145, 172
Afrikaner Weerstandsbeweging (AWB) 191–192
Ahern (Bosconian) 55
Alcock, Hylton 151
Alexander, Neville 21, 243
Alex, Uncle 27
Amandla Cultural Ensemble 152, 154
ANC-African Nationalist (ANC-AN) 183
ANC Youth League 132, 154, 160–161, 183, 185
Andersen, Bill 161
Anglo-Boer War 20, 69, 77, 189
Anti-Apartheid Movement 116, 140–141, 150
Antonio (Bull, Bosconian) 55
apartheid 16–17, 19, 21, 23, 25–26, 30, 36, 46, 49, 53, 57, 59, 62, 65, 69–75, 77–79, 83–84, 86–87, 89, 91, 94–96, 98–99, 114, 116–119, 127, 133–134, 136, 140–141, 148, 150, 153, 155–157, 159, 166–169, 171–172, 178–181, 183–184, 189, 209, 216, 234, 241, 243, 245, 249, 251–253
Arafat, Yasser 203–204
A Re Kopaneng ('Come Together') 161
Assemblies of God (AOG) 63, 64, 69, 82
Assmann, Hugo 59
Atmore, Eric 186, 197

Baardman, Ben 158
Balie, Philip 186
Barry, Meralyn 259
Barry, Michael 259
Barry, Shelly
Belton, Colin 147, 162

Ben (boy at Nazareth House) 42, 44
'Beware Comrade – the AmaMafiosi' 157
Bhengu, Nicholas 63, 69
Bhumibol Rama IX 247
Biko, Steve 25, 95, 187, 215, 248
'Black Fruits of the Vine, The' 220
Blair, Tony 203
Bleek, Wilhelm 74
Boff, Leonardo 59
Bonino, José 59
Bophuthatswana 191
Bosasa 234
Bosco, John 'Don' (also Bosconians) 55, 57
Botha, PW 79
Brecht, Bertolt 127
Bredekamp, Jatti 211–212
Brian (Bosconian) 55
Brickhill, Jeremy 123
Brickhill, Joan 123
Brigades Development Trust 103–105, 108, 115
Brink, Ray 195
Brown, Lynnette 151
Brown, Mannie 146
Brown, Merle 200
Brutus, May 149

Cadman, Beben 200, 207, 254
Câmara, Hélder 59
Camissa Africans, Museum 32, 46, 49, 63, 73–74, 90, 108, 131, 145, 152, 178–179, 235, 243–245
Cape Flats 53–54, 88, 92, 98, 175, 186
Cardenal, Ernesto 59
Carey, Mariah 9
Carneson, Fred 146
Carneson, Sarah 146, 151
Cassock, Prince 152
Castillo, Maite 260
Castle Bridge 51–53
Castle, Mervyn 210
Castle, Samantha 210–211, 216
Castro, Fidel 59, 203–204
Cawthra, Gavin 161
Centre for Early Childhood Development 186

INDEX

Challenges of Globalisation: South African Debates 243
Champion, AWG 63
Chiba, Govan 'Chips' 137
Chiba, Laloo 137
Chohan, Fatima 232
Cholozi (domestic worker) 127
Christopher, Russell 200–201
Churches Urban Planning Commission 97–98
Ciskei 191
Clarke, Maura 59
Clinton, Bill 203–204
Clinton, Hillary 204
Coetzee, Harold 186
Coetzee, Johann 148
colonialism, neo-colonialism 21, 74, 84, 127, 159, 181, 248
Committee on South African War Resisters 161
'Companero Printing Press' 163–164
Comrades Movement 90–91
Congress for Early Childhood Development 197
Congress of South African Trade Unions (Cosatu) 158, 168, 170
Congress of the People 159
Cook, Al 149
Couch, Beatriz Melano 59
Cuito Cuanavale, Battle of 115
Curly (storeman) 69–70
Curren, Brian 62

Dabengwa, Zodwa 149, 152
Dadoo, Winnie 151
Dadoo, Yusuf 146, 183
Dalindyebo, Sabata 133
Damara 178
Daniel (Bosconian) 55
Darwish, Mahmoud 141–142
Day, Dorothy 56
De Bruyn, Benny 'Natho' 118–119, 123, 130–131, 133
Deeying, Asirawan 'Leenah' 240–241, 264
Defend Our Democracy SA 242
De Goede, Alan 14, 17–18, 67–68, 76, 257–258
De Goede, Alan Jnr 17
De Goede, Annie (*see* Huntley, Annie)
De Goede, Anton 111
De Goede, Frances 257
De Goede, Henri 17, 66, 257
De Goede, John 17, 257–258
De Goede, Louisa (Toekies) 51
De Goede, May 17, 27–29, 46–47, 50, 60, 62, 111, 174–175, 254–255, 257
De Keiser, Ethel 149
De Klerk, FW 171
Dela (ancestor of author) 76
Deng Xiaoping 246–247

De Porres Velázquez, Martino ('Marty') 30–33, 211
De Smit, Graham 161
De Smit, Lorna 161
Dick, Nancy 151
Dilrosen, Bram 106
District Six 10, 19–22, 25, 27, 30, 32–33, 35, 41, 43, 47–48, 51–54, 75, 179, 199
Dlamini-Zuma, Nkosazana 225
Dodger (friend of author) 54–55, 57–58
Domestic Workers' Union 88
Dominic (Mole, Bosconian) 55
Dora, Aunty 26
Dora Valke Centre 98
Dosson, Teddy 88
Drosters 21
Dryja, Barbara 88, 112
Dryja, Chanel 174
Dryja, Gertie 174
Dryja, James (Jimmy) 88–89, 112, 174
Dryja, Stefan 174
Dube, John 46
Dube, Mandla 220
Duffy (Bosconian) 55
Dylan, Bob 93

Eddie, Uncle 77
End Conscription Campaign 82
Erentzen, Randy 195, 199
Evans, Ursula Oliphant 186, 192–193
Evans, Woody 193

Farelo, Maria (*see also* Mellet, Maria) 88
Farelo, Teresa 154
Farooq (Egyptian at Endymion Rd) 142
Feinberg, Barry 146, 148
Feinberg, Nick 149
Fireblade Aviation project 236
Food and Canning Workers' Union 127
Fortune, Somayah 207
Free Nelson Mandela campaign 169
Freire, Paulo 58
'Frontline Noise in the Night' 121–122

Gaetsewe, John 101, 119, 133, 145
Gang of Eight 183
Garner, Heather 97, 99, 161–162
Gastrow, Shelagh 208–211, 213–214
Gatsha Buthelezi: Chief with a Double Agenda 153
Gebara, Ivone 59
Genau, Macky 27
Geneva Protocols 95
Georgie (boy at Nazareth House) 43
Gigaba, Malusi 234, 236
Gilda, Aunt 28
Gilfellan, Calvyn 243

265

Ginwala, Frene 143, 200–201, 208, 250
Goldberg, Denis 158–159
Gomas, John Stephen 21
Gomez, Eli 142, 147
Gool, Cissie 21
Gqunukhwebe 21
Gracie, Aunt 27
Graham, Billy 63
Gramsci, Antonio 150
Grapes of Wrath, The 88
Grassroots 175
Grassroots Educare Adult Education and Training Trust 186–188, 192–193, 195, 197, 207
Griqua 73–74, 86, 178
Gross, Sally (Father Selwyn) 160
Group Areas Act 49, 53, 97–98, 251
Guevara, Che 59
Gupta, Ajay 233–236
Gupta, Atul 233–236
Gupta, Rajesh 233–236
Gutierrez, Gustavo 59
Gwala, Harry 154

Hadden, William 76
Hanekom, Derek 96–97
Hanekom, Kallie 96–97
Hanekom, Trish 96
Hani, Chris 153, 156, 184
Hannan, Alec 69
Harmel, Ray 151
Haron, Abdullah 62
Has Socialism Failed? 193
Has the Communist Party Failed? 194
Hawthorne, Tracey 264
Head, Bessie 108
Hendricks, Brian 41–42
Hendricks, Geneva 227
Hindley, Dr 165
Hitler, Adolf 69–70
Hodgson, Rica 151, 172–173
Hughes, Langston 26
human trafficking 190, 221–224, 227, 236
Huna, Bernard Matthews 93–94
Huna, Emily 93
Huna, Lumko 93
Huntley, Annie Gladys Frances (Mellet; De Goede, mother of author) 10, 13–18, 22–27, 29–31, 33–35, 43, 45–48, 51, 54, 58, 60, 65–68, 70–71, 75, 77, 111, 130, 149–150, 156, 174–175, 254–259, 261
Huntley, Bill (uncle of author) 13, 77, 259
Huntley, Bob 77, 259
Huntley, Charles (Charlie) 77, 259
Huntley, Doll (Mary van Rooy, aunt of author) 13–16, 26, 51–53, 72, 77, 139, 259
Huntley, Ma- (Mary-Anne) 13–15, 77

Huntley, Mabel 77, 259
Huntley, William (Willie) 13, 26, 77

Inauen, Lynette 255–256
Independent Electoral Commission 195
Industrial and Commercial Workers' Union 63, 127
Inkatha Freedom Party 191–192
inter-agency clearing forum (IACF) 225, 227, 232
International Confederation of Free Trade Unions 168
International Defence and Aid Fund (IDAF) 141, 149–151, 161
International Graphical Federation 87, 148
International Red Cross 188
Inyathelo – The South African Institute for Advancement 210–211, 213–214, 216
Izak, Uncle 25–27
Iziko Museums 211

Jacobs, Melanie 199–200
Jaffa, Abubaker 52–53
Jagers, Francina 76–77
James, Sergeant-Major 84–85
Jenkin, Tim 124, 149
Jensen, Peter 106
Jessica (infiltrator) 164
Jesus People Movement 63–64
Jethro, Rowland 200
Jimmy, Uncle 28
Joemat, Paul 175
Joemat, Rhoda 175
Johannes, George 152
Jones, Colin 243
Jordan, Isabel 127
Jugbaran, Nazli 260

Kabwe conference 183–184
Kadalie, Clements 21, 46
Kadalie, Kwezi 151
Kafaar, Razia Adams 200
Kahn, Sam 21
Kaplan, Bronwyn 146
Kaplan, Norman 146, 149
Karriem, Alf 200
Kasrils, Eleanor 146
Kasrils, Ronnie 146
Kaunda, Kenneth 132–134, 136
Kemp, Stephanie 146
Khanyile, Eleanor 135, 149
Khanyile, William 135, 149, 264
Khoe 21, 73–76, 178–179
Khuze, Ndonda *see* Mphahlele, Lazarus Hlekelo
King, Martin Luther 55
Kinloch, Alice Alexander 63
Kleinschmidt, Horst 146, 149

INDEX

Klopse Carnival 24
Kodesh, Wolfie 118–119, 124–128, 130–131, 139–140, 146, 162, 172–173, 188, 192, 205, 261–262
Koevoet 114
Koka, Drake 100
Korana 73, 178
Kotane, Moses 21
Krotoa 76

La Guma, James 21
Lancaster House Agreement 111
Laundry Workers, Cleaners and Dyers Union 23
Lawson & Kirk 21–22
Lebese, Michael (Sello Moeti) 159, 166, 264
Lee, Peggy 255–256
Le Cordier, Anna Maria 76
Le Cordier, Elsie Petronella 75–76
Le Cordier, Johannes 76
Le Cordier, Jurgen 76
Le Cordier, Susanna 76
Lee Kuan Yew 246–247
Lee, Stephen 124
Leendertz, Angus 243
Lenses on Cape Identities – Exploring Roots in South Africa 220
Lerole, Captain 126, 131, 133, 139
Lerole, Kenosi 152
Levy, Norman 146
'Liberated Africans' ('Prize Slaves') 20
Lie of 1652 – A decolonised history of land, The 242–243
Ling, Margaret 140, 142
London College of Printing 139, 147, 152
Lorca, Federico García 147
Lourens, Major 87
Louw, Colleen 207
Lumumba, Patrice 248

Mabhida, Moses 139
MacDonald, Patti 151, 159
Madiba *see* Mandela, Nelson
Maharaj, Mac 119
Mahlangu, Phil 200
Maja, Maurice 152
Makeni, Zambia 117–119, 122, 124, 128–129, 133, 136
Makgothi, Henry 'Squire' 101–102, 111–112, 122
Makona, Thembi 'Eva' 188–189
Mandela, Nelson 21, 53, 84, 96, 158, 169, 171–173, 190–191, 200, 204–206
Mangena, Alfred 21
Mangope, Lucas 191
Manzini, Manala 123
Manzini, Mavivi Mayakayaka 123
Mapungubwe: Echoes from the Valley 220

Marcus, Gill 140, 148, 151, 159, 164, 171
Marcus, Mollie 151
Margolis, Mrs 22–23
Marks, Robina 243
Maroons 21
Marshall, Anita 186
Martin, Gertrude 30
Martin, Mary 30–32, 211
Maru (ANC veteran) 137–138
Marx, Karl 146, 245
Maseko, Mandla 152, 161
Mashula gang 114, 134
Maslamoney, Laura 255, 257
Maslamoney, Noel 255, 257
Mason, Cedric 160–161
Mass Democratic Movement (MDM) 169–171
Matlou, Rebecca *see* Sankie Mthembi-Mahanyele
Matlou, Victor 123
Matshikisa, Esme 186
Matthews, James 98, 192
Matthews, Jimmy 192
Mayibuye, Peter *see* Netshitenzhe, Joel
Mayibuye 118, 123–124
Mayibuye, Dawn 123
Mayibuye, Voice of Women (Vow) 123
Mbange, Kenneth 207
Mbatha, Vernet 148
Mbeki, Govan 200
Mbeki, Thabo 118
McMaster, Lydia 88
Megwe, Ace 119–121
Meli, Francis 165
Mellet, Andre 255–256
Mellet, Aryan 260
Mellet, Ben 256
Mellet, Caleb 260
Mellet, Celeo 260
Mellet, Celeste *see* Naidoo, Celeste
Mellet, Dylan Mtshali 10, 93, 96, 100–102, 107, 118, 129–130, 135, 138–140, 143, 155–156, 160, 162, 174, 177, 179, 185, 187, 196–197, 203, 260
Mellet, Ella 260
Mellet, Francois 255
Mellet, Giel 254–255, 257
Mellet, Jimmy 255–256
Mellet, Lettie 254–255
Mellet, Manuel 10, 142–143, 162, 192–193, 196, 260
Mellet, Maria 88–93, 96, 98, 101, 103, 107, 116, 118, 138–140, 145, 147, 149, 154, 160, 162, 192, 196
Mellet, Patric
  1976 student uprising 89, 104
  Auntie Doll & Abubaker Jaffa influence of 52–53

birth 14
'Black Entrepreneurs in Tourism' 212
burn accident as child 18, 47
Camissa Museum co-founder 243
'Cleaner's Boy' 10, 27–28
Comrades Movement 90–91
Deng Xiaoping influence 246–247
foster homes 26–27, 256
genealogy 75–76, 254–261
El Mina and Cape Coast Castle visit 211
exiled, Botswana 95, 99–116, 139, 141, 153–154
exiled, Zambia 117–140
exiled, UK 140–174
fishing trawler, love for fishing; shelfpacker 60–62, 200, 225
Grassroots employment 186–188, 192–193, 195, 197, 207
growing up, District Six, Salt River 21–25, 51–54
health problems 165
Herzburg & Mulne maintenance fitter 87
Home Affairs manager 221–239
IDAF employee 149–151
Independent Electoral Commission voter education 195–196
inter-agency clearing forum (IACF) 225
Inyathelo 210–216
Jesus Movement involvement 63–64, 68
Latin American liberation theology, influence of 59, 63, 88, 96, 245
Lee Kuan Yew influence 246–247
Lenses on Cape Identities – Exploring Roots in South Africa 220
Lie of 1652 – A decolonised history of land, The 242–243
London College of Printing 139, 147, 152
'Long Road to Freedom' project 220
Mapungubwe: Echoes from the Valley 220
marriage to & divorce from Maria Farelo 88, 154
marriage to & divorce from Celeste Naidoo 162, 188
marriage to Ursula Oliphant Evans 192–193
marriage (Muslim-rites) to Zainie Misbach 197
marriage to and divorce from Cheryl Osborn 200, 233
marriage to Asirawan 'Leenah' Deeying 240
Mary Martin, influence of 30–32, 211
master's degree 193, 199, 207, 221, 261
military service, refusal to do 78–85, 120
Nazareth House (the Huis) 34–37, 43–44, 54–55
Nestor Paz and Camilo Torres, influence of 58–59
NGO for HIV/Aids 217–220
nicknames Mr Fix-it & Mr Maritime 206, 226

nom de guerre Oscar 126
Parliament, head of public relations, 199–207
Peninsula Workers Forum & Southern Socialist Working Youth 96
Phakamani editorial member 152
poem 'Frontline Noise in the Night' 121–122
political activism and influences 62, 70, 91–98, 246
precious-metalworker, jewellery 67–68, 199
printing training, experience, journalism 55, 87, 91–93, 96, 103–104, 106, 112, 116–117, 122–123, 125, 130, 135, 139, 147–148, 151–153, 159, 162–164, 172, 180, 193, 242–243
race classification 78–85
resignation from SACP 193–194
Rixaka editorial member 152
Salesian Institute 54–60, 62, 65, 104
Sechaba editorial member 152
self-education, reading habits 59
Slave Lodge Museum 212
South Africa 1st – For Constitution, People and Country co-founder 241–242
South African Heritage Resources Agency Council member 242
social advancement philosophy 23, 187, 214–216, 244, 247–249, 252–253
Spiderweb Press 148
storeman at hospital stores 69–70, 87
surname change 9, 71–72, 259–260
syncretic faith 33, 245
Thai health spa, guesthouse owner 241
Ties that Bind Us, The 212, 221
Umkhonto we Sizwe (MK) 87, 94, 103–104, 106–107, 111, 113–115, 117, 119–120, 124, 133, 135, 152, 154, 168, 172, 180, 206
Umsebenzi editorial member 152
University of Cape Town director fundraising 208–210
USA visit 204, 212
'Usual Suspects, The' 200
Worker's Unity editorial member 152
'Working Mom' drawing 45–46
Xi Jinping influence 246–247
Young Christian Workers 88, 93, 95–96
Young Voice & New Voice newspapers 96
Mellet, Petrus Francois (great-grandfather of author) —
Mellet, Pieter Francois (grandfather of author) 75–76
Mellet, Pieter Francois (father of author) 17–18, 67–68, 71, 75–76, 254–258
Mellet, Reg 255
Mellet, Ruby 254
Mellet, Tyler 260
Mellet, Vuyo 10, 149, 162, 192–193, 196, 260
Melly (Bosconian) 55

INDEX

Miller, Arthur 133
Miller, Gwen 118
Mini, Vuyisile 149
Miranda, José Porfirio 59
Mission to Seamen 62
Mneyele, Thami 159
M. Obler & Son 67, 199
Moche, Victor 123
Moeti, Sello *see* Lebese, Michael
Mogau, Awolowo 128–129
Mokeba, Uriah 126–127, 131, 139
Mokopo, Isaac ('Kopsie') 100–101
Molweni, Max 123, 129
Mompati, Ruth 101, 119, 143, 147
Mona (landlady) 45
Monday Paper, UCT 208
Moonsamy, Kay 126–127, 130
Morogoro 104, 112, 154, 160, 183
Morogoro Conference 112
'Mother to Son' 261
Motshabi, Doreen 126
Moumbaris, Alex 124
Mozambique, Angola, & Guinea Information Centre 141
Mphahlele, Lazarus Hlekelo 152
Mseleku, Bheki 161
Msimang, Mendi 168, 173–174, 176
Mthethwa, Nhlanhla 220
Mthembi-Mahanyele, Sankie 123
Mtshali, Oswald 93

Nagasaki, Kendo 137
Naicker, GM 183
Naicker, Sarah 151
Naidoo (Mellet), Celeste 152, 161–162, 173–174, 177, 185, 188
Naidoo, Lawson 200
Naidoo, Marcella 174–175
Naidoo, Neeran 200
Naidoo, Ramni 149
Naidoo, Shanti 149
Nama 73, 178
Nannucci Brothers 21, 23
National Education, Health and Allied Workers' Union (Nehawu) 187, 233
National Front (UK) 145
National Graphical Association (UK) 87, 148
National Liberation League 182–183
National Party 167, 170–171, 183, 191
National Union for the Total Independence of Angola (Unita) 84, 114
National Union of Mineworkers (UK) 145
National Union of South African Students (NUSAS) 102
Ndebele, Njabulo 208
Netshitenzhe, Joel 118

Netto, Miguel 142, 145, 147
Newman, Clive 195, 199–200
Newman, Denise 199
Ngeleza, Mafa 152
NGO sector culture 217–220
Nhlanhla, Joe 124–125, 129
Njokweni, Unathi 195
Nkadimeng, David 123
Nkadimeng, John 119, 123, 145
Nkobi, Thomas 122–123, 125, 130
Nkomo, Joshua 110
Nkrumah, Kwame 248
Nkula, Hector 133
Nlapho, Mavis (Thandi Ndlovu) 123
Nobrega, Maria 147, 162
'No Music' 135–136
Nxumalo, Jabulani 'Mzala' 153–154, 184, 250, 264
Nyerere, Julius 248
Nzo, Alfred 130

O'Donnell, Brian 64, 69
Oewies, Maggie 88
O'Gorman, Vinny 55, 58, 60
Oliver and Adelaide Tambo Foundation 220
Operation Vula 180
Orlam 21, 178
Osborn, Cheryl 199–200, 203
Oshkosh (askari) 134–135
Owens, Jesse 70

Pan African Association 63
Pan Africanist Congress (PAC) 171, 183
Pandor, Naledi 200, 230–232
Parsons, Neil 108
Patel, Kevin 173–175
Patrick (Bosconian) 55
Paul (Bosconian) 55
Paz, Nestor 58, 264
Paz, Octavio 9
Pelo, Miles 152, 264
Pembe, Aron 'Ben Bella' 158
Penton Street bombing 148, 151
People's Liberation Army (PLAN) 83
People's Movement for the Liberation of Angola Workers Party (MPLA) 84
Peregrino, Francis Zacharia 63
Pérez, José Julián Martí 59
Peter ('Motchie', Bosconian) 55
Petronella (Caatje Hottentottin Voortman) 76
Phakamani 152
Phillip (boy at Nazareth House) 44
Phillips, James 145–146
Phillips, Maud 145
Plaatje, Sol 21, 46
Plaatjies, Daniel 186, 197
Plum, Obed 207

'Politics of identity in post-apartheid South Africa, The' 243
'Prize Slaves' ('Liberated Africans') 20
Progressive Alliance 182
Public Servants' Association 70, 233

Qhali, Keitumetse 221

Rabie, Sergeant 86
race classification board 72
Radio Freedom (ANC) 87, 123, 129
Ramaphosa, Cyril 97, 202, 213, 252
Ramphele, Mamphela 208, 213
Randeree, Shaik Ahmod Goolam 118
Rasool, Ebrahim 175
Reinders, John 200
Renamo 114
Reynalds, Sharon 186
Rhoda, Veronica 207
Richards, Ginny 186
Richer, Pete 102–103, 105
Rixaka 152
Robertson, Ian 149
Robeson, Paul 145
Rodgers and Hammerstein 244
Romero, Oscar 59
Rose, Kathy 255–256
Ryan Commission 45

Saad, Helen 88
Salesian Institute 54–55, 57–59, 65, 104
San 5, 21, 74–75, 178
Scargill, Arthur 145
Schoon, Fritz 155
Schoon, Jeanette Curtis 102–103, 105, 154–156, 158, 264
Schoon, Katryn 102, 155–156, 264
Schoon, Marius 102–103, 105, 155
Schuller, Raymond 186
Sechaba 152, 164
security police 62, 70, 80–82, 87, 91, 95–96, 98, 102, 107, 114, 148, 155–156, 161, 176, 189
Sedgewick, Michael 98
Selebi, Jackie 185
September, Dulcie 21, 99, 130, 156, 184, 264
September, Reg 101, 111, 118–119, 129, 131, 176–177, 187, 242
Seria, Rashid 175
Serote, Mongane Wally 161
Serowe: Village of the Rain Wind 108
Shanley, Dorothy 151
shishita ('the cleansing') 132–144
Sibeko, Archie 94
Sigxashe, Sizakele 118, 139
Sikakana, Mbali 264
Sillen, Andrew 208–209

Simons, Jack 124, 126, 131, 139–140, 176
Simons, Ray Alexander 101, 119, 126–127, 139–140, 158, 176, 187
Sipalo, Milton 132
Sisulu, Walter 158
Skeef, Eugene 161
Slave Lodge Museum 212
Slovo, Joe 146, 180, 193–194
Smee family 47
Smith, Gail 199
Smith, Ian 110–111
Smith, Solly 164
Smith, Stephen 199–200
Snipes (Clinton security agent) 203
Snitcher, Harry 21, 23
Socialist International 182
Solomon Mahlangu Freedom College 104, 154, 159
Solomons, Rod 241
Sonto, Rose 186
South 175
South Africa 1st – For Constitution, People and Country co-founder 241–242
South Africa First 242
South African Coloured People's Congress 102, 146
South African Communist Party (SACP) 23, 81, 87, 94–95, 101–103, 106, 110, 119, 125–126, 134, 137, 139, 152–153, 164, 168, 171–172, 180–181, 183, 187, 193–194
South African Congress of Trade Unions (SACTU) 23, 67, 87, 94, 101, 103, 106, 110, 123, 125, 132–135, 139, 145, 147–148, 150, 152–154, 158
South African Defence Force 71, 79, 82, 84, 97, 107, 114, 120, 134, 189, 233
South African Heritage Resources Agency Council 242
South African Indian Congress 118, 137
South African Native National Congress 46, 182
South African Revenue Service 234
South African Typographical Union 87, 148
Southern African Development Community (SADC) 223–224, 251
Southern African News Agency 102
South Pacific 244
South West African People's Organisation (Swapo) 84–85
Soweto student uprising (1976) 89, 104
Spiderweb Press 148
Springbok Legion 119
Stander, Chrisman 64
state capture 241
State Security Agency (SSA) 230, 234, 236
Steenkamp (storeman) 69
Steinbeck, John 88

INDEX

Steve (boy at Nazareth House) 42–43
Stevenson, Peggy 149
Steyn, Susanna Catherina Francina 75
Streek, Barry 200
Sufficiency Economic Philosophy 214, 247
Swart, Suzie 88
syncretic beliefs 33, 245

Tambo, Adelaide 130, 220
Tambo, Dali 220
Tambo, Oliver 87, 95, 117–119, 124–125, 129–131, 134–135, 165, 172–173, 205, 220, 229, 232, 235–236, 239, 249
Thanomputsa, Cheyttha 264
Thanomputsa, Nongnaam 264
Thanomputsa, Watsana 264
Thanomputsa, Yao 264
Thatcher, Margaret 168
Thomas (Bosconian) 55
Thomas, Dylan 93
'Three Doctors' Pact' 183
'thuma mina' 252
Ties that Bind Us, The 212, 221
Tloome, Dan 102, 112, 119, 122
Toivo ja Toivo, Herman 84
Tom (Bosconian) 55
Torres, Camilo 58, 264
Trafalgar High School 179, 196
Transvaal Indian Congress 183
Tree Within, A 9
Trew, Tony 149
Truth and Reconciliation Commission 114, 148

Ujamaa African Socialism 248
Umkhonto we Sizwe (MK) 87, 94, 103–104, 106–107, 111, 113–115, 117, 119–120, 124, 133, 135, 152, 154, 168, 172, 180, 206
Umsebenzi 152–153
United Democratic Front (UDF) 169–171, 175
United Nations High Commission for Refugees 101, 111, 147
University of Cape Town's African Studies Library 185

Van der Ross, Richard 213
Vandross, Luther 19
Van Rensburg, Patrick 103–106, 108
Van Rooy, Christian Clarke 14, 16
Van Rooy, Clint 73
Van Rooy, Daisy (Falken) 73
Van Rooy, Edgar 73, 225
Van Rooy, Herbie ('Busy') 72–73, 225
Van Rooy, Joan 15–16
Van Rooy, Mary (*see* Huntley, Doll)
Van Rooy, Russel 73
Van Rooy, Vanessa 73

Vereenigde Oostindische Compagnie (VOC) 244
Verwoerd, HF 178
Victor (Bosconian) 55
Vincent (Vinny, Bosconian) 55
Vlotman, Lauren 102–103
Vuyani (activist) 94–95

Wankie/Sipolilo campaign 104, 115, 119
Williams, Henry Sylvester 63
Williams, Sophie 118
Williamson, Craig 155
Wolpe, AnnMarie 146, 160
Wolpe, Harold 146
Workers' Party of South Africa 182
Worker's Unity 152
World Federation of Democratic Youth 185
World Federation of Trades Unions 168
World Marxist Review 153
Wrankmore, Bernard 62

Xhosa, amaXhosa, isiXhosa 9, 21, 46, 73, 77
Xi Jinping 246–247
Xuma, AB 183

Young Christian Workers 88, 93, 95–96
Youth in Philanthropy South Africa 210

Zambian Defence Force 132, 134, 138
Zembe, Zola (Archie Sibeko) 94
Zimbabwe African National Liberation Army (Zanla) 104, 107
Zimbabwe African National Liberation Union (Zanu) 104, 107
Zimbabwe African People's Union (Zapu) 107, 110, 123
Zimbabwe People's Revolutionary Army (Zipra) 107
Zochling, Peter 161
Zondo Commission 241
Zondo, Raymond 241
Zuma, Jacob 97, 201–202, 234, 249

ABOUT THE AUTHOR

PATRIC TARIQ MELLET was born and raised in the Salt River, Woodstock and District Six districts of Cape Town. He is a former liberation movement cadre, who returned from exile in 1990. His MSc dissertation from Buckinghamshire New University is titled: Heritage Tourism – Cape Slavery and Indigenous People. In 2009 his work on the intangible heritage of the Cape received a Western Cape Provincial Honours award. In 2019 the Minister of Sport, Arts and Culture appointed him to the Governance Council of the South African Heritage Resources Agency. He is the content originator and founder of the Camissa Museum at the Cape Castle and author of the bestselling, *The Lie of 1652 – A decolonised history of land*.